Queen Victoria's central importance to the era defined by her reign is self-evident, and yet it has been surprisingly overlooked in the study of Victorian culture. This collection of essays goes beyond the facts of biography and official history to explore the diverse and sometimes conflicting meanings she held for her subjects around the world and even for those outside her empire, who made of her a many-faceted icon serving their social and economic needs. In her paradoxical position as neither consort nor king, she baffled expectations throughout her reign. She was a model of wifely decorum and solid middle-class values, but she also became the focus of anxieties about powerful women, and – increasingly – of anger about Britain's imperial aims. Each essay analyzes a different aspect of this complex and fascinating figure. Contributors include noted scholars in the fields of literature, cultural studies, art history, and women's studies.

CAMBRIDGE STUDIES IN NINETEENTH-CENTURY
LITERATURE AND CULTURE 10

# Remaking Queen Victoria

CAMBRIDGE STUDIES IN NINETEENTH-CENTURY
LITERATURE AND CULTURE

General editors
Gillian Beer, *University of Cambridge*
Catherine Gallagher, *University of California, Berkeley*

Editorial board
Isobel Armstrong, *Birkbeck College, London*
Terry Eagleton, *University of Oxford*
Leonore Davidoff, *University of Essex*
D. A. Miller, *Columbia University*
J. Hillis Miller, *University of California, Irvine*
Mary Poovey, *The Johns Hopkins University*
Elaine Showalter, *Princeton University*

Nineteenth-century British literature and culture have been rich fields for inter-disciplinary studies. Since the turn of the twentieth century, scholars and critics have tracked the intersections and tensions between Victorian literature and the visual arts, politics, social organization, economic life, technical innovations, scientific thought – in short, culture in its broadest sense. In recent years, theoretical challenges and historiographical shifts have unsettled the assumptions of previous scholarly syntheses and called into question the terms of older debates. Whereas the tendency in much past literary critical interpretation was to use the metaphor of culture as "background," feminist, Foucauldian, and other analyses have employed more dynamic models that raise questions of power and of circulation. Such developments have reanimated the field.

This series aims to accommodate and promote the most interesting work being undertaken on the frontiers of the field of nineteenth-century literary studies: work which intersects fruitfully with other fields of study such as history, or literary theory, or the history of science. Comparative as well as interdisciplinary approaches are welcomed.

A complete list of titles published will be found at the end of the book.

# REMAKING QUEEN VICTORIA

EDITED BY

## MARGARET HOMANS
*Yale University*

### and

## ADRIENNE MUNICH
*State University of New York, Stony Brook*

CAMBRIDGE
UNIVERSITY PRESS

PUBLISHED BY THE PRESS SYNDICATE OF THE UNIVERSITY OF CAMBRIDGE
The Pitt Building, Trumpington Street, Cambridge CB2 1RP, United Kingdom

CAMBRIDGE UNIVERSITY PRESS
The Edinburgh Building, Cambridge CB2 2RU, United Kingdom
40 West 20th Street, New York, NY 10011–4211, USA
10 Stamford Road, Oakleigh, Melbourne 3166, Australia

First published 1997

Printed in the United Kingdom at the University Press, Cambridge

Typeset in 11/12.5 pt Baskerville MT    [SE]

*A catalogue record for this book is available from the British Library*

*Library of Congress cataloguing in publication data*
Remaking Queen Victoria / edited by Margaret Homans and Adrienne Munich.
p.   cm.   – (Cambridge studies in nineteenth-century literature
and culture, 10)
Includes bibliographical references and index.
ISBN 0 521 57379 3 (hardback) – ISBN 0 521 57485 4 (paperback)
1. Great Britain – History – Victoria, 1837–1901 – Historiography.
2. Queens – Great Britain – History – 19th century – Historiography.
3. Women – Great Britain – History – 19th century – Historiography.
4. Victoria, Queen of Great Britain, 1891–1901.   I. Homans,
Margaret, 1952.   II. Munich, Adrienne.   III. Series.
DA550.R46   1997   941.081′092 – dc21   96–50285 CIP

ISBN 0521 57379 3 hardback
ISBN 0521 574854 paperback

# Contents

# Illustrations

# Notes on contributors

ALISON BOOTH, Associate Professor of English at the University of Virginia, is the author of *Greatness Engendered: George Eliot and Virginia Woolf* (Cornell, 1992), and editor of *Famous Last Words: Changes in Gender and Narrative Closure* (Virginia, 1993). Her study of Anglo-American collective biographies of women, entitled *Ruling Lives*, will include discussion of Victoria among other exemplary women.

ROBIN L. BOTT is an Assistant Professor of English at Adrian College in Michigan, where her current work is on representations of politeness and the instability of social identities in Renaissance drama. She has published on Chaucer and on Hawaiian ethnic humor and has an essay in a forthcoming Modern Language Association volume on teaching Shakespeare through performance.

DAGNI BREDESEN, a doctoral candidate in English literature at the University of Washington, is completing her dissertation on the meaning of widowhood in the narratives and culture of Victorian England. She has published an essay on widows in Dickens and has received grants in support of research and teaching from the University of Washington.

SUSAN P. CASTERAS, former Curator of Paintings at the Yale Center for British Art for nearly twenty years, now teaches at the University of Washington. She has organized many exhibitions on Victorian art and has written numerous books, catalogues, essays, and articles on this subject as well as on the iconology of women. She has also lectured extensively in the United States and abroad; her current projects include books on Pre-Raphaelitism and on Victorian religious painting.

KAREN CHASE, Professor of English at the University of Virginia, is the author of *Eros and Psyche: the Representation of Personality in Charlotte Brontë, Charles Dickens and George Eliot* (London, 1984), and *Of Middlemarch* (Cambridge, 1991). With Michael Levenson she is now completing a study of nineteenth-century domestic life, under the working title *Victorian Home/Works: the English Domestic Imagination at Mid-Century.*

MARGARET HOMANS is a Professor of English and Chair of the Women's Studies Program at Yale University. She is the author of *Women Writers and Poetic Identity* (Princeton, 1980), of *Bearing the Word: Language and Female Experience in Nineteenth-Century Women's Writing* (Chicago, 1986), and of numerous essays on Victorian literature and on feminist theory. Her next book is *Queen Victoria: Power, Representation, and the Woman Monarch.*

GAIL TURLEY HOUSTON, Assistant Professor of English at the University of New Mexico, has recently completed a book on Queen Victoria entitled *The Writer and the Queen: Victoria(n) Professions of Authority.* She is also the author of *Consuming Fictions: Gender, Class, and Hunger in Dickens' Novels* (Southern Illinois, 1994).

MARIA JERINIC teaches English at the College of Mount St. Vincent in the Bronx, New York, and is completing her dissertation on nationalism and nineteenth-century British women writers at the State University of New York at Stony Brook.

ELIZABETH LANGLAND is a Professor of English and Associate Dean for Faculty Affairs at the University of Florida. She is the author of *Society in the Novel* (North Carolina, 1984), *Anne Brontë: the Other One* (Macmillan, 1989), and most recently, *Nobody's Angels: Middle-Class Women and Domestic Ideology in Victorian Culture* (Cornell, 1995). She has coedited three volumes of essays in feminist criticism, and has published numerous articles in the areas of Victorian literature, theory of the novel, feminist theory, and women's studies.

MICHAEL LEVENSON is a Professor of English at the Unviersity of Virginia. His publications include *A Genealogy of Modernism: English Literary Doctrine 1908–1922* (Cambridge, 1984) and *Modernism and the Fate of Individuality* (Cambridge, 1991). He is coauthor (with Karen Chase) of the forthcoming *Victorian Home/Work: the English Domestic Imagination at Mid-Century.*

MARY LOEFFELHOLZ is a member of the English Department at Northeastern University. She is the author of *Dickinson and the Boundaries of Feminist Theory* (Illinois, 1991), and *Experimental Lives: Women and Literature, 1900–1945* (Twayne, 1992). She is working on a book on antebellum American women poets.

ADRIENNE MUNICH, Professor of English and Women's Studies, directs the Women's Studies Program at the State University of New York at Stony Brook and teaches courses in art and English and comparative literature. She is the author of *Queen Victoria's Secrets* (Columbia, 1996), and of *Andromeda's Chains: Gender and Interpretation in Victorian Literature and Art* (Columbia, 1989). She coedited *Arms and the Woman: War, Gender, and Literary Representation* and *Robert Browning: Critical Essays*.

NICOLA J. WATSON has written a number of essays on the literature of the romantic period, and is the author of *Resolution and the Form of the British Novel, 1790–1825* (Oxford, 1994) and co-author of *England's Elizabeth: National Fictions of Elizabeth I, 1603–1990* (forthcoming, Oxford). She served as an Assistant Professor of English at Northwestern University before returning to Britain, where she now lives.

SHARON ARONOFSKY WELTMAN, Assistant Professor of English at Louisiana State University, is currently completing a book on mythic discourse, gender subversion, and John Ruskin in nineteenth-century context. She has published essays on Ruskin, Christina Rossetti, and Robert Frost. She dedicates this article on the grace and dignity of domestic queenship to the memory of her mother, Molly Ruben Aronofsky.

JANET WINSTON is a 1996–97 American Fellow of the American Association of University Women Educational Foundation and a recipient of a 1996 Woodrow Wilson Dissertation Grant in Women's Studies. She has published essays on Virginia Woolf and empire and on the lesbian short stories of Woolf and Katherine Mansfield. Currently, she is completing her dissertation at the University of Iowa on Queen Victoria's image as an icon of imperialism in twentieth-century narrative.

CHAPTER I

# Introduction

### Margaret Homans and Adrienne Munich

Queen Victoria has been hidden in plain view for a hundred years. We propose to reveal her where we believe she always was, at the center of Victorian cultures around the globe. She was hardly obscure during her own reign: the author of best-selling books, the beloved "grandmother of Europe," the subject of a multitude of portraits disseminated in homes rich and poor, she is demonstrably as important to her age as Elizabeth I was to hers. Nonetheless, Victoria is generally viewed as having negligible importance for the political history of Britain because during her reign the last vestiges of monarchic political power were transferred to Parliament. Moreover, the newer social histories of Britain, which have brought to light much that was once considered unhistorical, have concentrated on the middle and working classes. Perhaps it is because Victoria embedded herself so firmly in the history of what she herself called the "people" that she has seemed indistinguishable from them. For multiple reasons, then, the term "Victorian" is not likely to bring the Queen herself to mind; even scholarly studies that use her name have next to nothing to say about her.

Where the Queen receives more than her share of attention has been in the genre of personal history – of biography. Members of her household began to publish illicit memoirs, beginning late in her reign; her two jubilees inspired scores of illustrated retrospectives of her reign and life. In 1921 Lytton Strachey's *Queen Victoria* permitted a less hagiographic view, and a new life is published every few years. Notable among more recent biographies are Elizabeth Longford's comprehensive study (1964); Cecil Woodham-Smith's biography of the years up to the Prince Consort's death (1972); David Duff's study of the relationship between Victoria and Albert (1972); Stanley Weintraub's "intimate" biography (1987); Monica Charlot's two volume study, only the first volume of which has been translated into English (1991); and Giles St. Aubyn's full-scale reassessment (1991). Yet this cult of royal personality isolates her from the cultural history of her era. Rich and full as these biographies are, as long as they remain the principal source of information and analysis, understanding of Victoria's historical and cultural importance will inevitably remain muted.

This volume makes few claims about Victoria's political power, narrowly construed as the execution of decisions taken about matters of state. It does, however, claim for her an expansive political role because we recognize that power is largely ideological and that social relations are power relations. In our view, and that of the contributors to this volume, Victoria was central to the ideological and cultural signifying systems of her age. She has disappeared from history not because she was unimportant but because her importance – like her monarchy itself – has been difficult to categorize. She was a monarch without precedent: neither consort nor king, she baffled expectations throughout her career. Never had England seen a reigning monarch so matrimonially devoted, so excessively maternal (nine children), and then so emphatically widowed. But these peculiarities nonetheless cast their influence over, and were in turn shaped by, the culture of a rapidly changing Britain and its increasingly colonized domain.

*Remaking Queen Victoria* takes a modern measure of Victoria's reign in terms of its cultural work. Victoria reflected back to her subjects their own values to reassure them about the comprehensibility of their lived reality; they in turn created her in their image to serve their social and economic needs. Queen Victoria, her subjects around the globe, and even those outside the empire collaboratively made her into a myth and an icon. The dynamic of these constructions produced those cultures that are collectively called Victorian. This volume recognizes the existence of many Victorias. It treats the diffusion of her image not as a problem to be solved by the creation of an illusory wholeness, but as a series of entry points into Victorian culture and into the nature of cultural formation. Each chapter shows how different "Victorias" created varieties of Victorian cultures and their disparate legacies. Taken together, the chapters remake Victorian cultural history.

Victoria's absence from histories and cultural studies of Britain is a twentieth-century phenomenon, although she had already begun to disappear and her image to fragment during her reign. She disappeared when she became a widow in 1861, declining for several years to open Parliament, to travel in an open carriage, or to make public appearances of any kind except to dedicate statues of Prince Albert. But she vanished in a different sense throughout her career into the varieties of representation by which she became known. One image became ubiquitous at the time of her jubilees: the impassive but maternal widow whose profile – as Thomas Richards (1990) demonstrates – became as identifiable as any commercial logo. Victoria, in publishing selections from her journals in 1868 and 1884, contributed to a persona that seems in keeping with this static expressionless image. *Leaves from the Journal of Our Life in the Highlands*, and *More Leaves*, which made her a best-selling author, often read like merely dutiful recordings of pleasant activities, drained of their pleasure. Although she was an accomplished amateur watercolorist, her descriptions of Scotland resemble little more than embellished cartographies: "The scenery in *Loch Linnhe* was magnificent – such beautiful mountains. From *Loch Linnhe* we entered *Loch Eil*, and passed the entrance of *Loch Leven* to the right, at the end of which is *Glencoe*, so famous for its beautiful scenery, and for the horrible massacre of the Macdonalds in William III's time" (Victoria 1868: 94; 20 August 1847). With this iconic image proliferating in the colonized territories and within the British Isles, Victoria seemed to validate imperialism and render it harmless, even comforting. Not only did official statuary in far reaches of the empire – South Africa, Australia, India – testify to Britain's power, small Parian ware busts of the Queen graced mantles from Dublin to Durban. Owing in part to the Queen's longevity, a color lithograph of her at her Golden or Diamond Jubilee was just as likely to be found in an American parlor as an image of any American president.

Despite the prominence of the familiar stolid icon, other muted images worked their way into Victorians' values. In place of a determinate identity of a singular Queen Victoria, many conflicting ideas of her increasingly came to be used to model or to justify a wide variety of cultural practices and personal self-fashionings. Writers on Victoria like to point to the paradoxes she encompassed. In Giles St. Aubyn's words, "Nobody can hope to understand the Queen without recognising that her nature abounded in contradictions, and it can only be misleading to seek rational explanations for what was essentially illogical" (St. Aubyn 1991: 58). Intensely private in her domestic relations, the Queen displayed her privacy for public consumption; she was alone and surrounded; autocratic and abject; charitable to the poor, egocentric and abrupt to others; immensely hardworking and immensely self-indulgent. Her writings include both classic statements of docile femininity – "we women are not made for governing" – and the utterances of a person long habituated to getting her own way. In 1892, for instance, a woman requests permission for her daughter to write an article on the Royal Mews and Kennels. The Queen responds to her secretary, "This is a dreadful & dangerous woman. She better take the facts from the other papers." The next year a painter asks leave to engrave one of the pictures he painted for the Queen. "Certainly not," she writes, "They are not good and he is very pushing" (Ponsonby 1942: 48). Adrienne Munich explains some of the difficulties in conceptualizing Victoria's power by mapping the doctrine of the separate spheres on to the medieval concept of two monarchical bodies: "the Queen's maternal body belonged to the private sphere while her sovereign body belonged to the public sphere." These ideologies, she argues, created a "gap in representability" (Munich 1987: 265) that could be usefully filled by a proliferation of different Victorias.

These Victorias often occurred simultaneously, for Victoria was capable of gesturing to both spheres at once. When she was widowed and flamboyantly sequestered, she explained her absence from public view by recourse not to the expected delicacy of a bereft widow, but to her royal duties. It was not "the Queen's *sorrow* that keeps her secluded," she explained to Sir Robert Martin, author of the six-volume authorized biography of the Prince Consort.

It is her *overwhelming work* and her health, which is greatly shaken by her sorrow, and the totally overwhelming amount of work and responsibility – work which she feels really wears her out . . . From the hour she gets out of bed till she gets into it again there is work, work, work, – letter boxes, questions, &c., which are dreadfully exhausting – and if she had not comparative rest and quiet in the evening she would most likely not be *alive*. Her brain is constantly overtaxed. (Martin 1908: 28–29, quoted in Strachey 1921: 215)

Victorians understood the ideology of work as well as that of true womanhood. The image of the lonely Queen laboring over the dispatch boxes despite her desolation fitted both plots at once. Victoria's style conveys her feminine superfluity of emotion while her action conveys the Victorian work ethic.

A handful of recent studies of Victoria have embraced her multiplicity. In *Defining Voices*, volume one of *The Woman Question: Society and Literature in Britain and America, 1837–1883* (1983), Elizabeth K. Helsinger, Robin Lauterbach Sheets, and William Veeder opened a feminist discussion of Victoria by examining how in her writing and her actions she both endorsed and undermined the so-called Victorian ideal of feminine asexual domesticity. Notably, this work succeeds by embracing Victoria's paradoxicalness: "She represents her era so adequately because the conflicting elements of her personality characterize the age itself" (Helsinger *et al.* 1983: 64). Cynthia Huff's 1988 essay on the Queen's diaries similarly finds paradoxes in the merging of public and private. Dorothy Thompson's *Queen Victoria: the Woman, the Monarchy, and the People* (1990) is the first extended study to ask feminist questions about Victoria and to explore her cultural significance from a historian's point of view. Thompson explains the almost universal acceptance of "a female in the highest office" in a "century in which male dominion and the separation of spheres . . . became entrenched in the ideology of all classes" by claiming that very separation enhanced her sway. At a time when the future of the monarchy was at risk, "her youth and gender . . . helped to reconcile many to traditional monarchical loyalties which, it should be remembered, included a strong folk memory – perhaps more a mythology – of good times for England under previous women rulers, from Boadicea through Good Queen Bess to Queen Anne" (Thompson 1990: xviii–xix).

Margaret Homans's work on Victoria discusses the paradoxes of her power. Early in her career, at a time of "enormous and sometimes self-contradictory anxieties about female rule," Victoria found in representations of her marriage "an effective strategy both for handling the public relations problem of female rule and, perhaps more important, for completing England's transition to parliamentary democracy and symbolic monarchy" (Homans 1993: 7, 2). Throughout her career, "Queen Victoria gave away her power in order to have it" (Homans 1994: 251); she achieved ascendency in her subjects' minds by appearing not to rule. As a widow, she maintained her monarchy by making a spectacle of her absence (Homans 1997). Adrienne Munich's *Queen Victoria's Secrets* (1996, incorporating Munich 1984 and 1987) investigates the way Queen Victoria performed the age's significant cultural codes, giving them her own personal signature. She meant different things to different groups, but her inspired performances ultimately made it possible for multitudes to think that they were doing the Queen's work, whatever they did – from explorations to ethnography, to "little" imperial wars, to having portraits made of their pets. Almost everyone attended in their imagination what Kipling called "the widow's parties," his term for the imperial wars but applicable also to the spectacular celebrations of her reign, including the jubilees in 1887 and 1897. Moreover, in the domestic and trivial connotations of "parties," one finds the kind of sexism that has made this extraordinarily complex figure easier to ignore as an active power in history. It is no accident that feminist scholars have been the first to take Victoria seriously. Her importance emerges with the emergence of feminist studies of culture.

This volume seeks not so much to assemble Victoria's diffused parts into a coherent whole – something that could be done only in an illusory way for any human subject – but to "remake" her diffuseness into a series of apprehensible and legible moments. Victoria is a model for middle-class women, as in Alison Booth's chapter on "role model anthologies" and in Sharon Aronofsky Weltman's chapter on Ruskin's domestic queens. On a larger scale, she serves to reflect ideals of nationhood, as in Elizabeth Langland's chapter on Victoria's role in shaping and promulgating the Victorian myth of ethnic Englishness; in Mary Loeffelholz's account of the "constitution of nineteenth-century American nationalism *vis-à-vis* Great Britain"; and in Robin L. Bott's chapter on how Liliuokalani, the Queen of Hawaii, imitates Victoria's style of rule to solidify her authority in the face of American colonization. Often, Victoria is ostensibly respected while being criticized indirectly, as in Dagni Bredesen's chapter on the insubordinate invocation of the "widdy" by Kipling's imperial soldiers or in Maria Jerinic's chapter on the dangers of female power when rendered exotic by the figure of the Rani of Jhansi. Sometimes her representation is entirely negative, as in Janet Winston's chapter on an Adrienne Kennedy work in which Victoria colonizes the mind of a present-day black woman. Other chapters emphasize the fashioning of her persona in positive or negative relation to cultural ideals of girlhood, womanhood, or queenship: Gail Turley Houston's chapter on the didactic fiction Victoria read as a child, fiction that modeled the law of female subordination that her reign was both to resist and to endorse; Karen Chase and Michael Levenson's chapter on her baffling of her subjects' and her ministers' expectations of her early in her reign; Susan P. Casteras's chapter on early portraits that both defy and conform to standard images of girlhood; or Nicola J. Watson's chapter on representations of Queen Elizabeth that indirectly and inversely create portraits of Victoria. But in all these cases, as in others, Victoria does not have a fixed identity to which others accede or object: instead, her image is created even as it is read, and destabilized even when it is treated as monolithic.

Of course there are common themes. Because Victoria was and is widely understood to be a domestic monarch who modeled ordinary middle-class womanhood even while she presided as empress over one quarter of the planet's territories, nearly all the chapters touch either on her utility for promulgating this ideology or on her failure to support it, or both at once. As a domestic, maternal, and seemingly middle-class queen she played out many aspects of the era's crucial yet self-contradictory ideology of "separate spheres." "Of all Victorian women," writes Houston, "the Queen had the greatest opportunity to resist but the most to gain by appearing to conform to the dominant Victorian pattern for femininity." For Americans in Loeffelholz's account, her role as peacemaker during the Civil War gradually merged with her tamer profile as ordinary matron, a role into which they saw her disappearing by the end of her reign. Casteras shows how portraits of Victoria represented her as both girlish and regal, and Chase and Levenson explore contradictions between her royal and domestic identities in an early crisis about her official household. Several chapters note the use of Victoria to criticize what some subjects saw as excesses of female power – hers or others': "the Rani's status . . . as primary insurgent," writes Jerinic, "indicates a British discomfort with ruling women and consequently with their own Queen." For the Queen of Hawaii, according to Bott, copying Victoria's glamorous excesses proved a political mistake. Conversely, Booth demonstrates that Victoria became a "role model" for female virtue only when writers downplayed her power and the narrative interest of her life story; for Watson, the Victorian denigration of Elizabeth I's sexual and political aggressiveness provided reassurance about their own queen's unthreatening virtues. For Weltman, by contrast, the power of domestic women is enhanced by their assimilation to a queen regnant. Two chapters – those by Langland and Winston – focus on her exemplary or oppressive whiteness, her imperial imposture as an Anglo-Saxon ethnic model. "As icon of empire," writes Winston, "Victoria comes to represent in twentieth-century literature both colonialism's excesses and the powers and limits of colonial representation."

Perhaps nowhere more vividly does Queen Victoria's influence live on than in the current English monarchy. The Victorian Queen haunts the English royal imagination; she has long shaped the idea of how good queens behave. According to their various dispositions, different members of the House of Windsor follow precedents set by Victoria. Consciously and unconsciously they pay her homage. Elizabeth II, Queen Victoria's great-great-granddaughter, seems at least partly conscious of her identification with her progenitor. The film honoring her fortieth year on the throne features her showing a visitor a page from Queen Victoria's journal. The explicit reference to Victoria brings to the fore what the entire film demonstrates: that Elizabeth's royal persona draws upon Victoria's methods of being a queen, from its carefully managed public appearances to its insistence upon the monarchy as an articulator of moral values. Elizabeth sets an example to her people by her restrained, moral behavior and her visiting of philanthropic institutions: hospitals, retirement homes, and orphanages. Projecting an image as asexual as Queen Victoria, Elizabeth II seems respectable by virtue of her always sensible shoes, her matronly handbag, and her seeming imperviousness to the winds of fashion.

By the end of her reign, Queen Victoria had become a shorthand for the firm virtues named for her age: family values, integrity of one's word, and earnest disapproval of levity. Considering her son irresponsible, she refused to give up the throne to him. Like Elizabeth II, she experienced trouble with her children's sexual escapades. Of her four sons, two, Edward Albert (Bertie), Prince of Wales, and Alfred (Affie) posed the most flamboyant problems. Bertie's taste for a fast set and for womanizing kept him in the public eye. "Beware of London and Marlborough House," Victoria warned her granddaughter, Princess Victoria of Hesse, about the houses where the Prince of Wales entertained what came to be known notoriously as "the Marlborough House set" (Victoria 1985: 282; 22 August 1883). The lesser-known Prince Alfred, without the charm but with the vices of his older brother, caused Victoria despair. Even the prospect of marriage to a good woman might not rein him in, she thought: "I wrote to him that I hoped and prayed he felt the very solemn and serious step he was going to take, how I prayed he would make the dear, amiable, young girl . . . happy and that she alone must have his heart and love – and all old habits must be given up. But he has said nothing in return! Oh if he only does break with old habits! It would be awful if he did not" (Victoria 1985: 234; November 13, 1873, to the Crown Princess of Prussia). Much like her descendant, Victoria found that her children did not follow in her virtuous footsteps: "You will find as the children grow up that as a rule children are a bitter disappointment – their greatest object being to do precisely what their parents do not wish and have anxiously tried to prevent" (Victoria 1985: 241; December 29, 1875, to the Crown Princess of Prussia). As if the two queens' own sexuality were transferred to their offspring, what seemed repressed in themselves returned in their children. Malcolm Potts and William Potts argue that Victoria was a bastard, fathered with the complicity of the Duke of Kent who knew that he was sterile and wished to produce an heir to the throne by any means. Apart from the story's possible interest to history, its journalistic coverage assimilates earlier royal behavior to tabloid reportage about the House of Windsor.

Despite their spectacular failure to live up to the model of marital felicity provided by Queen Victoria and Prince Albert's marriage, Diana, Princess of Wales, and Sarah, Duchess of York, nonetheless have included ingredients of Victoria's own recipes for royalty into their self-presentations. If Princess Diana cannot follow Victoria in her marital bliss, she can effectively portray herself as one who cares for ordinary people. A 1995 press release reported that the Princess sneaks out of her apartment in Kensington Palace (where Princess Victoria spent her childhood) disguised in jeans and a baseball cap to visit the seriously ill in nearby hospitals. Queen Victoria was often represented visiting wounded soldiers in Netley Hospital and sick cottagers in the Highlands. "I always feel drawn to the sick-bed of anyone, to be of use and comfort," Princess Diana's Victorian model confided to her Uncle Leopold, king of the Belgians, only a few years after the death of her husband (Victoria 1985: 189; 8 June 1865). Allowing for the slippage of time, Princess Diana's changed marital status allows her, also, to claim special connections to the unfortunate as she seems to echo Victoria in her words to a reporter: "There are hundreds of patients who are there without their own loved ones and need a human presence. I really love helping. I seem to draw strength from them" (*Newsday*, December 1995).

More surprisingly because more paradoxical, the Duchess of York claims a "psychic link" to Queen Victoria. Before the scandals that eventually led to her marital separation the Duchess coauthored a book, *Victoria and Albert: a Family Life at Osborne House*, because she was drawn to the Victorian royal family's intimate home life. Victoria represents more to the Duchess of York than simply the matriarch of a happy family. She believes that Victoria guided her while she researched for her book, *Travels with Queen Victoria*. "Several times she stopped to sketch a scene, only to discover the Queen had been there before. Once she impulsively detoured from her route to visit some villages – and found the Queen had done the same." From reading the Queen's diaries after her trip, the Duchess "realised obviously Queen Victoria wanted to show me where they had stopped." Like Princess Diana, the Duchess of York finds her imitation of Victoria therapeutic; and, after reading aloud the Queen's diaries, "in my Queen Victoria voice," she has fallen for her familiar: "I adore her," she confesses. "I think she's got this huge strength, this great will and yet this soft romantic side" (*International Express*, October 6, 1993: 2).

Victoria stood for the uprightness Princess Diana and the Duchess of York adopt, a trait that was, for the Queen, physical as well as moral.

"Promise me one thing, dear; don't stoop when you sit and write, it is very bad for you now, and later it will make you remember how straight I always sit, which enables me to write without fatigue at all times" (Victoria 1985: 106; June 29, 1858, to Princess Frederick William). Yet she has also been held responsible for the ills suffered by the inheritors of her reign. In her role as matchmaker of the royalty of Europe, Queen Victoria was seen as spreading contagion: the hemophilia descending through the royal genes was traced to her. Because Victoria's descendants populated the royal houses of Europe, the physical disease became a metaphor for a political one. Queen Victoria became the imagined cause of European disputes – between her grandson-in-law, Nicholas II, Tsar of Russia, and her grandson, Wilhelm II, Kaiser of Germany, for example. In addition, her imperialist sympathies became identified with the worst of British chauvinism. So powerfully has her image performed in its various theaters that she has been blamed for European – indeed for global – disorders. Queen Victoria's legacies continue to inspire new contradictory formulations, new paradoxical myths.

PART I

*Nation-making*

# Nation and nationality: Queen Victoria in the developing narrative of Englishness

## Elizabeth Langland

Recently, prominent politicians, Margaret Thatcher notable among them, have called for the English to return to Victorian values as a kind of shortcut for solving complicated national problems. What such appeals mask are the vexed complexities of the icon, Queen Victoria, and the age, England in the nineteenth century, to which they allude so simply. These appeals rely for their power on a simplification and codification of nineteenth-century images and narratives that are themselves internally fraught. And the figure that seems to ground these narratives – Victoria herself – is she that most disturbs ideas of what it means to be both English and Victorian. This chapter examines how representations of the monarch's position in English life and politics complicate developing narratives of Englishness and Victorianism in the nineteenth century. It explores intricate connections among images and ideas, foregrounding varied prominent strands of what is, necessarily, a rich and entangled network.

### VICTORIA AND ENGLISHNESS

In 1701 Daniel Defoe wrote *The True Born Englishman*, a verse satire which defended William of Orange against those who said that the English should not have a Dutch king. Defoe's proposition was that no such thing as a true-born Englishman existed. In his words, "We have been Europe's sink, the jakes where she Voids all her offal outcast progeny." However, ideas of "Englishness" and the "Englishman" could not be eradicated simply through mockery, and they took only a firmer hold throughout the eighteenth and nineteenth centuries, achieving a new clarity and definition through representations of Queen Victoria.

In Victoria, a national idea finds its articulation through gender, race, class, and ethnicity. As woman, mother, wife, and widow, Empress of

India, and Queen of England, Victoria becomes a site for the concept's simultaneous consolidation and contradiction. Certainly, her father, the Duke of Kent, alive to the significance of nationalistic sentiment, early recognized the importance of birthing and raising his daughter in England, exposing his pregnant wife to danger through insisting that his child would "at whatever cost first open her eyes on English soil." And the Duke's measures – which included eliciting a promise from her mother that, whatever the hardships, Victoria would be raised in England – produced a monarch who was, in her biographer Elizabeth Longford's words, "uncompromisingly English" (Longford 1964: 263). Stanley Weintraub echoes this assessment in claiming that during her reign Victoria "became England," a conclusion cited recently by John Lucas in support of his argument that "the queen became identified as an embodiment of England during the latter half of the nineteenth century," a process involving "not merely the creation of Victoria as England but of England as Victorian" (Lucas 1987–88: 64). I find the latter proposition – "England as Victorian" – more troubling than the former, but both must be more carefully examined for the cultural conflicts these formulations elide. Lucas sets out to argue that Victoria as "a complex female figure is produced as the emblem of England and of what are identified as English values" without acknowledging that to be an emblem of England and to embody the essence of Englishness (which is how I read his phrase "identified as English values") are not the same thing.[1] I will argue that the concepts of "Victorianism" and "Englishness" have a different scope in the nineteenth century and a different investment in Victoria as icon.

Victoria's contradictory inscription as ruler and mother/wife facilitated the process by which women, and the domestic sphere they "governed," were amalgamated to England's imperialist mission yet also excluded from it by a positioning of the female body as ground and origin for male achievement. In this development, England itself emerges as a feminine Britannia, the fertile soil of her English sons' achievements, and Englishness takes on an increasingly masculine construction. Certainly, by the early twentieth century, the association of England with ground or soil is very well established. In "The Soldier," Rupert Brooke readily amalgamates earth with England and posits his own body as English soil:

> If I should die, think only this of me:
>   That there's some corner of a foreign field
> That is forever England . . . (Brooke 1941: 23)

Thomas Hardy's "Drummer Hodge" proleptically parodies such sentiments:

> Yet portion of that unknown plain
>   Will Hodge for ever be;
> His homely Northern breast and brain
>   Grow to some Southern tree . . . (Hardy 1925: 83)

Lucas cites an episode in which "Eleanor Farjeon asked Edward
Thomas why he had decided to fight in the First World War" and "he
explained himself by kneeling down, scooping up some earth, and
holding it out to her" (Lucas 1987–88: 63–64). However, such connections did not wait until the early twentieth century to be articulated.
Victoria's father, in fact, anticipates all of these in boasting that he had
"fulfilled [his] duties in establishing the *English birth* of my child, and
giving it material nutriment on the soil of Old England."[2]

Certainly, English identity was at issue when Victoria assumed the
throne and chose as husband the German-speaking Prince Albert of
Saxe-Coburg-Gotha. Lytton Strachey's 1921 biography of Queen
Victoria captures national fears in its remark that "what was immediately and distressingly striking about Albert's face and figure and whole
demeanor was his un-English look" (Strachey 1921: 154). Contemporaneous anxieties about the royal family's national allegiance find expression in the journal *Punch*, which revealed itself to be particularly
xenophobic in its satiric depictions of Albert: "Mr. Punch's criticism
of Victoria and the court stemmed in part from . . . his 'Anti-
Albertianism,'" which originated largely in "Albert's Germanism and his
attraction to foreign cultures" (Fredeman 1987: 51). Mr. Punch also suffered some spasms of anxiety on the birth of the Princess Royal, whom
he satirically depicted as being instilled with "'an utter contempt for
everything English, except those effigies of her illustrious Mother which
emanate from the Mint'" (Fredeman 1987: 50). However, the subsequent
arrival of the Prince of Wales elated him because there were now "'two
cradles between the Crown of England and the White Horse of
Hanover'" (Fredeman 1987: 50). Mr. Punch's antagonism toward Albert
abated only after the success of the Great Exhibition in 1851, a celebration that Victoria, like *Punch*, credited at once to Albert and to England,
enthusing in her journal: "God bless my dearest Albert, and my dear
Country which has shown itself so great today" (*Victoria* 1985: 84).

Victoria's own determined linking of Albert and English interests
perhaps facilitated gradual refigurations of the Queen and her Consort
as Anglo-Saxons, "guardians of ancient British liberties" in British

paintings of the 1850s and 1860s (Strong 1978: 44). Art Historian Sir Roy Strong points out that "The Anglo-Saxons were after all German. No wonder that at the tail end of the cult William Theed should have chosen in 1868 to depict Albert and Victoria in an "astounding tableau" that "could as easily be relabeled 'Alfred the Great and his Queen', so interchangeable had they become" (Strong 1978: 118). This representation of Victoria both fueled and fed off a popular impulse at mid-century to locate the very essence of Englishness in Anglo-Saxon roots. But it is important to note what Strong does not remark – that in the refiguration of the royal couple as Anglo-Saxons, Victoria is consort, Albert the king. Theed reconceives Victoria as clinging wife rather than stalwart monarch, an imagery that resonates with other iconic depictions of the royal family as embodying the "bourgeois ideals of family life" (Strong 1978: 44): "Kemble, the Anglo-Saxon historian, described her as 'fearless in the holy circle of her domestic happiness" (Strong 1978: 152). Stanley Weintraub dubs Victoria "queenly yet middle-class at heart" (Weintraub 1987: xii).

Images that depict Victoria as middle-class mother derogate from representations of her as queen regnant. They position her within Victorian culture as ground for her sons' achievements and adventures rather than the stimulus for them. Roy Strong notes differences between representations of the Elizabethan and Victorian ages, calling attention to the freedom and status enjoyed by Elizabethan women of the upper classes, "a freedom and status unknown to the women of Victorian Britain." He adds, "*Pace* Victoria herself, [Victorian women's] kingdom was the fireside and the nursery" (Strong 1978: 154). But Strong's exemption of Victoria is somewhat illogical because representations of the Queen herself serve as a prominent source of depictions of "Victorian" women. At least we must acknowledge the degree to which representations of England's "maternal monarchy," in Adrienne Munich's coinage, are iconographically complicated (Munich 1987: 265).

A significant literary work of this period plays with similar tropes, figuring contemporary England through an Anglo-Saxon past and at the same time establishing a gendered ethos of Englishness that becomes instrumental in empire-building. I refer to *Tom Brown's Schooldays*, published in 1857. Thomas Hughes's novel is born of the same conception of national character that produced the apocryphal "Wellington *mot*," as it is called: to wit, that the battle of Waterloo was won on the playing fields of Eton.[3] The year that *Tom Brown's Schooldays* came out, the *Saturday Review* noted that, "It is in these sports that the character of a

boy is formed. It is from them that the readiness, pluck, and self-dependence of the British gentleman is principally caught" (quoted in Haley
1978: 161). In *The Healthy Body and Victorian Culture*, Bruce Haley explains
that, "In 1857 that line of thought was quite new but was catching on
everywhere: the function of a public school was to turn out gentlemen;
a gentleman was a man of character; character consisted of readiness,
pluck, and self-dependence; and these virtues were best learned on the
playing field" (Haley 1978: 161).

If those were initially the attributes only of gentlemen, they quickly
became rearticulated and expanded as the elements of a national character. E. M. Forster identified the character of the English in his 1928
essay, "Notes on the English Character," as "essentially middle-class,"
embodying such traits as "solidity, caution, integrity, efficiency. Lack of
imagination, hypocrisy" (Forster 1936: 3). That is his "First Note"; his
second stipulates that "Just as the heart of England is the middle classes,
so the heart of the middle classes is the public school system. This extraordinary institution is local. It does not even exist all over the British Isles.
It is unknown in Ireland, almost unknown in Scotland . . . it remains
unique, because it was created by the Anglo-Saxon middle classes, and
can flourish only where they flourish" (Forster 1936: 3–4). In Forster's
articulations we notice some significant, and by now familiar, conjunc-
tions: English character takes its shape from Anglo-Saxon roots, finds its
embodiment in the Victorian middle classes, and locates its most distinctive expression in English public schools and imperialism.[4]

What, then, of a queen who has been successfully refigured as Anglo-
Saxon and bourgeois? Can she be made to embody an Englishness that
is articulated through a public school ethos? Although questions of race,
ethnicity, and class could all be reinterpreted, gender, it seems, creates a
fault line along which national identity is precariously established.

*Tom Brown's Schooldays* sets forth several dimensions of a developing
narrative of Englishness in the mid-Victorian period. The novel opens
with a history of the Browns that positions the family as responsible for
the greatness of England: "For centuries, in their quiet, dogged, home-
spun way, they have been subduing the earth in most English counties,
and leaving their mark in American forests and Australian uplands"
(Hughes 1971: 13). At the point the narrative begins the Browns are
"scattered over the whole empire on which the sun never sets" and
their general diffusion is "the chief cause of that empire's stability"
(Hughes 1971: 15). The tale is set in the Vale of the White Horse, a
locale dear to the hearts of those who "care for England," a "sacred

ground to Englishmen . . . For this is the actual place where our Alfred won his great battle" (Hughes 1971: 16, 19). The invocation of a heroic Anglo-Saxon past constitutive of England and English virtues recalls the positioning of England's monarch in that same frame. And Hughes's novel further underscores the ways in which women are reduced within that frame (as was Victoria herself) to wives and mothers. Women figure only minimally in Tom Brown's world, as individuals against whose "petticoat government" the boy conducts a "war of independence," so that his mother finally acknowledges his "inaptitude for female guidance" (Hughes 1971: 33). This is a world shaped by old country "veasts" with backswording and wrestling and racing, "something to try the muscles of men's bodies, and the endurance of their hearts," a world of "old English home duties" and the "healthy sound expression of English country holiday-making" (Hughes 1971: 42, 43). A world where "English mothers," as ground and material nutriment (like the soil of old England), fortify their sons with a love "as fair and whole as human love can be," in order that a "young and true heart" can achieve the full realization and expression of English values (Hughes 1971: 57).

Englishness is here articulated differentially through gender. For women it consists in passive virtues like perfect self-sacrifice, "love and tenderness and purity" (Hughes 1971: 288); Englishmen, in contrast, are invested with all the active virtues that have formed the empire. Mr. Brown stipulates as specific goals for Tom's education that his son turn out "a brave, helpful, truth-telling Englishman" (Hughes 1971: 66). The narrator remarks of Tom's journey to Rugby that he has "the consciousness of silent endurance, so dear to every Englishman – of standing out against something, and not giving in" (Hughes 1971: 67). And the first rugby match at school is imaged in terms of battle and heroic tradition: "Meet them like Englishmen, you School-house boys, and charge them home. Now is the time to shew what mettle is in you – and there shall be a warm seat by the hall fire, and honour, and lots of bottled beer to-night, for him who does his duty in the next half-hour" (Hughes 1971: 93). This pattern culminates, perhaps predictably, in a celebration of fighting and Englishness: "After all, what would life be without fighting, I should like to know? From the cradle to the grave, fight, rightly understood, is the business, the real, highest, honestest business of every son of man" (Hughes 1971: 218). Further, "fighting with fists is the natural and English way for English boys to settle their quarrels" (Hughes 1971: 231). And, finally, "if you do fight,

fight it out; and don't give in while you can stand and see" (Hughes 1971: 232).

At this point, women, as embodiment of the mother country England, have been written out of the script of Englishness; the public school world exists oblivious to them except as the occasional angelic inspiration; they are mothers, wives, and widows who bear England's sons, and then suffer silently and endure patiently.

This representation is not very far from those of Victoria as mother of her nation. Two poems by Barrett Browning on the occasion of Victoria's coronation and a poem and jubilee ode by Tennyson several years later demonstrate a remarkably similar imagery. In "The Young Queen" and "Victoria's Tears," Barrett Browning images the child-queen as mother of her nation – whose "grateful isles / Shall give thee back their smiles / And as thy mother joys in thee, in them shall *thou* rejoice" (Barrett Browning 1973: 11, 108) – and as the embodiment of feminine sympathy whose tears influence her nation more effectively than the "tyrant's sceptre" (Barrett Browning 1973: 11, 109).

First fourteen, and then fifty years later Tennyson draws on the same tropes when he celebrates Victoria in "To the Queen" (1851) and "An Ode in Honour of the Jubilee of Queen Victoria" (1887). The former poem ostensibly praises Victoria as ruler, entrusted with the "care that yokes with empire," but it concludes by emphasizing her role as static feminine icon ("Mother, Wife, and Queen") while the responsibility for initiating policy devolves on her "statesmen":

> Her court was pure; her life serene;
> > God gave her peace; her land reposed;
> > A thousand claims to reverence closed
> In her as Mother, Wife, and Queen;
>
> And statesmen at her council met
> > Who knew the seasons when to take
> > Occasion by the hand, and make
> The bounds of freedom wider yet
>
> By shaping some august decree
> > Which kept her throne unshaken still,
> > Broad-based upon her people's will,
> And compass'd by the inviolate sea. (Tennyson 1898: 1–2)

Victoria is directed by her statesmen, who represent "her people's will."

The "Jubilee Ode," much parodied in its day, is probably some of Tennyson's worst poetry – prosy and preachy – but it is significant for us in the ease with which it trots out clichés of Victorian womanhood.

Tennyson celebrates Victoria for possessing

> Nothing of the lawless, of the despot,
> Nothing of the vulgar, or vainglorious,
> All is gracious, gentle, great and queenly.
>
>                 . . .
>
> Queen, as true to womanhood as Queenhood,
> Glorying in the glories of her people,
> Sorrowing with the sorrows of the lowest!
>
>                 (Tennyson 1898: 529)[5]

These poetic images resonate with the portrayals of the Queen in portraiture of the early and middle Victorian period. In his article "Portraits
of the Queen," Ira Nadel comments that "Victoria's portraits . . . are
conscientious efforts to record the certainty and assuredness of the
Queen and what she and her family represent: the domestic, bourgeois
values of stability, comfort, and security" (Nadel 1987: 170). Nadel,
however, identifies three distinctive phases in the development of
Victoria's portraits, "each related to a different period of her life, and
emphasizing a different set of iconographic elements" (Nadel 1987: 173).
The first phase, "Princess/Queen," "suggests domesticity as well as sentiment" (Nadel 1987: 175); the second, "Queen and Mother," becomes
"insistently historic and domestic," emphasizing Victoria and Albert as
Anglo-Saxons guarding ancient British liberties (the icon Sir Roy Strong
also identified), an image which "reflected the domestic bliss they projected on to the nation." Curiously, the third phase appears to contra-
vene the previous images. Following the widow's seclusion and
withdrawal from public life, portrait painters felt it imperative to respond
explicitly "to public criticism over Victoria's neglect of public duties following the Prince's death" and to depict the Queen no longer as "idealized regent or mother," but as "the resolute guardian and embodiment
of English power" (Nadel 1987: 179). Thus, portraits of Victoria in this
last phase would seem to contradict what I have been arguing about the
way the Queen is portrayed in a developing narrative of Englishness.
And, indeed, Nadel acknowledges that, "The image of the stern
monarch, renewing her claim on the monarchy, contradicts, of course,
the maternal and self-conscious figure in the portraits from her middle
period" (Nadel 1987: 182).

Surprisingly, too, the iconography of the late portraits seems to run
counter to literary representations, which, as we have already seen in
Tennyson's "Jubilee Ode," tended to deploy conventional feminized
images. Is there a profitable way to explore these apparent contradic-

tions? In fact, the 1875 von Angeli portrait of the Queen, in which Nadel locates the new iconography of regal power, also embodies these same contradictions, a fact Nadel acknowledges but does not investigate. Nadel notes that "wearing a black dress accentuated by a double strand of pearls, large ruby bracelet, and white handkerchief, Victoria is a portrait in contrasts. At once she is the grieving widow and the Empress exerting her power" (Nadel 1987: 179). Thus, if she is an icon for England, it is still mother England, the Britannia to which John Lucas points in his essay "Love of England: the Victorians and Patriotism." Lucas argues that the successive images of Victoria became "merged in other significant images: of Liberty and Britannia" (Lucas 1987–88: 64): "Victoria as Liberty may be under threat and so expect chivalric defense; Victoria as Britannia may have a warrior-like invulnerability and so command deferential awe" (Lucas 1987–88: 65).

Portraits of Victoria as Liberty and Britannia find literary echoes that suggest how even this puissant icon becomes complicit in conventional feminine values when England is articulated separately from Englishness. As we have seen, in this gendered division woman becomes the body that nourishes true Englishmen and that subsequently demands their loyal defense.[6] George Eliot's essay "The Modern Hep! Hep! Hep!" provides a narrative of this process. Purportedly from the hand of Theophrastus Such, this essay sets forth Englishness in terms derived from the "seafaring, invading, self-asserting men [who] were the English of old time" (Eliot n.d.: 131) because "the eminence, nobleness of a people," depends on "this living force of sentiment in common which makes a national consciousness" (Eliot n.d.: 132). It is, however, the immediately succeeding comment that is most telling here: "Nations so moved will resist conquest with the very breasts of their women" (Eliot n.d.: 132). Apparently, nation is so precious that men will sacrifice even their women in its defense. Logically, then, nation is herself that most sacred feminine figure requiring defense, and her men enact their pride of nationality in defending her. This passage and others like it work at a differential gendering of nation and nationality that accords well, I would argue, with the iconography of Queen Victoria. Woman, Queen, Mother England – Britannia is that which must be defended by stalwart sons animated by a consciousness of their "national life" or Englishness:

The only point in this connection on which Englishmen are agreed is, that England itself shall not be subject to foreign rule. The fiery resolve to resist invasion, though with an improvised array of pitchforks, is felt to be virtuous, and worthy of a historic people. Why? Because there is a national life in our veins.

Because there is something specifically English which we feel to be supremely worth striving for, worth dying for, rather than living to renounce it. (Eliot n.d.: 144)

A woman and a queen, Victoria was gradually shaped into an icon of England in ways that left the narrative of Englishness to be articulated through discourses of masculinity.

### VICTORIA AND VICTORIANISM

The first part of my argument has forwarded the proposition that in Victorian England different and gendered sites developed for the cultural investments that inform the concepts of nation and nationality. But what, then, we might inquire, of the age to which she gave her name: the Victorian? How is the concept of Victorianism related to Victoria herself and how is it differently inflected from the idea of Englishness in the nineteenth century?

Obviously this question cannot be easily or comprehensively answered and its very formulation poses the danger – one also present in my discussion of Englishness – of encouraging oversimplification and generalization. Victorianism itself has become a catch-all term for movements, behaviors, and beliefs that extend beyond England's borders. G. M. Young, looking back on the Victorian age from the perspective of the early twentieth century, admits that "the more carefully one studies the years between the death of William IV and the accession of Edward VII, the more difficult it becomes to find anything to which the word Victorian can be correctly and exclusively applied. Much to which we commonly give the name turns out, on a closer acquaintance, to be simply nineteenth century, or simply European" (Young 1962: 158–59). Or he reminds us that "the Victorian age, as we call it, is the insular phase of a movement common to the whole of Western Europe and its offshoots beyond the seas" (Young 1962: 110–11). In fact, the concept has become so broad that its association with the person Victoria may seem purely adventitious – a historical convenience. Although aware of the dangers of generalization, Margaret Homans has recently called attention to a corollary problem, the fact that little, if any, notice has been paid to the figure who gave her name to an age. Indeed, the Victorian period is persistently and commonly discussed without even an allusion to Victoria.[7] Homans argues that "while Victoria may have been subject to an ideology over which no individual had control, it is impossible not to think that she had some active hand in shaping the ideology that bears her name" (Homans 1994: 245). Homans's goal, therefore, as well as my own cautious attempt here, is to begin "to put Victoria back into Victorian" (Homans 1994: 258n11).

I have already indicated that early portraiture of Victoria cast her as mother – of a nation, of a family, of a nation as family. The domestication of the monarch helped produce and was itself produced by an ideology of domesticity that is often seized upon when commentators seek something quintessential to define the last half of the nineteenth century in England. And, certainly, here we may locate one prominent intersection of Englishness and Victorianism. In his essay "Tempus Actum," Young puzzles over the concept of Victorianism and confesses that "the truth is that much of what we call Victorianism is a picture at second hand, a satirical picture drawn by the Victorians themselves. The word does undoubtedly mean something, but what it means has to be built up by going behind the criticism, the invention, and the caricature, and examining the originals" (Young 1962: 159). What Young calls an "origin" is precisely that generally privileged construction of the concept that we are looking for. His search culminates, perhaps predictably, in "the ordinary educated, evangelical household [as] in many ways the pivot of Victorian life" (Young 1962: 160), by which he also means the "respectable" family (Young 1962: 122).[8] Later he claims of this period that the "family counts for everything" (Young 1962: 122). This ideology has been remarkably durable; in his book *Victoria's Year*, Richard Stein has identified this adulation of domesticity as the heart of Victorianism and its parodies.

Certainly Victoria has lent her name to *this* familial ideology of Victorian life. Indeed, the virginal young queen embodied a dramatic change from her predecessors, and she was readily seized upon as an icon of emergent bourgeois values. Writing in 1937 on the centenary of Victoria's accession to the throne, Young remarked of the period that the "transference of the Crown from an elderly, undignified, and slightly crazy sailor to a girl endowed with remarkable self-possession and much force of character, could hardly be without its picturesque circumstances" (Young 1962: 24). For him, it represented a "waft of Arcadia" (Young 1962: 25).[9] Associations of conventional propriety and familial devotion accumulated around Victoria despite the fact that, as Dorothy Thompson points out, "if the stereotypical Victorian woman was well-mannered, self-effacing, demure and devoid of passion, Queen Victoria was so far from the stereotype as to be almost its opposite" (Thompson 1990: 44). Indeed, Victoria is memorable for her distress at being forced repeatedly to bear children; she described herself as "furious" when she learned of her first pregnancy, complained that an "ugly baby is a very nasty object," and always expressed distaste for "that terrible frog-like action" of newborns (Victoria 1964: 191). Albert, more maternal, was continually admonishing the Queen to be more of a mother and less of a monarch with her nine children. But the public conferred upon Victoria an image of itself which confirmed both the emergence and importance of middle-class domesticity. That self-portrait was facilitated by the "diffusion of cheap printed words and pictures [that brought] the image of the monarch and her family regularly into the consciousness of her subjects" (Thompson 1990: 139). In 1867 Walter Bagehot summarized the effect of familiarizing the populace with a wifely and maternal Victoria: "A *family* on the throne is an interesting idea. It brings down the pride of sovereignty to the level of petty life."[10] Albert's death in 1861 further solidified Victoria's bourgeois image because she "refused ever again to wear the robes of state, appearing in versions of widow's weeds" (Thompson 1990: 141).

Thus, as this analysis suggests, the markers of domesticity that helped define Victorianism for both the nineteenth and twentieth centuries also ultimately distinguished it from emerging concepts of Englishness that accumulated around more imperial and masculine representations. To the extent that Victoria embodied wifehood and maternality, she became the imagined essence of Victorianism but, therefore, not the quintessence of Englishness.

We may examine more fully the way gendered qualities were shaping a split between Victorianism and Englishness by continuing with the writings of Young and Lytton Strachey. These two prominent intellectuals were both born in Victorian England: Strachey in 1880, and Young in 1882. They thus experienced the last two decades of Victoria's rule but also lived through the early modern period during which images of the Queen and her age continued to be consolidated along certain gender lines. In his biography of Queen Victoria, Strachey writes of her early life that "it was her misfortune that the mental atmosphere which surrounded her during these years of adolescence was almost entirely feminine. No father, no brother, was there to break in upon the gentle monotony of the daily round with impetuosity, with rudeness, with careless laughter and wafts of freedom from the outside world" (Strachey 1921: 45). He adds, "henceforward, female duty, female elegance, female enthusiasm, hemmed her completely in" (Strachey 1921: 45). While Strachey focuses on the misfortune of Victoria's personal development,

Young sets out to define what he sees as the great misfortune of the Victorian age: its failure to develop a national secondary school system. He says, "Fundamentally, what failed in the late Victorian age and its flash Edwardian epilogue was the Victorian public, once so alert, so masculine, and so responsible" (Strachey 1921: 6–7). It is, frankly, hard to know what to make of this statement; it is so confident in its sweeping generalization. It implies that the Victorian public had become self-absorbed, feminine, and insular – all adjectives which could easily have described the Queen – first by training and then through her reclusive mourning for Albert. Significantly, these two ostensibly different commentaries both play on gender tropes to develop their meanings. Strachey positions Victoria as effectively crippled by her femininity, and then Young depicts the age as crippled by its feminization.

The differentiation between Victorianism and Englishness receives its most interesting and compelling articulation in relation to the Great Exhibition in 1851. Tracing the earliest example and subsequent popularization of the term Victorian, Richard Stein notes that "the adjective came into use in 1851, the year of the Crystal Palace and the founding of the Australian colony of Victoria" (Stein 1987: 274). Significantly, Strachey's biography locates the consolidation of the Victorian age and Victorianism in the Great Exhibition. Defining Victoria as having "surrendered her whole soul to her husband," Strachey depicts her as upholding a "standard of moral purity with an inflexibility surpassing, if that were possible, Albert's own" (Strachey 1921: 169, 195). Strachey then launches into peroration, introducing the concept of a Victorian age through what he terms its "living apex," Victoria:

But she was no longer Lord M.'s pupil: she was Albert's wife. She was more – the embodiment, the living apex of a new era in the generations of mankind. The last vestige of the eighteenth century had disappeared; cynicism and subtlety were shriveled into power; and duty, industry, morality, and domesticity triumphed over them. Even the very chairs and tables had assumed, with a singular responsiveness, the forms of prim solidity. The Victorian Age was in full swing. (Strachey 1921: 195)

This passage then segues into a discussion of the Crystal Palace: "Only one thing more was needed: material expression must be given to the new ideals . . . It was for Albert to supply this want. He mused, and was inspired: the Great Exhibition came into his head" (Strachey 1921: 195–96).

The opening of the Crystal Palace was, as I noted earlier, a pivotal point in England's embrace of Victoria's German consort, Albert. His achievement brought distinction to England and, therefore, national gratitude to him. Again, Strachey comments, "In 1851 the Prince's fortunes reached their high-water mark. The success of the Great Exhibition enormously increased his reputation and seemed to assure him henceforward a leading place in the national life" (Strachey 1921: 204). Then the reader is informed that "before the year was out another triumph, in a very different sphere of action, was also his": during a country visit, he "had ridden to hounds and acquitted himself remarkably well" (Strachey 1921: 204).

Certainly, although subtly parodic, this assessment remarkably conflates events of enormously different magnitudes, thereby providing a pressure point for analyzing concepts of Victorianism and Englishness. Strachey goes onto remark that "This was a serious matter." It seemed to suggest that Albert "was a good fellow after all" (Strachey 1921: 205). But then he failed to follow up his advantage because hunting bored him, and, although it was agreed that he "could keep in his saddle well enough," he was pronounced "no sportsman" (Strachey 1921: 205). Or, in Strachey's rendition of the popular sentiment, "The Prince, in a word, was un-English. What that word precisely meant it was difficult to say; but the fact was patent to every eye" (Strachey 1921: 206). Strachey then constructs an archetypal struggle between Albert and Lord Palmerston, then foreign secretary. Strachey represents Palmerston as "the very antithesis of the Prince" and "English through and through." There was "something in him that expressed, with extraordinary vigour, the fundamental qualities of the English race" and thus, "all the mysterious forces in Albert's soul leapt out to do battle with his adversary, and, in the long and violent conflict that followed, it almost seemed as if he was struggling with England herself" (Strachey 1921: 206). This remarkable narrative creates out of Lord Palmerston a kind of democratic imperialist, who had "an English gentleman's contempt and dislike of foreign potentates deep in his heart" and enjoyed protecting "the interests of Englishmen abroad" (Strachey 1921: 219, 210). The phrase that is supposed to capture his Englishness is "happy valiance," expressed in conduct at once bold and prudent in the pursuit of national and international affairs (Strachey 1921: 209). Albert, in Strachey's narrative, remains tied to monarchical interests throughout Europe and committed to "due order, with careful premeditation" (Strachey 1921: 222). In short, Albert was Victorian but not English, not even after Victoria, asserting that "'The Queen has a right to claim that her husband should

be an Englishman,'" won for him the title of Prince Consort (1857):
"Albert remained as foreign as before."[11] And the Consort's position
helped construct the frame in which the Queen would be understood
and interpreted: Victorian to the core, the image of England herself, but
not possessed of "happy valiance," that masculine insouciance that
makes one quintessentially English. That trait belonged to her foreign
secretary, who would later rise to the post of prime minister.

### VICTORIA AND ELIZABETH I

This is, of course, an inflection of Englishness similar to that touted in
*Tom Brown's Schooldays* and elaborated in the public school mythology
that Hughes's novel helped to create. But, in touching on the relations of
true Englishness to conflicts with foreign potentates, it introduces the
third context – a subtext of Victorianism – in which I wish to consider
Victoria's place in the narrative of nationality: that is, in the Victorians'
construction of the Elizabethan age. By participating in defining
another age in terms of its queen – the designation "Elizabethan is a
nineteenth-century coinage" (Ormond 1987: 30) – the Victorians forwarded and justified their own project of nation and empire building
under Victoria. Just as Queen Elizabeth faced down Spain and Parma,
so, too, England, under Victoria, would achieve international
supremacy.

The comparative project of English queens began immediately with
Lord John Russell's expressed hope on Victoria's accession that she
would be an Elizabeth without her tyranny, an Anne without her weakness.[12] It is notable, however, that similarities between the sixteenth- and
nineteenth-century rulers that may seem apposite "from the vantage
point of the late twentieth century," did not readily present themselves
to the Victorians, who focused on the differences between the women
(Ormond 1987: 30). Although the women themselves were perceived to
be different, the fact that they were both female monarchs facilitated
comparisons between the two ages and the discovery therein of similarities.

Victoria on the throne encouraged contemporaneous commentators
to construct a link between the period of her reign and Elizabethan
England, and to imagine in the two ages a shared English heroism and
sense of English destiny. In "'The Spacious Times of Great Elizabeth':
the Victorian Vision of the Elizabethans," Leonée Ormond points out
the extent to which the Victorians self-consciously constructed the

Elizabethan age, often ignoring historical accuracy in the interest of certain heroic myths (Ormond 1987: 34–35). For the Victorians, "the Elizabethan age had two great strengths: one being its writers, the other its seamen" (Ormond 1987: 32). To the Victorians, language and its uses were as central in creating national identity as was bold and heroic action.[13] They brought them together in their choice of Elizabethan worthies: Shakespeare, Spencer, and Sidney on the one hand; Grenville, Raleigh, and Drake on the other. In evolving an English vernacular, the literature and language of the Elizabethans forged the beginnings of a national consciousness; the exploits of their sea heroes created foundations for national supremacy and empire building.

Charles Kingsley's novel *Westward Ho!* and James Anthony Froude's essay "England's Forgotten Worthies," in particular, helped to popularize new versions of England's past, in contradistinction to Macaulay's *History of England*, which opens with the Glorious Revolution of 1688 and the establishment of constitutional monarchy as "the event from which the true development of the English people could be traced" (Ormond 1987: 37). In "England's Forgotten Worthies," Froude so effectively contended that Englishmen of the sixteenth century forged an indispensable link in the chain of English national identity that he set in motion a process through which "the Elizabethans were no longer regarded as a barbaric and unfortunate element in England's history, and an increasingly celebratory attitude began to emerge," culminating in an "almost mythic status" for Elizabeth and her age (Ormond 1987: 43, 46). Ormond convincingly traces this process in her essay but stops short of what interests me here: the necessity of the Elizabethan myth to developing Victorian myths of empire. That connection emerges clearly in Froude's and Kingsley's accounts of England's relations to the West Indies.

In *At Last! Christmas in the West Indies*, Kingsley chronicles his own journey from Southampton to the Spanish Main, celebrating that he is "on the track of the old sea-heroes; of Drake and Hawkins, Carlile and Cavindish, Cumberland and Raleigh . . ." As he passes the Azores, he recalls and quotes Richard Grenville's famous words after his 1591 defeat in valiant battle,[14] and poses the question, "There were heroes in England in those days. Are we, their descendants, degenerate from them? I, for one, believe not" (Kingsley 1871: 6). This, as Kingsley joyfully prepares to touch ground in the "New World" of England's West Indian colonies, is nation building tied to empire building.

In *The English in the West Indies*, Froude refers to those same seafaring men, and he closes the first chapter of his book with a warning that for England to allow the West Indies to "drift away" from her power "because they have no immediate marketable value would be a sign that she had lost the feelings with which great nations always treasure the heroic traditions of their fathers" (Froude 1888: 10). He concludes: "When those traditions come to be regarded as something which concerns them no longer, their greatness is already on the wane" (Froude 1888: 10). The argument, although couched in the language of fathers, is implicitly *ad feminam*, gesturing for its logic to two queens who embody Britannia herself.

This connection between a heroic past and a present condition recalls passages in George Eliot's "The Modern Hep! Hep! Hep!" where Theophrastus Such locates the origins of Englishness in an even earlier tradition of seafaring men, praising the "language and genius" of those "old English seamen, who, beholding a rich country with a most convenient seaboard, came, doubtless with a sense of divine warrant" (Eliot n.d.: 130). Mr. Such concludes: "Let us know and acknowledge our common relationship to them, and be thankful that, over and above the affection and duties which spring from our manhood, we have the closer and more consistently guiding duties that belong to us as Englishmen" (Eliot n.d.: 131). The presence of Victoria has been all but swallowed up in a narrative of nation, ages, and empire, but that narrative found its initial impetus in the meaningful coincidence of queens on England's throne: two distinctive women, two heroic periods, one great nation.

This chapter only begins what must be a longer project: teasing out Victoria's complex relationship to developing, interwoven narratives of Englishness and Victorianism in nineteenth-century England. The terms necessarily resist simple codification. Even a preliminary study reveals the complex relationship between the figure of Victoria and the articulation of key elements of nation and national identity. Where she seems most tangential – in the Victorian creation of the Elizabethan age – she is perhaps most central because her very longevity as queen increasingly fed notions of similarities between the ages and helped to nurture a vision of imperial destiny played out over centuries. The Victorian age is thus thoroughly imbued with the figure who gave it her name, although that individual has often been effectively erased from accounts of the period. To return her to those stories of national identity, however, is not to stabilize them. The figure that seems to ground these narratives – Victoria herself – is she who most disturbs ideas of what it means to be both English and Victorian. Because both nation and national identity are associated with specifically masculine virtues, the monarch's gender clouds the very concepts she supposedly crystallizes. Gender tropes facilitate an intricate cultural mapping of the concepts "Victoria," "Englishness," "Victorianism," and "Elizabethanism," but at the cost of a resolution in which we can see the possibility for the radical destabilizing of every element in this iconography.

NOTES

1 Lucas adds of Victoria's cultural construction that "Moreover, this loved body is largely put together by and for male consumption. (Victorian patriotism had little to offer women beyond their being encouraged to develop as images of the queen, in which sign husbands might conquer.) This requires some comment" (1987–88: 65). However, he fails to comment on the explicit contradiction of the maternal monarch, confining his discussion instead to the gradual emergence of Victoria from the 1870s onward as a figure "somehow 'above' politics" (1987–88: 65).

2 Quoted in Strachey 1921: 27.

3 Bruce Haley notes that "The Duke of Wellington did not, we now know, claim that the battle of Waterloo was won on the playing fields of Eton. But the authenticity of the 'Wellington mot' . . . was accepted by almost everybody, and the myth inspired a sort of lugubrious pride. It is hard to say when the story got started, but it is at least as old as the Comte de Montalembert's remarks on Eton in 1856" (1978: 260).

4 Bruce Haley notes that the "process begun with *Tom Brown* culminates with 'Vitaï Lampada': the highest values of the schoolboy become the guiding principles of the adult" (ibid.: 260). Haley explains that the phrase "'play the game' was immortalized in Henry Newbolt's poem 'Vitaï Lampada.' An ex-schoolboy soldier, his regiment under bloody siege, rallies his comrades with inspiriting words recalled from his days on the cricket field:

> This is the work that year by year,
>    While in her place the School is set,
> Every one of her sons must hear,
>    And none that hears it dare forget.
> This they all with joyful mind
>    Bear through life like a torch a flame,
> And falling fling to the host behind –
> 'Play up! play up! and play the game!'" (1978: 260)

5 It is interesting that parodies of Tennyson's ode often debunked the image of Victoria as tender "mother" and guardian to her people, depicting her instead in images of familial partiality, cupidity, and malfeasance:

> Fifty times the rose has flower'd and faded,
> Fifty times it would have bloomed without her –
> Smelt as sweet without "the crown, the sceptre.

Or,

> Fifty times the State has fooled and blundered,
> Fifty times the royal pension's risen
> Since the Queen assumed the globe, the sceptre.

The final stanza is revised thus,

> Are there thunders moaning in the distance? –
> 'Tis the German band of near relations;
> Trust the mother Queen to guide her people
> Where they'll live in plenty without labour,
> And her Alberts, Victors, Georges, Henries,
> Families raise for Jubilees for ages. (cited in Fredeman 1987: 20, 21)

6 Again, Lucas automatically conflates the concepts of England and Englishness, as in this claim: "That was why it was so important to promote images of the monarchy as 'above' politics or party interest, and as reconciling opposing points of view in a single, seamless concept of 'Englishness'" (1987–88: 66).

7 It is notable, for example, that Walter Houghton's magisterial *The Victorian Frame of Mind* alludes to Victoria only four times, all passing references, i.e. "Frederic Harrison, brought up from the country at the age of seven to see Queen Victoria's coronation . . ." (1957: 308), or, "Levity is what Queen Victoria found 'not amusing'" (ibid.: 357). For Houghton, Victoria is not a relevant figure to discuss in assessing the Victorian frame of mind.

8 Young explains this concept at length:

> The great dividing line in 1860 is not rich and poor, but the respectable and the others. You may be rich, but if you are not respectable you will not pass muster in the eyes of society. The Queen will not have you at Court. Mothers will not let their daughters dance with you. On the other hand, you may be poor, but if you are respectable the world will think well of you. And what are the outward and visible signs of respectability? Well, by now I think you know: cleanliness – the children at school – sobriety (a pint of beer may pass, the respectable man never enters a gin shop) – the benefit club – the family walk of a Sunday afternoon – the weekly magazine, like the *Weekly Welcome* or the *British Workman*. You can complete the tale yourselves (1962: 122).

9 It is interesting to note the structural and stylistic similarities between Young's description of this transition and Strachey's, from his biography:

> What, above all, struck everybody with overwhelming force was the contrast between Queen Victoria and her uncles. The nasty old men, debauched and selfish, pig-headed and ridiculous, with their perpetual burden of debts, confusions, and disreputabilities – they had vanished like the snows of winter, and here at last, crowned and radiant, was the spring" (1921: 72).

Here we have a glimpse of ideology in the making.

10 Quoted in Thompson 1990: 139.

11 Victoria's letter, quoted in Strachey 1921: 288.

12 Cited in Strachey 1921: 72.

13 Macaulay's "Minute on Indian Education" (1835) famously recommends unequivocally that English, instead of Arabic or Sanskrit, be employed in the instruction of Indians. He argues that, "Whether we look at the intrinsic values of our literature, or at the particular situation of this country, we shall see the strongest reason to think that, of all foreign tongues, the English tongue is that which would be the most useful to our native subjects" (1952: 723). He adds, "The literature of England is now more valuable than that of classical antiquity" (1952: 724). Macaulay's goal is to "form a class [of Indians] who may be interpreters between us and the millions whom we govern; a class of persons, Indian in blood and colour, but English in taste, in opinions, in morals, and in intellect" (1952: 729). Language and national identity go hand in hand.

In a similarly nationalistic vein, George Eliot's Theophrastus Such argues that "it is a calamity to the English, as to any other great historic people, to undergo a premature fusion with immigrants of alien blood; that its distinctive national characteristics should be in danger of obliteration" (n.d.: 142). He "groans" over the threatened danger manifest every day in the foreigners' corruptions of English:

> To one who loves his native language, who would delight to keep our rich and harmonious English undefiled by foreign accent . . . it is an affliction as harassing as the climate, that . . . we must expect to hear our beloved English, with its words clipped, its vowels stretched and twisted, its phrases of acquiescence and politeness, of cordiality, dissidence, or argument, delivered always in the wrong tones, like ill-rendered melodies, marred beyond recognition" (Eliot n.d.: 142–43).

14 "Here die I, Richard Grenville, with a joyful and quiet mind; for that I have ended my life as a true soldier ought, fighting for his country, queen, religion, and honour" (Kingsley 1871: 5).

CHAPTER 3

# Crossing the Atlantic with Victoria: American receptions, 1837–1901

## Mary Loeffelholz

The cover of *Fifty Years a Queen*, written by Katherine Hodges and published in the United States in the year of Victoria's 1887 jubilee with the aim of giving, "from an American standpoint, a brief and unbiassed [*sic*] resumé of the events of Queen Victoria's time, and of her reign of half a century," is illustrated with a line drawing entitled *Victoria Refusing to Sign Recognition of Southern Confederacy*. Standing in the foreground of the drawing in ermine-trimmed robes of state, an outsized Victoria imperiously refuses the blandishments of her own minister and two other bearded men, more plainly dressed, in the background – her own cowed lesser officials, or disappointed spokesmen for the Confederacy. The minister in the foreground gestures agressively with his right hand, its index finger pointed directly at Victoria and positioned over the official document on the table behind them, its seal dangling toward the floor, while his left hand is opened more supplicatingly toward the Queen. Half turned away from the confrontation, Victoria raises one hand in rejection of the document and the minister's pointing finger, while the other protectively or retreatingly gathers her veil up to her waist, a gesture that also, along with her sash, calls attention to her ample maternal bosom.

This retrospective 1887 construction of Victoria as the imperial but feminine savior of American union implies a good deal about the axes of gender, nation, and empire upon which Victoria's reception turned in the United States during her long reign. The year 1861, the year of Victoria's first jubilee, had indeed emerged as the canonical moment for her reputation in the United States, the fulcrum on which American attitudes toward Britain and its monarch were conventionally seen to turn. The cover design for *Fifty Years a Queen* condenses the tangled events of British–American relations in 1861/62 – Great Britain's decision in early 1861 to remain neutral in the Civil War, the resolution of the *Trent* affair at the end of 1861, and Britain's continued refusal to endorse France's agitation for European states to recognize the Confederacy – into a

33

visually coherent, accessible form. Here Victoria acts alone, out of her royal prerogative, to protect the young American republic in its most difficult hour. As she acts to protect American union, so, too, her figure and her gestures symbolically subdue, after the fact, the fierce conflict among competing interests that erupted in Great Britain itself as the Union blockade kept the South's cotton from reaching Britain's mills. Acting as queen and woman on her autonomous conscience (or so the drawing suggests), Victoria preserves an image of Great Britain as in some way united above the fray of male party ambitions and economic interests; at the same time, her hinted-at feminine vulnerability or retreat, coupled with maternity, implies for American readers in 1887 that England in its true symbolic heart could never act aggressively toward its figurative child.

Yet the events of 1861 also permitted other retrospective constructions that proved attractive in other ways to Americans interested in Victoria. Although *Fifty Years a Queen* canonizes Britain's decision for neutrality as Victoria's decisive intervention at the beginning of the Civil War, other late nineteenth-century American interpretations of Victoria's role in the Anglo-American crisis of 1861 tend to focus on the *Trent* affair of November/December 1861, in which Victoria and Albert together modified the hostile language of Britain's formal complaint to the United States over the seizure of Confederate representatives journeying to England aboard the British ship *Trent* and so averted the very real risk of war between Great Britain and the US.[1] Victoria's recollection of the *Trent* crisis appeared shortly after the end of the Civil War in *The Early Years of His Royal Highness the Prince Consort*, published on both sides of the Atlantic in 1867, and American readers immediately seized upon the story. "In the last public act of the Prince," wrote a reviewer of *The Early Years* for *Harper's Monthly*,

> we have a special interest. It is thus told:
> "On the 1st of December, 1861, when suffering under the extreme prostration of his last fatal illness, the Prince roused himself to write a memorandum for the Queen, on the communication which the Government proposed to make to the United States on the affair of the *Trent*. This memorandum was adopted by the Queen, and influencing, as it did, the tone of the Government communication, had a material effect in preventing a rupture between the two countries."

Everyone who knows of the history of the time, is aware that there was the most imminent peril of hostilities growing out of this affair. Had the British ministry acted as they were disposed to act, we can hardly see how war could have been avoided. What would have been the result no man can say. (review of *The Early Years* 1867: 654)

American commentators would bring out this narrative over and over again in the closing quarter of the century. Frequently joined with accounts of Victoria's condolences offered to the widows of Lincoln and Garfield after the assassinations of both presidents, the vignette of the Queen's and Prince Consort's collaborative efforts toward peace would become the single most durable *topos* of Victoria's reception in the post-Civil War United States.

In contrast to the cover design for *Fifty Years a Queen*, this way of retrospectively framing the 1861 canonical moment of Victoria's America reception locates the decisive action in the private realm of domesticity and deathbed writing, rather than the public realm of royal visual spectacle, and most versions of the story make the Prince Consort at least as responsible as Victoria, if not more so, for the course of Anglo-American history. Rather than attributing historical agency to the visibly queenly, single figure of Victoria, the vignette represents Victoria's effects as a closeted, collaborative project to which the material work of writing is essential. At the same time, of course, the domestic tableau of Albert's deathbed writing is inescapably public and historical, the writerly counterpart of what Margaret Homans, analyzing royal family portraiture, has labeled "the spectacle of royal domestic privacy" (Homans 1993: 4). Albert revises Palmerston's memorandum; Victoria adopts Albert's language as her own; her ministers take the memorandum-now-palimpsest over as the state's collective intention; when Victoria authorizes the compilation of Albert's biography after his death, the whole project of royal collaborative writing circulates back in the other direction. Subsequent biographies of the Prince Consort continued the work of canonizing Albert and Victoria's final scene of collaborative writing: Martin's 1875–1880 five-volume *Life* of Albert actually reproduced for American and British readers Albert's handwritten reply to the original, hostile draft memorandum – written by the Prince in the Queen's voice, with Victoria's further corrections in her own hand (Martin 1875–80: v, 348–49).

For American readers especially, perhaps, the various models and genderings of historical agency derivable from the *Trent* narrative seemed to have been attractive or usable from any number of nationalist perspectives. Walt Whitman, possibly America's greatest nineteenth-century literary specialist in floating agency across and athwart gender identifications, seized on some of the story's appeal in the quatrain and accompanying note he composed for the Queen's birthday in 1890. The quatrain's floral tribute, "A bunch of white and pink arbutus, silent, spicy,

shy, / From Hudson's, Delaware's, or Potomac's woody banks," bears
Whitman's signature floral mixings of feminine with phallic associations.
Its explanatory note grafts Whitman's tribute directly onto the still-green
memory of the *Trent* episode:

> Very little, as we Americans stand this day, with our sixty-five or seventy mil-
> lions of population, an immense surplus in the treasury, and all that actual
> power or reserve power (land and sea) so dear to nations – very little I say do we
> realize that curious crawling national shudder when the "Trent affair" promis'd
> to bring upon us a war with Great Britain – follow'd unquestionably, as that war
> would have, by recognition of the Southern Confederacy from all the leading
> European nations. It is now certain that all this then inevitable train of calam-
> ity hung on arrogant and peremptory phrases in the prepared and written
> missive of the British Minister, to America, which the Queen (and Prince Albert
> latent) positively and promptly cancell'd; and which her firm attitude did alone
> actually erase and leave out, against all the other official prestige and court of
> St. James's. On such minor and personal incidents (so to call them) often depend
> the great growths and turns of civilization. This moment of a woman and a
> queen surely swung the grandest oscillation of modern history's pendulum.
> (Whitman 1973: 620–21)[2]

As Whitman's note suggests, the *Trent* story was richly capable of sus-
taining a variety of constructions.[3] Unlike the *Harper's* reviewer,
Whitman makes Victoria much more than a conduit of Albert's writing,
but in doing so he also, interestingly, cancels out the spectacle of Albert's
sentimental deathbed. Albert is not deathly ill but "latent," a sort of
retired textual ground on which Victoria "positively" acts, but acts negatively, by canceling and erasing. A curious train of association links
Whitman's "latent" Albert to the "silent, spicy, shy" arbutus branch
hidden in the American woods, and to the "reserve power . . . so dear to
nations," in possession of which Whitman's America of the 1890s is the
envy of the world. The Queen's "firm attitude," even if exercised in
what seems to be the "personal" sphere, mediates between the public,
masculine realm of history and a masculinity even more retired and
"latent" than Victoria's existence as "a woman and a queen." The
popular American construction of Victoria's action in the *Trent* affair, as
personal and domestic, obviously allows Whitman to hail Victoria
without compromising his own democratic understanding of history.
Less obviously, perhaps, the figure of Victoria with Albert "latent" fur-
thers Whitman in representing a doubled version of masculine power
and ultimately of American nationalism: like masculinity in Whitman's
poetry, the United States is both engorged with public power and shy,
reserved, isolationist in its retired woods, historically innocent.

This chapter will read some of the important currents of Victoria's reception in the United States, before and after Victoria's canonical 1861 "moment of a woman and a queen," with the questions raised by Whitman's tribute to Victoria in mind: with a view, that is, to how nineteenth-century American interpretations of Victoria help elaborate changing notions of what kind of world history the United States participates in, and how individual Americans, women and men, are agents of that history. During the course of her long reign, Victoria came to be identified more consistently by Americans as the "mother" in "the mother country." But like other mothers, this one could be repudiated and condescended to as well as venerated. The viscissitudes of Victoria's American reception thus trace out some of the contending vectors of religion, race, and gender in the constitution of nineteenth-century American nationalism *vis-à-vis* Great Britain.

In the antebellum United States, the cult of Queen Victoria initially made slow headway against several opposing currents of American cultural nationalism, underlined by ongoing territorial disputes between the United States and Great Britain and US anxiety over Britain's imperial designs in the Western hemisphere. The earliest years of Victoria's reign and the pomp and ceremony of her marriage to Albert coincided with a bitter feud between Great Britain and the United States over the boundary between Maine and Canada, followed a few years later by the crisis in Anglo-American relations over the Oregon border. Some Americans were prepared to go to war over the border, while many saw the eventual annexation of Canada, with or without war, as the logical outcome of the two countries' common English-speaking culture. More rabid republicans in the United States rejoiced at Britain's internal troubles in the 1840s and forecast the end of the monarchy with little special deference to Victoria. A writer in the *Southern Literary Messenger* in 1842, offering up his "Speculations Upon the Consequences of a War with Great Britain," turned the tables on British anticipations of the ultimate break-up of the United States by forecasting "'humiliation, dismemberment, and ruin' to the British monarchy, and we will add as a consequence, liberty, abundance and happiness to the British people" ("Speculations" 1842: 447).

At the same time, however, nearer relations with Great Britain were essential to other strains of American nationalism. Emergent discourses of racial "Anglo-Saxonism" in the 1830s and 1850s United States promulgated a nationalist myth of origins that tied American republican institutions back to the supposed ancient liberties of the mother country.[4] This discourse in the United States nevertheless paid rather little attention to Victoria during these early years of her reign. Antebellum American Anglo-Saxonism for the most part idealized not Britain's ancient queens, but the barons who signed the Magna Carta and the energetic religious men who kept the true church alive in England. Its macho flavor is suggested by an essayist writing in 1848 for the *American Whig Review,* who, after nodding to "*the social elevation of women*" as one key to Anglo-Saxon racial "pre-eminence," goes on to celebrate King Alfred and President Washington as "the extreme links (as it were) to a chain of powerful, brave, and high-souled men," exemplars of the racial genius of Anglo-Saxondom guarded in Britain through the ages and fulfilled in "the period of our own political origin, when the democratic principle was proclaimed to the world as the natural and inalienable safeguard of human authority, of governmental supremacy" ("Anglo-Saxon Race" 1848: 29, 41). For this writer, as for many other antebellum American theorists of Anglo-Saxondom, Victoria held no necessary place in the chain of vigorous Anglo-Saxon masculinity binding the United States to Britain.

It is not that British queens were invisible or absent in American culture in the years immediately preceding and following Victoria's accession; far from it, as the steady stream of antebellum periodical essays and poems treating Elizabeth and especially Mary, Queen of Scots, underlines.[5] But they were present in ways that left many Americans, women and men, slow to receive Victoria's emergent image as a modern bourgeois female monarch: virtuous wife, mother, and queen. Americans frequently used queens, or their idea of queens, to define antebellum American womanhood by contrast – yet not by simple negation. "American womanhood" incorporated and transformed some traditionally queenly qualities as Americans sought a vocabulary for what they saw as the special virtues of American, or Anglo-American, culture and the special characteristics of Americans as subjects of history.

From the standpoint of antebellum American ideals of "republican motherhood," queens no less than kings belonged to a generically dissolute aristocracy; they were negative historical examples to be set against models of the republican matron past and present. In this respect American republicans, especially evangelical Protestants, held much in common with their dissenting English relatives. Writing in 1845 on "Female Character and Education" for an American Methodist audience, British Methodist preacher Samuel Galloway drew what had become a familiar contrast between "Mary, the Mother of Washington" and Cornelia, "mother of the Gracchi," on the one hand, and queens like Cleopatra and Queen Elizabeth on the other. The virtuous republican mother "rears the pillars of her country's greatness, and her deeds are unnoticed and unknown. The history of the world abounds with her commanding influence" (Galloway 1845: 154). By contrast, the negative power of history's queens is constituted by ostentatious public display and erotic scheming, rather than private self-discipline and motherly instruction:

Where is the admirer of that Egyptian queen whose art once conquered Roman arms, and the music of whose voice drowned the trump of ambition! Egyptian spices, perhaps, yet embalm her lifeless body; but where, in the world's great heart, has she a choice recollection? Where is she who once held supremacy on Britain's throne? The record of her deeds is on the page of history; but in the pure intellect of a virtuous posterity, Elizabeth holds no dearer place than the disasters of her country's wars. (Galloway 1845: 168)

Neither to this British citizen nor to his American audience in 1845 did it yet occur that Queen Victoria was a figure in which the contradiction they assumed between monarchy and domestic female virtue might be reconciled, or cultural bonds maintained between the United States and the mother country on the grounds of a common middle-class standard of femininity.

American cultural nationalism in the years 1830 to 1860 often preferred that England's queens keep their place in this standard republican morality play, for which Victoria was an unpromising candidate from the start. Even in their more sympathetic avatars, queens or other royal women in the antebellum United States tended to be cast as dark protagonists of tragic old world political and religious histories, exactly the histories many antebellum Americans hoped and thought they had transcended in the new world's providential nation. Mary, Queen of Scots, despite or because of her intractable allegiance to popery, was endlessly popular as a tragic heroine. Her famous beauty endeared her to sentimental readers; her romantic entanglements, her political ambitions, and the cruelties of her reign could be dilated upon freely because all was paid for by her spectacular death.[6] To readers of American women's periodicals, Mary was time and again painted as

> a theme
> To touch the coldest heart – to send the soul
> Upon a mission to the pathless track
> Of former ages, there to seek, in airy thought,
> One sweet, sad moment, dreaming o'er thy lot! (Cumming 1842: 46)

– or as another American writer explained Mary's appeal, her "youth, her rare attractions, and native gentleness of character . . . excite our kindliest sympathies, and awaken a tender consideration for her during her brief but eventful and unhappy career." Mary's fate "thrills upon the heart of a woman" who rewrites her story as that of incipient sentimental Protestant bourgeois heroine tragically born in the wrong time and place: "'The last words that I speak,' said she, 'shall be the words of a queen.' O, had she known the rich harmonies slumbering within her bosom, she would have scorned a note so low" (Barker 1850: 133).

As subjects of history, what queens in this antebellum sentimental American mode do best is remember, and incite others to remember – to wander "the pathless track of former ages." And queens remember best on the eve of execution, "Wrapt in the scaffold's gloom" (Sigourney 1849: 247) and its private thoughts; Lady Jane Grey and Anna Boleyn turn up frequently in this situation, along with Mary, Queen of Scots, in American representations.[7] What matters about these queens is not their actual deeds, nor their doctrinal affiliations, nor the political consequences of their reigns, but the way their gender frames English history in terms of a pathos of distance for American readers: as the object of sentimental identification, but at a safe remove from effectiveness in the present. "Doomed" in her hour of reflection "to know / How far a mother's grief transcends a martyr's woe" (Sigourney 1849: 248), Lydia Sigourney's Anna Boleyn dramatizes what Ann Douglas has called the nineteenth-century American "feminization of theology," with its replacement of doctrinal matter by domestic feeling. Where queens like Cleopatra and Elizabeth stage their power in their public and erotic bodies, their sentimental queenly counterparts witness privately and reflectively to their own suffering.[8]

Yet this way of understanding queens as sentimental subjects of history is in certain ways not so distant from antebellum American understandings of the educated republican matron. Galloway's apostrophe to the educated woman in "Female Character and Education" suggests how American women might inherit and transform the sentimental queenly subject of history. Like the sentimental queen, the educated woman is a creature of memory, of inward historical theater and reflection; unlike her, the educated American woman possesses the vision of a future as well as a past, witnesses to hope as well as to personal injury, and can pass her knowledge on to others, at least within the domestic sphere:[9]

She quits the narrow sphere of prejudice and passion, and is borne aloft, by the impulses of a new and sublime life, to a loftier theatre, where a range opens up adequate to the aspirings of a nobler spirit. She watches the tide of emigration that rolls over the land – contemplates the rising grandeur of her country . . . – unrolls the map of the world, and, as from an observatory, looks abroad upon the various moral conflicts which are agitating its interests – sees kingdoms rising and falling . . . and in the spirit and practice of a kind instructress, interprets to her family and friends the varied signs of the times, and the mighty events which cluster around the movements of the age. Nor is she confined to the *present* in her sources of gratification; for the same power which confers the privilege of a delightful participation in the movements of this age, lifts the curtains which shroud the *past* from view, and secures a rich inheritance in its choicest possessions. The scenes of other days rise at the bidding of her will, and memory throws them before her vision . . . [A]s she marks the traces of mighty events and ancient glory, the illustrious dead of centuries troop up before her, and alike rivet the steady gaze and warm emotion of her enraptured intellect and heart. (Galloway 1845: 159–60)

This inward Protestant theater of history (belated compensation, one might say, for the vision of history from which Eve is excluded in *Paradise Lost*) makes the American matron queen of her own consciousness, a Victoria reviewing the troops of all time.

But again, the comparison is not directly to Victoria. The American matron's British counterpart is not Queen Victoria, for Galloway, but rather the Protestant sisterhood of female authorship: "Ah! how do the queens of other times sink, in comparison with the humbler pretensions, and yet more majestic achievements of such spirits as Mrs. Hemans, Miss Carter, and Hannah More! . . . And who of you, that has communed with the writings of your own countrywoman – Mrs. Sigourney – has not felt the power of education combined with the loveliness of piety!" (Galloway 1845: 168–69).[10] Addressing these women writers collectively as "American matrons," even though Sigourney is the only literal American citizen among them, Galloway not only conflates the roles of mother and writer but implies that the "American matron" is a kind of supernational category: a new subject or author of history in whom the older power of queens and nations is both canceled and preserved.

Perhaps it makes sense, then, that what I have called Victoria's canonical moment in the United States, the post-Civil War construction of her queenly role in keeping the American Union together and at peace with Britain, would depend for much of its power not only on Victoria's widowhood but on her writing from the position of widowhood.

Widowhood would eventually unite in Victoria's person the queen of historical pathos and the good bourgeois matron; writing her widowhood would connect her to "the humbler pretensions, and yet more majestic achievements" of transatlantic Protestant literary womanhood. Yet this queenly subjectivity for Victoria was some time coalescing in the United States, and even as it came together its sources in antebellum American women's culture would be drying up or shifting their courses.

American observers in the 1840s and 1850s who took notice of Victoria, even from sympathetic perspectives, nevertheless tended not to see the sentimental queenly subject of history in Victoria. If Elizabeth Barrett, in her poem "The Young Queen," had cast Victoria very much in this role of reflection and remembrance, Americans – especially those writing about English travels for audiences at home – were more often moved to write about Victoria from the position of onlooker than from the position of sentimental identification. Their curiosity was engaged as much by the popular spectacle of royal power, particularly in the context of London's urban crowds, as by Victoria herself. Writing for *The Family Circle and Parlor Annual* of 1848 (of which he was also the editor), the Revd D. Newell closed his account of a visit to London "by alluding to a topic in which every Englishman takes a peculiar pride. We were struck, as it is impossible not to be, with the immense POPULAR-ITY OF THE QUEEN. But one feeling seems to pervade the great mass of the British Nation and that is a feeling of enthusiastic, idolatrous attachment to VICTORIA." Joining the crowd waiting for Victoria at the dedication of Lincoln Inns, Newell saw

the tide of living beings [begin] to flow from all directions; the gathering and still increasing multitudes seemed like the unnumbered waves of the ocean when agitated by a storm . . . The desire of seeing the queen, drew them together . . . We tried to get a glimpse of her majesty, BUT IT WAS IMPOSS-IBLE, yet, the occasion was not lost to us, since, in the midst of this mighty confluence of Britons, we could, in a sense see and feel the strong pulsations of a nation's heart. (Newell 1848a: 156)

Newell, absent a personal Victoria, infers the invisible cause from her effects – or is it the other way round: the effect, "Victoria," from its cause, the crowd's idolatry? In terms of Newell's historical narrative, either relationship is possible: "Victoria" is both her people's link to their mighty origins and the symptom of London's unfamiliar mass modernity.

Even Americans who came closer to Victoria's domestic life and to

individuals among her subjects often maintained some skeptical nationalist and republican distance from Victoria's bourgeois, popular, familial modernity. Harriet Beecher Stowe heard a good deal about Victoria
during her 1850s travels in England and Scotland following upon the
international success of *Uncle Tom's Cabin*. Like Newell, she was struck by
the Queen's popularity, but she insistently frames her account of the
Queen's reported virtues as hearsay rather than as direct intuition of
Britain's heart:

> [T]he impression seems to prevail among her Scottish subjects, that she never
> appears to feel herself more happy or more at home than in this her Highland
> dwelling. The legend is, that here she delights to throw off the restraints of
> royalty; to go about plainly dressed, like a private individual; to visit in the cot-
> tages of the poor; to interest herself in the instruction of the children; and to
> initiate the future heir of England into that practical love of the people which
> is the best qualification for a ruler.
>
> I repeat to you the things which I hear floating of the public characters of
> England, and you can attach what degree of credence you may think proper.
> (Stowe 1854: I, 126)

Attractive as the rumored queenly domestic virtues clearly are to Stowe,
she also points directly to the paradox of a royal domestic privacy that
is, and is intended to be, public property.[11]

Another American observer of the early 1850s, writing on "Queen
Victoria" for the *Southern Literary Messenger*, revelled in the incongruity
he saw between the Queen's personal, private being and her royal role.
This writer judges Victoria as a wife and erotic object, and from this
perspective makes Victoria's gender into a vehicle for his own
American ambivalence about royalty as an institution. "We
Americans, when abroad, are anxious to see a live monarch," he
claims, "simply because the species is not to be found in our own lati-
tude, and not because of any suddenly inspired reverence" ("Queen
Victoria" 1852: 186). Yet, he admits, there is something more: the
English monarchy earns "a sentiment apart from that of curiosity"
from Americans, as the "representative part of Saxon manhood." If
the current representative is a woman, all the better: in that case, she
can summon forth "that chivalrous loyalty, which is the instinct of
generous bosoms" but which is not incompatible with manly American
"independence" ("Queen Victoria" 1852: 186). Chivalrous but conde-
scending, this writer follows Victoria through the Crystal Palace and
various royal progresses, assessing her teeth ("very pretty"), upper lip
("a trifle too short") and general demeanor in the job ("I wondered that

she had not more composure" ["Queen Victoria" 1852: 187–88]).
Republican America, he concludes, could supply better queens than
European high breeding: "I could find more than one young lady in
Virginia, who, if called upon, could bear her part in such a pageant,
as well as, it may be better, than the granddaughter of George III"
("Queen Victoria" 1852: 189). Reducing the ancient dignities of British
monarchy to the position of wallflower at a Virginia ball, this writer
fully exploits for nationalist purposes the paradoxes of Victoria's
queenship – exploits, to put it from a twentieth-century psychoanalyt-
ical perspective, what happens when a woman can *be* but not *have* "the
representative part of Saxon manhood."

He also exploits for nationalist purposes Victoria's lack of fit with the
sentimental American stereotype of queenship. Looking at an unfin-
ished statue of Victoria set up in front of Scotland's Holy-Rood Palace,
he muses on the contrast between Mary and Victoria:

> As I gazed upon this statue of a young Queen, upon whom every blessing seems
> to have been showered down, I thought how different had been the lot of her
> whose mournful history gave Holy-Rood Palace its chief interest. More gifted
> by nature with personal charms and mental endowments, amiable in disposi-
> tion and of a loving heart, she led a life of incessant terror, to suffer a cruel death
> at last. Certainly she had not the steadfast principles of the pure Victoria, but
> then poor Mary had been differently brought up, and she was sorely tempted.
> Poor Mary – happy Victoria . . . And, therefore, while we join with those who
> cry, "Victoria, whom God preserve," we will not forget the while to sigh, Alas
> poor Mary, beautiful Mary! ("Queen Victoria" 1852: 190)

Mary, the reader infers, would have held her own among the Virginia
belles. As a locus for sentimental revery, she preserves the English past
as something safely past and yet romantically available for this American
male viewer. Victoria, by contrast, bears in her no "mournful history";
instead, her name and her only modestly desirable body together mark
the place where British royal history might consume itself.[12] Anticipating
the comments of many subsequent observers, both American and
British, this writer judges that the very middle-class virtues Victoria exercises in the monarchy are destined to bring about the monarchy's end.
"[I]f the English ever get so fairly into the current of the Progress of the
Age, as to attempt a real Republic," he ventures, "there could never be
a better time for the movement, than would be presented at the death of
the present Queen"; in that case "monarchy itself would undergo a sort
of apotheosis, and the sainted memory of Victoria, first and last of the
name, be revered forever" ("Queen Victoria" 1852: 192). Dismissed in

the flesh, Victoria rises again in the spirit as the madonna of a future Anglo-American republican heaven.[13]

Not every antebellum American thought the republican heaven needed a British madonna. Although Victoria continued to be popular with American audiences, and the 1859 visit of the Prince of Wales to the United States generated an outpouring of favorable publicity, many Southerners and Westerners – or in not quite overlapping party terms, many Jacksonian Democrats – were more hostile, not only to aristocracy and monarchy as such, but to British moralizing over American slavery. In this context the rabidly nationalist and anti-British *Democratic Review* asked itself in 1855 "A Pertinent Question" – "Who is Victoria?" Tracing her pedigree back through William the Conqueror, "the bastard son of the Duke of Normandy, by a tanner's daughter, of Falaise" ("A Pertinent Question" 1855: 216), the *Review* wondered whether Victoria or "any of the crowned heads and potentates of the old world" were "heaven descended" ("A Pertinent Question" 1855: 218) or otherwise entitled to hand out the moral law to republican Americans. Drawing heavily on the old saws of republican morality, but without their characteristic stress on the education and elevation of women, it tarred sober Victoria with its condemnation of Northern elite Whiggery: "the higher law, and abolition, has become the anti-marriage, amalgamation party, tending to the subversion of every wholesome doctrine in politics and religion" – "women's rights men, foolishly supposing that anarchy means liberty" ("A Pertinent Question" 1855: 218). American independence, according to the *Review*, entails the domestic subordination of women and slaves, along with the humbling of Northern elites; despite her own personal morality and lack of interest in women's political rights, Queen Victoria is more than apt as a scapegoat for this work.

Strikingly, "A Pertinent Question" is directly followed, in the March 1855 *Democratic Review*, by a poem celebrating "Palmyra's beauteous queen, Zenobia" ("Zenobia" 1855: 219). It is impossible to know with certainty whether the juxtaposition of Victoria and Zenobia was intended, but possible to read in "Zenobia" an allegory of relations between Britain and the United States, perhaps coupled with the European revolutions of 1848:

> Rome had passed her noon – her tyranny
> Was overgrown – an earthquake was at work
> At her foundations, and new dynasties,
> Striking their roots in ripening revolutions,
> Were soon to sway the destinies of realms. ("Zenobia" 1855: 219)

With "all the anxious cares / Of an unstable and capricious throne" cast on her by her husband's death, Zenobia rears a capitol "whose towers and domes / Vied with proud Rome in architectural grace,"

> and betrayed
> Her bold ambition, and her rivalry
> With the imperial mistress of the world.
> But 'tis the gaudiest flower is soonest plucked.

Captured and "led in chains" through the streets of Rome as a trophy of war, Zenobia falls into the revery typical of sentimental queens, her "dim reminiscences of former days / . . . like a dreamy deluge on her mind." But the inward eye of remembrance is also the eye of prophecy:

> in the wreck of her magnificence,
> With eye prophetic, she beheld the doom
> Of the proud Capitol of all the world.
> She saw the quickening symptoms of revolt
> Among the nations, and she caught their cry
> For freedom and for vengeance. ("Zenobia" 1855: 221)

Rome, the poem concludes, will fall to "the Goth" whose "reckless sword" unknowingly "avenge[s] / The cause of the oppressed." In the republican nationalist context of the mid-1850s *Democratic Review*, it is no great leap from imperial Rome to Great Britain. But what to make of Zenobia's relation to Victoria? Or of an American political conscious-ness that defended American slaveholding and American independence against perceived British encroachments by manipulating images of Queen Victoria's tainted royal bloodline on the one hand, and on the other an exotic Eastern queen enslaved and led captive through Rome?

It is the very malleability of queenly sentimental pathos, I would suggest, that made tragic or exotic queens so ubiquitous for the work of antebellum American national and historical consciousness – and the historical Victoria in some quarters so equivocal a figure for this work. As the subject of pathos and prophecy, Zenobia functions for the 1855 *Democratic Review* rather as conventions of noble Indians and "Indian prophecy" were coming to function in the antebellum eastern United States: like noble Indians, tragic queens in the antebellum United States lend their powers to their republican successors (who might also be their exterminators or enslavers). At the same time, however, the vigorous 1840s and 1850s transatlantic traffic between the US and Great Britain in literary and artistic representations of queenly women as captives and slaves (Kasson) seems to have registered an American anxiety that the old world imperial histories embodied in American images of tragic queens might prove not so easy to sublate in nationalist terms as many Americans hoped: too many real African bodies were enslaved on the land for any number of enchained queens to cancel out.

As monarch of Great Britain, officially opposed to the slave trade yet deeply dependent on cotton from the slave states, Victoria stood in a complicated symbolic and actual relationship to the American struggles leading up to the Civil War. The narrative that eventually emerged in both England and the United States of her actions in the early days of the war, especially in the *Trent* affair, would help reconcile popular feeling in the once-again United States with Great Britain. It would also help some Americans – mainly white, Protestant, preferably native-born Americans – reframe their understanding of the Civil War and of what actually united the United States. Following the Civil War, with the resumption of active trading and technological relations with Britain and with boundary disputes between Great Britain and the United States on the North American continent a thing of the past, the cult of Queen Victoria became more assimilable to the universalizing aspirations of white, English speaking, Anglo-American bourgeois society. As the mother in the "Mother Country," Victoria could be reverenced without undue discomfort to post-war American national-ism, and cast as the progenitor of a racially united "Anglo-Saxon" civilization invested in a common worldwide empire of technology and progress. In this very role, however, Victoria's image became the focus of rising modern anxieties about the imperial bourgeois subject's agency in history.

Like all such developments, the consolidation of Victoria's post-Civil War American image was uneven. Victoria herself influenced its development decisively by the well-timed (from an American per-spective) postwar publication of *The Early Years* of Prince Albert, fol-lowed by her own *Leaves from the Journal of Our Life in the Highlands*. While some American readers of both books, taking their cue from *The Early Years*, immediately mythologized Victoria and Albert's peacemaking collaboration in the *Trent* affair, others were content simply to celebrate the domestic virtues of Victoria and Albert, and implicitly to celebrate the healing of American domestic wounds.

The Cincinnati *Ladies' Repository*, for instance, a middle-brow, anti-slavery Methodist periodical only cautiously interested in Victoria before and during the Civil War,[14] printed in 1866 "The Queenly

Power of Woman," an extract from John Ruskin's "Of Queens' Gardens," followed shortly by an editorial celebration of Queen Victoria "as the sovereign of a powerful empire, as a Queen revered and beloved by her subjects, as a woman, wife, and mother . . . as a model of excellence" (Ruskin 1866: 551). In October 1867 the *Repository* noted the publication of *The Early Years*, and the following month's "Betrothal of Victoria," extracted from *The Early Years*, completed the *Repository*'s conversion of Victoria into a sentimental heroine for an American women's audience without ever explicitly mentioning the *Trent* affair or incidents of the war. The picture depends crucially on Victoria's "latent" (as Whitman might have said) but widely acknowledged authorship of Albert's life as well as of her own journals. Only she can "exhibit," under authorization of her "irrepressible grief" ("Queen Victoria" 1866: 552) the intimate domestic evidence required to satisfy the *Repository*'s audience "that, after all, the Queen of England is very much as other women are, and that among his other great qualities the Royal Prince had a genuine human heart" ("Betrothal" 1867: 677). To discuss the Civil War *Trent* affair in any detail, for this audience, would have been to violate the *Repository*'s genteel mid-century taboo against women's knowing too much of the actual workings of political power; the ideal of Victoria's peacemaking influence as promulgated here actively repels any such historical specificity. Rather, both Victoria and the 1867 American female audience of the *Repository* have in common their dedication to the work of mourning that is communal as well as private.

Different conclusions could be drawn in the United States, however, from the *Highland Journal*'s implicit lesson that a queen is a woman, and from the increasing distribution in the United States of Victoria's domestic photographs. Sentimental American receptions, like those of the *Repository*,[15] contended with emergent modernist readings of Victoria's image and writings – which is to say, readings of the gender (as well as the race and nationality) of modernity. By 1868 – only a few months after celebrating "the last public act" of Prince Albert in saving the Union from war with Britain – *Harper's* wondered whether Victoria's revelations of her domestic life would not bring British monarchy to an end. Unlike the *Southern Literary Messenger*, the 1868 *Harper's* saw this possibility not as a triumph for the historical logic of the republican ideal, but as one of "the inevitable questions" raised by "an epoch of photographs and general suffrage and books by the Queen" – the epoch of mechanical reproduction ("Editor's Easy Chair" 1868: 664). As

Victoria's withdrawal from public affairs stretched on, Americans some-times joined in revived British republican speculation about the possible end of the monarchy (Thompson 1990: 104–19), but not always with the same antebellum nationalist exaltation.

For one thing, American and British interests in world affairs were coming to seem more congruent, especially from American commercial and industrial perspectives. For another, some American native-born elites clung to Victoria's image as a bulwark against the rising tide of Eastern European immigrants to the United States in the final decades of the nineteenth century. When Joseph Chamberlain floated his dream of an "Anglo-Saxon Union" between Britain and the United States, noting that Americans had already "Anglo-Saxonized California, Louisiana and Texas" and would "someday Anglo-Saxonize Mexico" even more effi-ciently than Britain had its own overseas empire (Chamberlain 1877: 789), he both flattered and reassured American elites (even those who objected to the tone of his proposals) of their common racial destiny with the Queen's England – whatever its eventual form of government. The point was not lost on Americans who did not come of the preferred racial stock; Irish-Americans in Boston, for instance, organized vigorous opposition to celebrations of Victoria's 1887 jubilee, which implicitly made allegiance to Victoria's cult an emblem and test of "whiteness."[16]

By the time of her 1897 Diamond Jubilee, and even more so follow-ing her death, salutes to Victoria as the "race mother" of Anglo-Saxondom would be commonplace on both sides of the Atlantic.[17] The transatlantic *Review of Reviews*, for instance, published a tribute to "Her Majesty the Queen" in the 1897 Jubilee year that juxtaposed a photo-graph of Abraham Lincoln with one of Victoria and proudly claimed that "the high water-mark of realised success in the Evolution of Humanity" could be seen in "the production of the supreme American man in the person of Abraham Lincoln and the supreme English woman in the person of Queen Victoria" ("Her Majesty" 1897: 15). Although many readers of the time would immediately have recalled the actual historical events of the American Civil War that linked Lincoln to Victoria, the essay defers its obligatory narration of the *Trent* affair to the very end ("Her Majesty" 1897: 30), as if to ensure that whatever his-torical knowledge of the war's crises it presents will be interpreted through the stylized racial-family romance of the mother–father por-traits. (And the *Review*'s 1897 version of the *Trent* story sinks Albert's role almost entirely: perhaps one symbolic husband, Lincoln, is enough.) Still further racializing history in the figure of the Queen, a 1901 American eulogy for Victoria in *The World's Work* celebrated her reign as "The Rule of the English-Speaking Folk" and drew the conclusion that the "right measure of events whether past or future is always the race-measure" ("The Rule" 1901: 479). The essay's series of illustrations begins with a global map designating in black "the domains of English-speaking people" and ends with a reproduction of the massy, flat, black-robed Nicholson portrait of the aged Queen that stylistically seems to echo the imperial map ("The Rule" 1901: 482, 494). If not so immediately striking a juxtaposition as that of the Lincoln and Victoria portraits in the *Review of Reviews*, these visual bookends nevertheless suggest how fully Victoria's individual face had become interchangeable for American readers with the racial face of global "Anglo-Saxon" empire.

At the same time, however, the dissolving of Victoria's face into her empire's demography implies the disappearance under her aegis of certain kinds of historical agency or subjectivity, a disappearance that vaguely haunted observers of modernity in the United States as well as in Great Britain. While still concerned at times to maintain the old antagonism between monarchy and republicanism and the nationalist logic of history according to which Britain's ancient free institutions were revived and fulfilled in the United States, Americans found in Victoria and the Anglo-Saxon concord of the 1890s rather less material to work into these familiar narratives. As race-mother and benign constitutional monarch, she smoothed over what the 1901 *World's Work* eulogy dismissed as the "old-time enmity between the United States and the mother country" ("The Rule" 1901: 479). But as the old teleological narrative of relations between mother country and republican child lost its drive, as meaningful distinctions between the political workings of the post-Civil War United States and late Victorian constitutional monarchy seemed few and far between, some Americans began to wonder instead about the historical forces or conditions of modernity that might be acting on republic and monarchy alike, and about the wider implications for individual agency that might be drawn from Victoria's equivocal fate as a subject of world history.

Helen Hunt Jackson's sonnet "Memoir of a Queen" (first published in 1870) looks back to sentimental queenliness with its trademark pathos of memory, but also, perhaps, forward to Victoria's modernist sublation as an individual subject. Although it may well have been inspired by Victoria's recently published *Journal*, the Queen of Jackson's poem is by definition anonymous and unwritable: "When she was crowned, her kingdom said,

'The Queen!' / And, after that, all other names too mean / By far had seemed. Perhaps all were forgot / Save 'Queen, sweet queen.'" Like Victoria, this Queen saves a warring land. Unlike Victoria, she leaves no written record of her reign: "All curious search is wholly vain / For written page or stone whereon occurs / A mention of the kingdom which obeyed / This sweet Queen's rule" (Jackson 1888: 58). Ostensibly devoted to memory, Jackson's "Memoir" actually hymns forgetfulness; what makes queens sentimentally memorable as well as troublingly modern is that their agency is both all-pervasive and self-erasing.

Writing on "The Queen of England" for the elite *North American Review* during Victoria's 1887 jubilee, Moncure Conway also found himself intrigued by the paradoxes of the Queen's self-undoing agency. Taking a Brahmin's superior tone toward the English–Irish brawls in Boston over the 1887 festivities – "the ghostly conflict between St. George and St. Patrick," as he calls it, "which made the mild sensation of the Queen's Jubilee in America" (Conway 1887: 120) – Conway sees history itself, as summed up in Victoria, in spectral terms. The woman idealized by Victoria's cult and the queen demonized by Irish-Americans are alike "phantasmal" shadows (Conway 1887: 121) from an (elite, native-born) American perspective. Indeed, all of European history loses substance in the light of America's common day: "the American atmosphere seems to change transatlantic forms to phantoms" (Conway 1887: 120).

If all these are "phantoms," however, who is the writer? Who or what is the American subject of history? Conway's essay never faces this question directly. Instead he births a modern machine out of the ghost of old monarchy, observing that the "apparent antiquity" of English institutions "is unreal, and that amid archaic walls, names, decorations, machinery of a modern and even advanced kind is at work" (Conway 1887: 123). If Victoria "has made her throne the tomb of every last relic of personal authority" (Conway 1887: 121), she has also rendered the state machinery more efficent by enabling "[t]he tinsel and the powers of chieftainship" to be "bestowed in separate estates" (Conway 1887: 124). As the political representative of aristocratic "high breeding," she presides over a social reservoir of eugenic potential "in which there is something scientific, something Darwinian": "An aristocracy of birth . . . would be a phenomenon not without philosophical interest in this time when the 'survival of the fittest' has become an familiar law, while survial of the unfittest seems a no less familiar fact" (Conway 1887: 126). Although Conway's conclusion protests in Darwinian terms that

England's arrangements are the evolutionary "development out of certain conditions of its own" and "can no more be transmuted to our America than its chalk cliffs can be changed to granite hills," the logic of his argument runs full circle upon the essay's beginnings. If Victoria in one sense is but the ghost of an individual historical agent, "the homely representative of a disfranchised [*sic*] sex" (Conway 1887: 127), "Victoria" in another way names a modern configuration of force and substance in which, Conroy half fears, Great Britain may be historically in advance of the United States.

Visiting Great Britain in the year of Victoria's Diamond Jubilee, American reporter Richard Harding Davis also went searching for Victoria in Britain's imperial substance. "As the day for celebrating the Diamond Jubilee drew nearer," his account begins, "the interest in it increased in proportion, and fed on itself, spreading and growing until it overwhelmed every other interest in the Empire" (Davis 1903: 261). Feeding is indeed, literally, the issue, as Davis details the arrangements made to ensure that enough potatoes arrived from Ireland and beef from New Zealand to nourish the visiting hordes. Like the American Reverend Newell, visiting London in the 1840s, Davis feels Victoria through her effects on the urban crowds rather than sees her directly. Yet his late-century Victoria is not so much her people's heart, in Newell's terms, as their collective belly – or even more mechanically, a statistical disturbance in the ether of world commerce. Her festivities cause a global rise in freight rates, "suggest[ing] how far-reaching were the effects of the Jubilee, and also how tightly the world is now knit together, since a street parade in London disturbs traffic in Auckland and on the Bay of Plenty" (Davis 1903: 262).

Has this vast web of modern power a subject at its center, one that an American could see? On his hunt for the subject, Davis takes his cue from "[o]ne of the English papers," which informs him "that each step of [Victoria's parade] route was a lesson in English history . . . and it was these points of interest that gave the route and the procession its great dignity and its magnificent significance" (Davis 1903: 283). The sheer demography of empire – the "three millions of loyal subjects and crown-princes of foreign and barbarous course, ambassadors and Christian archbishops, field-marshals and colonial premiers, red-coated Tommy's [*sic*], costers, and publicans" expected to line the parade route – gives the spectacle number and weight. "But greater than any of these," Davis proclaims, "were the dumb statues and silent signs of those who had gone before" (Davis 1903: 283–84).

Victoria is the subject in whom imperial demography and the pathos of history – the dumb statues and silent signs – should legibly unite if the spectacle is to have dignity and significance. Yet the grammar of this subject, as Davis imagines the Queen's progress, is elusive and conditional. Unlike sentimental antebellum American queens, Victoria's reminiscences are opaque to observation; indeed, it is not altogether clear that Victoria herself sees or remembers the historical pageant of which she is nominally the center and subject. "In those six miles the Queen would have passed over earth hallowed by memories of men so great that queens will be remembered because they reigned while these men lived – men whose memories will endure for so many years that a monarch's 'longest reign' will seem but an hour in the vast extent of their immortality" (Davis 1903: 288). Who actually remembers whom in this almost parodically decentered sentence? As in Helen Hunt Jackson's "Memoir of a Queen," the subject-position from which queens might remember and be remembered – the position from which antebellum American sentimental queens did their work as the suffering subjects of history – seems to be canceled in Davis's very gesture of pointing to it. The woman missing from the spectacle of the Diamond Jubilee is the queenly subject of history conjured in 1846 by the Reverend Galloway: "as she marks the traces of mighty events and ancient glory, the illustrious dead of centuries troop up before here, and alike rivet the steady gaze and warm emotion of her enraptured intellect and heart." Galloway thought this subject was to be found not in history's queens but in the educated American matron. By the time Richard Harding Davis goes to London for Victoria's Diamond Jubilee, perhaps she is not to be found anywhere; or again, as Jackson's "Memoir" suggests, she is to be found, unrecorded, everywhere.

According to Nancy Armstrong, "the modern individual was first and foremost a woman" (Armstrong 1987: 8); following Armstrong, Margaret Homans argues that "the modern British monarch was first and foremost a woman" (Homans 1993: 3). The evidence of Victoria's reception in the United States from her accession in 1837 to her death in 1901 suggests that nineteenth-century Americans often made sense of their emergent nationalism, their racial destiny, and their place in world history through the figures of woman and queen, figures that eventually coalesced in Queen Victoria. If not first and foremost, nineteenth-century Americans at least frequently imagined the subject of history as woman, queen, and Victoria. In taking on this role, however, Victoria also became a figure for growing American anxieties about individual historical agency in modern mass culture at the turn of the century. A sermon preached by Howard Brown in King's Chapel, Boston, following Victoria's death predictably eulogized Victoria's success in learning to "bear [her]self like the simple-hearted mother of all these lands and peoples" (Brown 1901: 9) but also used her both to confirm and to counter fears that "the tendencies of our mechanical age have seemed distinctly adverse to the free development of the individual life" (Brown 1901: 7). The age of the Great Man "has not passed away" in 1901, Brown's sermon proclaims (Brown 1901: 14), but the model Great Man for the age is a woman, Victoria, whose nineteenth-century woman's mode of exercising power by "influence" may survive the age of mechanical reproduction better than traditionally masculine forms of individual historical agency. The terms of Brown's eulogy anticipate those of his Boston contemporary, Henry Adams, who famously tried to tame his own bafflement at understanding "neither the formula nor the forces" of history at the beginning of the twentieth century by reducing them to the opposition of the Virgin and the dynamo (Adams 1961: 379). In Brown's American Victoria, however, the nineteenth-century mother marries the machine.

NOTES

1 Although modern diplomatic historians tend to be more cautious, twentieth-century biographers of Victoria and Albert agree with nineteenth-century estimates of the tension between the US and Great Britain over the *Trent* and the importance of the Queen's and Prince Consort's intervention. "It is hardly to exaggerate that a totally unnecessary major crisis was thereby averted, which could easily – indeed, almost certainly – have resulted in conflict" (James 1984: 271); see also Woodham-Smith 1972: 421.

2 "For Queen Victoria's Birthday" and Whitman's accompanying note first appeared in the Philadelphia *Public Ledger*, May 22, 1890, and in *The Critic* May 24, 1890: 262.

3 For other American versions of the "extremely romantic and, in the true meaning of the word, sensational incidents" (Merrill 1901: 286) connected with the *Trent* affair and the surrounding events of Victoria's role in the Civil War, see Merrill 1901: 286–93; Bartlett 1901: 14; May 1901: 12; Chamber of Commerce 1901: 10–13.

4 On the emergence of racial Anglo-Saxonism in the antebellum United States and its role in Anglo-American boundary disputes in North America, see Horsman 1981, especially 23–97, 219–28.

5 See Alice Carey's 1848 poem "Death of Cleopatra" (Carey 1848) and the

anonymous essay on "Queen Elizabeth" in the *Eclectic Magazine* ("Queen Elizabeth" 1859: 290–92) for echoes of Galloway's censure of Cleopatra's and Elizabeth's penchant for bodily self-display in the exercise of queenly power.

6 Nina Baym notes antebellum American women tourists' "obsession with murdered queens" (Baym 1995: 222) and their tendency to value Mary, Queen of Scots as sentimental martyr over Elizabeth's more equivocal femininity (ibid.: 143, 219–22); without considering Victoria herself as a queen in this period, Baym connects martyred sentimental queens with the larger "ideological mutation from Enlightenment to Victorian values" she sees in American women's history writing (ibid.: 219).

7 See, for instance, Lydia Sigourney's "Anna Boleyn" (Sigourney 1849: 246–48) and Newell's "Lady Jane Grey" (Newell 1848: 165–71).

8 Compare the illustrations to the 1859 *Eclectic Magazine*'s companion pieces on "Mary, Queen of Scots" and "Queen Elizabeth": Elizabeth, in an engraving taken from the Zucchero portrait, faces the viewer (as the essay notes disapprovingly) panoplied with the self-authored allegorical devices of her royal power. Mary, on the other hand, seen "On the Evening Preceeding her Execution," weeps over her bible in the standard pose of young women's sentimental reading, illuminated from above by the light of a single window. That the essay immediately preceding "Mary, Queen of Scots" in the September 1859 issue is a violent British-authored attack on popery only underlines how independent sentimental queenliness had become from actual historical controversy.

9 On the importance of women's historical knowledge to their role as domestic teachers in republican ideology, see Baym 1995: 29–45.

10 Galloway's vision is not eccentric; during the antebellum years, sketches of Felicia Hemans, Joanna Baillie, and other British women writers keep company with Queen Mary and Queen Elizabeth in middle-brow American women's periodicals more often than does Queen Victoria.

11 A later glance at Victoria in *Sunny Memories* seems more ready to credit the "example the Queen sets in the education of her children," since Stowe remarks on the many families she herself has seen following Victoria's lead. Still, Stowe carefully notes here that her information on the royal household comes from a personal talk "with Lord Wriothesley Russell" (Stowe 1854: 11, 17–18) – which establishes both her solid American skepticism and the access her authorship gave her to the British aristocracy.

12 For another American view from the 1850s that also dwells on the Queen as woman rather than as mother, and that sees monarchical history as *literally* consumed in her, see "Our Foreign Gossip" in the 1855 *Harper's*, which metonymically indicates the Queen's erotic womanhood through her imagined consumer desires as a visitor to Paris: "We are in the way of forgetting that the Queen is, after all, a woman, with womanish curiosity and loves, with womanish whims and fancies, with womanish weaknesses and tea-drinking, with womanish resolves and skirts, with a womanish eye for colors

and Paris hats" ("Our Foreign Gossip" 1855: 848). Playing on Victoria's role as "the chief consumer in a nation of consumers" (Homans 1993: 2), the *Harper's* editor jokes about the Queen having "to spend a week in Paris, and in that time never go shopping!" ("Our Foreign Gossip" 1855: 849). The antiroyalist moral of Victoria's Paris trip is that "men are growing to be men, and women to be women. Individuality is gaining voice" (ibid.: 849) – individuality as measured by consumer preferences; the queen who wants to shop is the gauge of modern individualism.

13  Munich suggests that "By being so confoundingly physical and fecund, Victoria's female body does not lend itself to translation as a madonna, to assimilation into a personification, such as Britannia, or to veneration as a mortal sage" (Munich 1987: 256). This American observer focuses on Victoria's erotic rather than maternal body in imagining her "apotheosis."

14  During 1863, for instance, the *Repository* concluded a traveler's tour of "The Sacred Places of England" with the ringing call, "Let the temporal power be taken from the Queen and the temporal tax from the people, and Christianity would soon sweep away England's formalism, and probably England's throne" (Haven 1863: 174). Another *Repository* writer, however, who denounced British ambitions for "*dominion* over all the world for the great, selfish, Arrogant Anglo-Saxon nation" during this dark year of the war, also praised "the almost republican simplicity" of Buckingham Palace: "It is about what was to have been expected of this true, simple-hearted, almost domestic English matron" (Tefft 1863: 616, 521).

15  For later examples of the postwar sentimental American Victorias that continued to be drawn from Victoria's own writings, see "Queen Victoria's Private Character" and the 1880 "Queen Victoria" in *Harper's*.

16  See the British–American Association's indignant account of its efforts to hold a banquet for Victoria's 1887 jubilee in Boston's historic Faneuil Hall, against the objections of Irish–American citizens, who charged that honoring Victoria betrayed the revolutionary history of the building. On the equivocally "white" position of Irish Americans in nineteenth-century American racialism, see Roediger 1991.

17  On the "race mother" as an important figure of modernist discourse, see Laura Doyle, who observes that "the race or group mother is the point of access to a group history and bodily grounded identity, but she is also the cultural vehicle for fixing, ranking, and subduing groups and bodies" (Doyle 1994: 4).

PART II

*Queen Victoria and other queens*

# CHAPTER 4

# Illustrious company: Victoria among other women in Anglo-American role model anthologies

## Alison Booth

The happiest women, like the happiest nations, have no
history.                              George Eliot, *The Mill on the Floss* (1860)

Western nations in recent centuries have seen an increasing demand –
in the name of the pursuit of happiness – for biographies of women who
have a history or who play a part in a national narrative. While the token
mistress of a king surfaced among collected lives of men, biographers
often collected exemplars who share the presumptive attributes of
womanhood, whatever else has set them apart from the "ahistorical"
sex. Since its origins in classical and medieval catalogs or legendaries
(McLeod 1991: 1–6), collective female biography has proliferated under
different historical pressures, increasingly opening the ranks of fame to
middle-class women of letters or of social action. Among the martyrs for
love, faith, or the nation, there has always been a place reserved for
queens.[1] The representation of Queen Victoria in varied assortments of
eminent womanhood provides a fine example of the ideological and
rhetorical tensions in exemplary biography.

Collective biographies of historical women, or what I term role model
anthologies, have been published steadily since the eighteenth century,
but there was a Victorian outpouring of these works from respectable
publishing houses in London, New York, and elsewhere. Such volumes
ironically underscore the claims to representative status of examples that
simultaneously break the mold they are said to exemplify. The queen is
like women (for example, those grouped in a particular collection) who
are unlike other women. At the same time, comparison of representations within and among these anthologies threatens any claim to either
mimetic likeness or individual distinction. Victoria is one of a kind, preeminent, the very *type* of Anglo-Saxon progress, maternal rule, the
empire of duty; yet, repeated in various guises, she tends to resemble
each other woman in a particular series.

As "the most splendid monarch of the nineteenth century" (Abbot

1913: 197), as a woman "conceived, born, and bred . . . to mount to the summits of greatness" (Sitwell 1936: 115), Victoria is perhaps most readily imagined *alone*. "Alone" was a quality she frequently attributed to herself in her journals, whether as a declaration of independence or bereavement, from her accession to her widowhood (St. Aubyn 1991: 65, 362). Yet as the representative of a nation whose women were encouraged to emulate queenliness, Victoria could scarcely claim to stand alone; her public life and the proliferation of "lives" of her ran the risk of dissolving the difference between her and her middle-class female subjects.[2] Well-known biographies of Victoria have established the commonplace that she was the quintessential sovereign yet the archetypal middle-class Englishwoman. Indeed, her power as a representative figure derives from the conjunction of differences, as in Stanley Weintraub's tally of contradictions: "Victoria was pleasant and unpleasant, selfish and selfless, democratic and dictatorial, . . . queenly yet middle-class at heart . . . She contained multitudes" (Weintraub 1987: xii; Langland 1995: 62–63; Strachey 1921: 415–16; Munich 1996: 12–13).

I will examine a selection of collective biographies that feature Queen Victoria, to demonstrate some of the functions of this mode of publication. Victoria, synecdoche of multitudes, both shapes her audience and is shaped by the company she keeps: according to the volumes' different forms, contents, and ideological orientations. In what follows, I entertain the various Victorias constructed in different assortments of notable women, not the woman whose life occasioned these constructions. After introducing the designs of role model biographies, I will examine several ways in which Victoria's story stands apart from those of queens as well as eminent commoners, particularly in her unwavering goodness and in her claim to coincide with the spirit of her age without losing her middle-class integrity. Different selective serial arrangements reshape the Queen's life in remarkable ways, at times rendering her comparatively unremarkable. When the Queen is immersed in a diverse assembly of renowned and obscure women through the ages, when she presides at the end of a gallery of English queens, or when she sets the stage for strong-minded "Victorian" women, her narrative takes on the coloring appropriate to different habitats, yet the story always stands out in its simplicity, felicity, predestined historical prominence, and in some perspectives, its lack of distinct achievement.

Representations of this most bourgeois of queens exemplify the ideological ambiguity of collective female biography or role model anthology. This subgenre of biography, which includes wide formal variation as well as shifting tables of contents, meets greater demand during periods when gender roles and social strata appear in flux (from Christine de Pizan's *The Book of the City of Ladies* [1405] to Shari Benstock's *Women of the Left Bank* [1986]). The composite structure of individual volumes, as well as the slightly varied repetition of such publications, tends to challenge conventions of singular identity, including those of gender. "Famous types of womanhood" (the title of an 1892 volume by Sarah Knowles Bolton) are sequential – serially displaced – as well as consequential, setting precedence that may actually be followed and ultimately replaced. Like conduct books and novels in the perspective opened by Nancy Armstrong and others, collective biographies of famous women have assisted in the cultural work of shaping bourgeois subjectivity in feminine terms. The excessive, slightly modulated reproduction of biographical assortments seems to superimpose restrictive codes of female virtue or heroism upon the audience, yet at the same time to offer fungible varieties of celebrity and achievement (compare Braudy 1986: 1–14; Munich 1987: 266). Certain names crop up perennially, yet there is a wide scope for new, perhaps hybrid personalities.[3] The differences among models and collections betray the instability of every foundational term in this arena, from exceptionality and fame to women and history. The standards of exemplary conduct for European and American middle-class women, far from being determined and timeless, require perpetual redefinition.

Queen Victoria appears in diverse collective biographies of women from mid-nineteenth century to between the wars, often with emphasis on her function as a role model to women of her race and nation. William Henry Davenport Adams, in his *Celebrated Englishwomen of the Victorian Era*, praises Victoria's "nobly useful life" – both ontological and textual:

a character which all English girls may well do their best to imitate, and a life which, in their lowlier spheres, they may rightly attempt to follow. Her moral courage, her fortitude, her industry, her elevation of aim, and her tenacity of purpose – these are qualities which they may successfully cultivate, even if they cannot hope to equal their Queen in perspicuity, in soundness of judgment, in breadth of intellectual sympathy, and in artistic feeling. They may take the woman as their exemplar, though they cannot approach the Queen. (Adams 1884: 1, 86)

Besides its curious division between qualities that are attainable and those that are beyond reach, this tribute exemplifies the structure of role models in general. The term "role model" is often taken to refer to a commendable person (or, in some contexts, entity), but, more properly, it indicates a relation among three figures: the target audience, the model, and the presenter or narrator (who may nearly coincide with the model in autobiography). In practice, a role model entails an interaction among these three figures that is expected to enable a recreation of the audience in the model's image. This effect is expected only if model and audience share certain attributes, usually those of sex and race or nationality, if not class[4] (notice that common English girls may emulate the Queen). The resemblance between model and audience, and often presenter as well, nevertheless requires a marked difference; the model must metonymically figure its field (an eminent *woman*), yet stand apart (an *eminent* woman). Much as in the triangulations of sexual rivalry and homosocial exchange of women that dominate Western drama and fiction, the constituents of a role model are drawn to each other by desire for sameness with a difference.

If a role model is working at all, it helps to destabilize the ranking of differences; this effect of gradual social remodeling is compounded by the serial form of the many provisional lists of exceptional examples. If there are multiple models of eminent womanhood, as each volume affirms, and shifting principles of inclusion in the ranks, as the succession of different collections indicates, then the audience begins to sense something like an equal opportunity to earn a place in this flexible register. Yet the desirability of any register, from collective biographies to restricted clubs, derives from vigilant gatekeeping. Well before present-day multiculturalism, Anglo-American anthologies frequently included one Asian princess, one Native American, one Jewish street urchin turned actress, or other nonconformities. Though potentially these are role models to their own marginal group because they resemble the heroines of the dominant race, the volumes are more often aimed at readers who take their own racial privileges for granted; a certain exoticism renders the implied norms all the more compelling. The effect of identification (Doane 1987: 13–19, 32–33), the approximation of audience to model, is all the greater for this obliteration of differences in a composite portrait of female eminence. In texts that seem caught between the democratizing tendencies of self-help and the closed kinship rules of *Who's Who* or Debrett's, representations of Victoria epitomize a productive ambivalence.

Role model anthologies present an illustrious company of women who have a history. Their tales are retold to conform to narrative conventions, yet the typical narratives entail trespasses which must in some way be exonerated. As Mary Cowden Clarke acknowledges, instead of "models," famous women are often "beacons of warning" (Clarke 1858: 3). Many women of record have crossed class barriers with a mobility that transgresses gender codes as well. Given the well-known penalties of female quest narrative, we are hardly surprised that Victorian or post-Victorian presenters of conspicuous women feel they have some explaining to do. All the more remarkable, then, that Victoria and a select few of her true peers in these volumes, contemporary middle-class women of letters or social reformers, evade what I will call the Nell Gwyn problem.

The significance of the Nell Gwyn problem is best indicated by examining Willis J. Abbot's *Notable Women in History* in some detail. Subtitled *The Lives of Women Who in All Ages, All Lands and in All Womanly Occupations Have Won Fame and Put Their Imprint on the World's History*, the volume presents Victoria among seventy women illustrating the inevitable "upward and onward movement of womankind" (Abbot 1913: 1–4). Such complacency does not resolve a presenter's difficulties when exemplary women have moved upward and onward in ways that should not be followed. Abbot responds to improper deviations with what might serve as the caption for most pre-nineteenth-century examples in these collections: "'Other times, other manners.'" Take for instance Nell Gwyn:

If in this day of a more superficial, or, it may be actual, morality, a girl could come from the slums of New York, proceed through the stages of street peddler, orange girl in the theatre, be an inmate of a brothel and finally wind up as the mistress of a king, and possibly his wife, the world would stand aghast.

Manifestly, the famous woman of pre-Victorian Europe who did *not* pass through a sexualized apprenticeship must have been a saint, a nun, very wealthy, highly educated, or combinations of these. Abbot cannot condone but simply admire Nell Gwyn as a brilliant light of her day, the toast of great literary men (Abbot 1913: 328). In his preface she is the antithesis of a pure American heroine, Martha Washington, though both contribute to "the composite picture of eternal woman" (Abbot 1913: 3). In his table of contents Abbot groups Nell Gwyn with several more respectable "Women of the Footlights," and sets Martha Washington apart with Dolly Madison and Joan of Arc as three

"Women Who Stand Alone" – Victoria being placed not "alone" with these three, but among "Many Queens and Some Martyrs." The inclusion of twelve "Women of Wit and Pleasure" (e.g. Ninon de L'Enclos, "A Typical Parisian Parasite") suggests that the Nell Gwyn phenomenon encroaches on other grounds for female historicity; indeed, some collections are entirely dedicated to historically remote adulteresses (e.g. Bleackley 1909). Yet with few exceptions, no woman whose lifespan overlapped with Victoria's could succeed at Nell Gwyn's metamorphosis *and* be included in the lists of commendable biography.

Some Victorian models seem to require no polishing. Victoria, Florence Nightingale, Harriet Beecher Stowe, and their like never appear to cross class, racial, or "moral" boundaries as do so many of their predecessors in history. Among chaste women who remain within their class, Victoria assumes a place in history with exceptional ease. Among regnant queens, moreover, she is unique for retaining her status as moral model, as I shall show. In spite of her long reign, Victoria's story is rather short and straightforward, from birth to accession to marriage, motherhood, and widowhood; the granddaughter and niece of kings avoids both the perils and the career opportunities of a Nell Gwyn. Such brevity may signal virtue (Lady Jane Grey sets a strict standard for the blameless queen, executed days into her reign), but it is not the greatest attraction in female role model biography. Even so, certain crossings of boundaries call for explanation. Instead of "How did a common woman become great?" or "How did a deviation become historically representative?," the questions would be, "How did a woman come to inherit the throne?" "How did a German mother give birth to an English girl, and the Hanoverian line yield yet another English monarch?" After the fact, she is supposed to have been *born* to be the best example of both English sovereign and woman, though biographies focus on the strangely static yet cataclysmic moment in which she *became* both.

For Victoria, the Nell Gwyn problem of unchaste social mobility is moot, as she never had to stir to attain her sovereignty. It was a short journey, indeed, from girl to queen: "I got out of bed and went into my sitting-room (only in my dressing-gown) and *alone*, and saw" the messengers bearing news that the king had died, "and consequently that I am *Queen*." The annunciation scene is replayed in most collected biographies (e.g. Adams 1884: 1, 6; Abbot 1913: 201–2; Carey 1899: 28–29; Howitt 1868: 513). The detail of her dressing-gown (some add that her hair was down) focuses on the vulnerability of an ordinary girl meeting several men in a private room, and heightens the contrast with the grandeur of a transfer of regal state. Victoria and her witnesses collaborate in sanctifying her feminine embodiment as a kind of discipline for her subjects rather than a monstrous transgression of sovereignty.[5] Biographers recall a magic transformation of innocent girl into queen: "A Royal Idyll indeed! – . . . like a fairytale . . . heard first at our mother's knee" (Carey 1899: 28). Victoria's most heroic achievement is to remain an authentic English lady in settings and situations indeed suited to fairytales. Genealogical fate, not her ability to captivate a king, placed her on the throne; in this, she not only transcends the Nell Gwyn problem but the several problems of the biographies of queens.

THE BAD QUEEN/GOOD QUEEN MODEL

Though Victoria takes a prominent position in anthologies of queens, she appears less at home in this illustrious diachronic company than among good women of ordinary rank in collections of contemporaries. In all varieties of collection, queens either were very very good or they were horrid – the same queen's biography becoming either saintly or villainous in different volumes. A rarity among queens, Victoria never appears as the bad queen. Rather than exemplifying the temptations of wealth and power or the vulnerability of her sex, Victoria demonstrates judicious discipline and domestic virtue. In encyclopedic collections that include any woman of note and that discover feminine virtue in every woman, Victoria can lose her distinction. Such sweeping collections may even claim the moral superiority of any and all queens, though anthologies that exclusively scrutinize queens know better.

Sarah Hale, in her encyclopedic *Woman's Record*, maintains that womanhood is a universal sign of moral superiority, transcending racial, religious, or individual defects. Thus even the "odious" African queen Anna Zinga (1582–1663), who feigned conversion to Christianity, is said to have had "better dispositions than any king of her race" (Hale 1870: 560–63). In the vanguard of Christian womanhood is Queen Victoria, "the best sovereign . . . , morally speaking, that ever sat on England's throne," a sign of Anglo-Saxon fitness to rule "the destiny of the world" (Hale 1870: 806, 563–64). Hale's Victoria, the epitome of "the reign of feeling and intellect, of industry and peace," becomes a static emblem of feminine rule, leaning on her husband's arm at the Crystal Palace (Hale 1870: 809; Homans 1993).

The precedents among female monarchs, however, would not encourage Hale's sanguine view of the queen as model to her people and her age. According to two of the many writers included in Hale's volume, Anna Jameson and Agnes Strickland, queens have offered an unflattering sample of womankind (Hale suggests they have at least been better than kings, who "have usually been very poor specimens of humanity" [Hale 1870: 799]). According to Jameson, Queen Christina of Sweden was the "more conspicuously wretched" because of "her sex, her learning, and her splendid situation"; similarly, Catherine II was warped by her "one overmastering passion – ambition," which should have devoted itself "to shining in a drawing-room" (Jameson 1832: 5–6, 214). In Strickland's account, many an English queen was likewise corrupted by unfeminine power: Isabella, wife of Edward II, became "a vindictive political agitator, and finally branded her once-honoured name with the foul stains of adultery, treason, and murder" (Strickland 1851: 91). Thus the two writers who did most to awaken biographical interest in queens during the nineteenth century encouraged readers to relish stories of queens' catastrophic defiance of strict standards of feminine conduct. The young woman who came to England's throne in 1837 – too late to be featured in Strickland's *Lives of the Queens of England, from the Norman Conquest to the Reign of Queen Anne* (London, 1840–48), or Anna Jameson's *Memoirs of Celebrated Female Sovereigns* (1832) – promised to obey those standards perhaps too well, her virtue nigh on unnarratable.

Portraiture of Victoria, whether in anthologies of mixed rank or of queens only, submits to several pressures: not only do judgments of queens gravitate to saint–virago extremes, but, as I have suggested, the judgment of manners and morals becomes more strict in the more contemporary biographies of role models. Thus, like the courtesan who has become part of the spirit of her age, many earlier models have been whitewashed by history, whereas any woman in close-up must be maculate. Another pattern in sequential modeling, however, aligns history with teleology, and equates the later with the better. In collections of English queens where Victoria takes the ultimate position, history's linear plot suggests that she is best or most advanced, though not actually higher ranked than her fellow "subjects." The age demanded that the living or recent Queen of England be the good queen, sponsor of Britain's deserving domination of the world. All the better that Victoria made discipline appear voluntary; the biographies repeat her performative utterance, "I will be good" (Carey 1899: 21, 33). Willis J. Abbot spells out the typical alternatives: "Catherine of Russia was an unspeakable libertine; Victoria a wife and a mother without blemish. But as queens they were equally great," equally sponsoring the expansion of empire (Abbot 1913: 3).

Victoria's story stands apart among the queens of England for its good fortune and its compatibility with an English public narrative; she can appear as a kind of ubiquitous influence, an anticlimax at the end of a series of violent or woeful tales. Many of Victoria's royal predecessors had to flee their husband's enemies or friends and forfeit their children; they were relatively powerless genetic vessels except in instances of regency or military leadership such as Margaret of Anjou's. Most often foreign-born, they were frequently viewed as alien to their people. Agnes Strickland finds a source of civilizing influence in the stories of exotic royal brides: "Our Queens . . . have been brought from foreign climes to plant the flowers and refinements of a more polished state of society in our own" (as quoted in Hale 1870: 799). But such a Victorian conception of the proper role for a queen scarcely accords with the treatment of queens such as Anne of Bohemia and Isabella of Valois as pawns in attempts at royal endogamy and territorial consolidation, or with the English attacks on the "foreign influence" of such queens as Johanna of Navarre (Thornton-Cook 1927: 85–96, 100–3). Yet while some biographers stress Victoria's German derivation – "the English crown . . . was 'made in Germany,'" and Albert was part of a "German invasion" (Abbot 1913: 200, 204) – most accept her English birth, and lavish praise on the Duchess of Kent and Baroness Lehzen as her excellent role models, and on Albert as her "Prince Charming" (Parton 1869: 425).

A pair of volumes, *The Queens of England* (Strickland 1851), and *Biographical Sketches of the Queens of England* (Howitt 1868), illustrate Victoria's privileged placement yet diminished allure in an unromantic age. Both are massive books for presentation, conspicuously illustrated to serve as a *Royal Book of Beauty* (the 1868 subtitle). In the earlier book, twenty-eight full-page engravings accompany as many biographies adapted "from Agnes Strickland" (the three latest queens had to be added where the Strickland series ends). The later *Biographical Sketches*, edited by Mary Howitt, includes twelve more unillustrated biographies interspersed with the same engraved series of full-busted, wistful or imposing antique beauties reproduced with the same potted "lives" (there is no acknowledgment of the earlier collection). The New York and London versions both end with nearly the same biography of Victoria, but in 1868 the frontispiece also represents Victoria (a classical bust), and her biography displays an extra engraving of the young queen; all three unmatched images of the Queen are out of keeping with "the Royal Book of Beauty" sequence. *The Queens of England* announces the aims of both volumes: to "portray equally the grandeur of the queen, the attachments of the wife, the affection of the mother, and the charms and the infirmities of the woman" (Strickland 1851: 4). The last words alert us that these models, beautified and almost beatified in the engravings if not in the text, cannot always be made good.

The biographies of Victoria's predecessors portray extremes of suffering and vice, heightened by contrasts. Thus in *Biographical Sketches*, Mary, Queen of Scots becomes a saint gazing heavenward, the "vicissitudes" of her life serving as "extenuation for" her "faults" (Howitt 1868: 349), whereas her sister Elizabeth, engraved as a stern equestrienne in pearls, becomes "heartless, treacherous," a "wanton" old woman stiffly "dancing . . . and ogling striplings . . . she was all that even the least rigid man would most abhor to detect in wife, sister, or mother" (Howitt 1868: 389). Though this suggests that the bad-queen type serves to reinforce the prohibition on female agency and desire, it is by no means true that all triumphant queens are censured in these collections. In *Biographical Sketches* Katherine of Arragon (*sic*), for example, is rated as high as the best English queens. Her "queenly dignity" and "womanly piety" daunted "her most deadly enemies. Her masculine abilities, and her lofty and assured temperament, set at defiance all the arts of her savage husband." Neither saintliness nor middle-class domesticity are being praised here, and yet Katherine is said to have gained, as Victoria later did, her nation's "deepest sentiments of respect and affection" (Howitt 1868: 271).

The more prosaic life of Victoria appears necessarily last in both collections of English queens. Its static quality could be due to the fact that there was no source in Strickland for this biography, but it is also an effect of Victoria's proximity. The text, closely corresponding in both volumes, acknowledges its superfluity: "The name of Victoria is on every lip, and imprinted on the heart of each of her subjects, yet would the memoirs of English royalty be incomplete, without a brief outline of the life of the reigning sovereign" (Strickland 1851: 337; Howitt 1868: 511). Outline it is, listing travels and assassination attempts, recalling how the public rejoiced at her accession and felt for her at the births of her children and, in Howitt's longer account of 1868, how they grieved at the death of her husband. Howitt's last paragraph seals the series of queens in the whole volume with a rather characterless encomium:

Queen Victoria presents the noblest example of domestic purity and social propriety. She has always been ready to second the plans of sound reform . . . ; and
with the blessings of cheap bread, of literature, commerce, . . . her reign is . . .
one of the most beneficently great, in the English annals. (Howitt 1868: 516)

Both the 1851 and 1868 biographies end with a ritual tribute to the
generic Queen of England in the volumes' preceding series of portraits.
The 1868 version, hinting at the lapse in Victoria's popularity with her
prolonged mourning, is more fulsome: "her subjects throughout the
world hail with joy and delight her reappearance in public. 'THE QUEEN!
GOD BLESS HER!' resounds on all sides as echo to the national prayer: 'GOD
SAVE THE QUEEN!'" (Howitt 1868: 516).[6] The surplus of three engravings
of Victoria in 1868, like the repeated national declamations of her
generic title echoed round the world, suggest that she has become more
elusive yet more ubiquitous over time and the expansion of the empire.
Born and trained for her oxymoronic role as feminine dependent and
supreme ruler, Victoria more easily conforms to prevailing gender differences of the industrialized middle classes than the many queens plucked
young from foreign courts or the native queens untutored in family life.

### VICTORIA AS THE SPIRIT OF THE AGE

In spite of the conflicting demands upon the persona of a queen, she is
expected like other monarchs to stamp her name and spirit upon the
period of her reign. Biographies of queens before Victoria, however,
observe a discrepancy between the character of the sovereign and her
times. Abbot, for example, sets Queen Anne at odds with her day: "After
all Anne was commonplace. Her era was glorious; . . . but . . . she was
[not] in any sense the animating force" (Abbot 1913: 96). Elizabeth's
"success and glory were probably as much the effect of chance as of
talent . . . the sources of the public prosperity will be found more in her
vices than in her virtues" (Abbot 1913: 405). Notably, Victoria's consistency with the norms of her middle-class subjects, not her outstanding
leadership, seems to be the "animating force" of her age; even as biographers deny her direct credit for industrial, imperial, or intellectual
progress, they regard these as sponsored by the benevolent female sovereign.

Collective portraits of Victorian womanhood frequently include the
Queen, whether as one among many examples of the age or as the pre-
siding spirit. She may lead the way in a mixed-rank selection such as
Rosa Nouchette Carey's *Twelve Notable Good Women of the* XIX *th Century*,

also figuring in the frontispiece (as she sometimes does in collections of queens, e.g. Howitt 1868; Thornton-Cook 1927). Prominently as she may be figured, however, she can appear comparatively characterless. The extra burden on the Queen as role model to all aspiring commoners of the empire and beyond tends to suppress the particulars of an individual life, while the pioneering achievements of strong-minded women can overshadow Victoria's career of self-control in fairytale circumstances.

Victoria comes first in William Henry Davenport Adams' two-volume *Celebrated Englishwomen of the Victorian Era*, which I cited for its designation of Victoria as model for English girls; she is followed by Harriet Martineau, Charlotte Brontë, Mary Russell Mitford, Mary Somerville, Sara Coleridge, Mary Carpenter, Adelaide Anne Proctor, George Eliot, and, finally, Jane Welsh Carlyle. Within her own biography Victoria is undoubtedly supreme, yet her effects are diffused by Adams's desire to convert a gentle-hearted English wife and mother into the spirit of the age. As though her narratable life ceased with Albert's death two decades before, this 1884 biography shifts midway to become a portrait of the era.

Adams traces what might be called the global reproductive capacities and indirect economic and political effects of the eponymous heroine of the period ("we already speak . . . of 'the Victorian age'" [Adams 1884: 1, 25–26]). "Cabinets come and go, but the Queen remains, and by her presence guards against any sudden arrest of the wheels of government" (1, 69). The calm repository of British memory, Victoria also personifies the benevolent dominion over India and Ireland. As feminine inertia, she has ensured "the peace, prosperity, and contentment of the empire," which in turn ensure progress in the railway system, the telegraph, the Post Office, and other measurable improvements during her reign (1, 73–78). Adams concludes with a paean to the "intensity and universality" of Victoria's popularity, at its height in 1884 (the "final stages" of her reign; 1, 80–86).

Willis J. Abbot in 1913 still attributes national prosperity and pre-eminence to female rule: "during the three most glorious epochs of English history the crown was worn by a woman" (Abbot 1913: 197) – though I noted above how little credit he gives Anne and Elizabeth for the glory of their own eras. Abbot repeatedly stresses the expansion of empire while Victoria anchored her nation: "During the calm reign of the British sovereign the national red was far-flung over the map of the world" (3). Victoria, "The Most Splendid Monarch of the Nineteenth

Century, 1819–1902 [*sic*]" as the subtitle of her biography has it, might be the genius of technology conquering the world. "When she was crowned it took months for her Foreign Office to communicate with her most distant possessions: when she died the news was flashed over mountains and under oceans to the very antipodes in a few seconds" (198; compare Thornton-Cook 1927: 372). Victoria influenced a worldwide advance in humanitarian principles as well as communications:

Mankind progressed in brotherly love . . . Child labor was regulated . . .; women were no longer permitted to work in mines; the negro, however savage, was free wherever the British flag waved; her ships were the chief factors in suppressing the African slave trade on the high seas and her influence was thrown on the side of the anti-slavery forces in our own war between the states. (Abbot 1913: 198)[7]

Victoria assumes the agency of the entire British government, which is then personified as a liberal reformer instead of the contentious set of institutions that helped enforce British dominion (and for a time attempted to support the slaveholding states). Though Abbot emphasizes Victoria's imperial might, he also capitalizes on the view of woman as weaker sex. The "fundamental fact that [Victoria] was a woman" eased the progress of democracy (similarly, Parton suggests that her "chief service" to her country may have been to postpone revolutionary protests against the "costly pageant" of monarchy [Parton 1869: 438]). Abbot implies that a dominion so mild and self-disciplined insinuated itself into every corner of the world (Abbot 1913: 202–3). In closing, Abbot affirms Victoria's effective fusion of national destiny with an exemplary female life: "All London, all England, was draped in the purple hue fixed upon for mourning, but all the world sincerely mourned . . . a good queen, a good wife and a good mother" (206). So representative that she is hard to distinguish, Victoria is ultimately far from alone, a spectacle witnessed by all the world.

In such programmatic modeling, the Queen appears as though in a stereoscope that pairs the close-up of a domestic middle-class woman with the outline of a global force. Curiously, Abbot, Adams, Hale, and others exalt Victoria as model to the world, yet never consider what might happen if this spirit of the age succeeded in modeling an audience equal to itself. The British Queen can be commended not just to English girls, or women, or her nation, but to any spectator across the globe as a model for self-improvement, even by presenters who appear dedicated to immutable racial or class hierarchies. Yet we can observe in volumes such as Abbot's, ostensibly supportive of liberal progress and women's rights, that the fiction of a universal passport to eminence is easily reconciled with a conservative rather than a democratizing agenda. Though volumes that present women of many ranks appear to promise more options for social transformation, they present their own codes of exceptionalism and trickle-down majesty.

### A TRUE MIDDLE-CLASS HEROINE

As the spirit of her age, Queen Victoria can serve as a mere backdrop for women who make a name for themselves. Indeed, in collections that require documented life works, Victoria's only ticket for admission is her royalty. In most cases Victorian notable women meet the same standards of domestic virtue, accomplishments, and learning as Victoria; the Queen's main achievement is that *in spite of sovereignty* she is just like an ordinary good woman. Although a woman's reign is said to encourage the expectation of female achievement in wider fields of endeavor, Victoria herself hardly led the way. Thus, presenters often appear to recommend her as a model to reproduce the run-of-the-mill. According to Carey, Victoria's daily schedule as a young queen exhibited "that untiring industry and remarkable aptitude for business that was to set such a noble example to her subjects" (Carey 1899: 33, 43). Whether the Queen is most constrained to resemble her subjects or the other way around is never quite resolved, however.

Undoubtedly the image of Victoria is shaped by the increase of opportunities for middle-class women during her century, and some of those who led the way, her closest *semblables*, at times seem to overshadow the Queen. Adams's *Celebrated Englishwomen* is particularly instructive in its application of the dual scales for women's preeminence, those of domestic virtue and intellectual achievement or public service. He represents Victoria as the spirit of the age, as we have seen, and places her first, but the effect of the whole volume is to cut the Queen down to size. She may become a historical signpost at the beginning of several of the biographies – "Queen Victoria had been eighteen years on the throne when Mary Russell Mitford closed her useful and honourable career" (Adams 1884: 1, 189) – or an incident in contemporary memoirs, as in Charlotte Brontë's recollection of seeing Queen Victoria in a carriage on the Rue Royale in Brussels: "She looked a little stout, vivacious lady, very plainly dressed; not much dignity or pretension about her" (Adams 1884: 1, 154).

Biographical realism, in Adams's collection as in others, further contributes to the image of the Queen as a plain middle-class woman.

In keeping with the detailed physical descriptions of each biographical subject, Adams observes Victoria closely:

In stature her Majesty is below the average height, and of late years has shown a decided tendency to *embonpoint*; but . . . she has the air of command natural to her lofty station, with the refinement of bearing that comes from high culture . . . Deep furrows, traced by affliction, experience, and meditation, mark the thoughtful face. Altogether, one who saw the Queen without knowing who she was, would look at her again and again, as at a woman of strong character, of high position, and accustomed to great responsibilities. (Adams 1884: 1, 67)

What at first appears unmajestic – a short, fat woman – is read more carefully as an authentication of upper-class excellence that would command attention regardless of the rank of queen. Such scrutiny of the qualities of a revered global influence invites closer comparison with other high-minded women of her day. She meets their highest standards in domestic matters, yet in other respects she fails to measure up.

The Queen's own biography in Adams's collection, the second longest after George Eliot's, seems to exhaust the representative qualities of her domestic life: "The Queen to perfect husband was perfect wife" (Adams 1884: 1, 39). She has "set her family a noble example," reproducing her own excellence in children and grandchildren (1, 62–66). Eyewitness accounts of marital interludes lead to glimpses of the many elaborate shrines to Albert (1, 42 and 50–56). Adams condones the widowed Queen's prolonged absence from the public (lessening by 1884) because "the nation . . . gain[s] by the lofty example she has set of conjugal devotion" (1, 60–61). But more than family devotion is required for entrée to this collection, and in instances of sufficient achievement such virtures may even be waived.

All Adams's exemplars besides Victoria have committed themselves to action or authorship, and some even verge on the Nell Gwyn problem of unchastity. Adams seems compelled to acknowledge defective models. Harriet Martineau – "the first of the notable Englishwomen of the nineteenth century," a "pioneer" (Adams 1884: 1, 89) – exemplifies more strongly than the queen "the highest development of the intellect of women," a characteristic of the Victorian age (11, 86–87). Adams has misgivings about this woman of intellectual enterprise, however. In contrast with Victoria's soothing influence, Martineau's career is "typical of the unrest and feverishness of the nineteenth century" (1, 88) – a symptom also of Charlotte Brontë, though the latter is a true genius and pious Christian (1, 156, 123). No "woman of genius," Martineau succeeded through "a colossal self-confidence" and ambition (1, 89 and 92), rather like a bad queen. Among Martineau's errors are her atheism and her desire to set the terms of social visiting: "she should have accepted the homage paid to her [as literary celebrity] . . . instead of insisting on being brought down to the level of ordinary womanhood" (1, 107; see Langland 1995: 31–34).

Adams encounters a nearer repetition of the Nell Gwyn problem in his biography of George Eliot, who exceeds Charlotte Brontë in artistic achievement, but falls far short of Victoria's and Brontë's examples of virtue. Victoria is unnamed in nearly 100 pages on Eliot, as though the two models occupy separate worlds due to the novelist's unforgivable breach of "conduct," her "so-called marriage." Adams supposes that Eliot's novels stress "the sanctity of domestic ties" to counteract "the injurious effect" of "laxity . . . on the part of individuals [Eliot and Lewes] so conspicuous by their genius and general elevation of character" (Adams 1884: 11, 108). The works themselves become the proper role model when the woman threatens to encourage pernicious behavior. When the standard of cultural achievement is invoked, Eliot ranks supreme and Victoria sinks below the horizon.

These and other collected portraits suggest that while ordinary Englishwomen have learned to resemble each other, *notable* Englishwomen have somehow gained public confirmation for certain deviations from the norm. Such confirmation is then wrought backward to the birth or nature of these heroines, who are said to be as chosen and removed from common service as Queen Victoria. Genius should exempt Charlotte Brontë from "arbitrary social conditions"; Adams sees Brontë's labor as a governess as a debasement of almost sacred powers, as though "the waters of Niagara are expended in turning a petty mill-wheel" (Adams 1884: 1, 141). The most fortunate examples encounter circumstances that concur in their exceptional nature, the equivalent of being chosen for coronation. Thus James Parton sees a providential design in Florence Nightingale's life: "Inheriting from nature a striking and beneficent talent, she was able, . . . finally, to exercise it on the grandest scale in the sight of mankind" (Parton 1869: 11).

The Lady with the Lamp has often been aligned with the Queen; the two role models, often appearing in the same collection (Carey 1899), share the function of codifying Victorian femininity (Poovey 1988: 171). A glance at this preeminent Victorian lady suggests not only how readily Victoria was outdone by enterprising female subjects, but also why anthologized biographies of Victoria tend to swerve from narration of a particular life to congratulations either on the Queen's extraordinary ordinariness or on her benign worldwide effects. In a word, Victoria has done too little alone; solitary yet surrounded, her every action has the air of being pre-scripted. Though Nightingale's model career was similarly constrained by proprieties and myths, it was indisputably also self-made, and helped directly to initiate other women's careers.

Lady and Queen both figure in *Eminent Women of the Age*, edited by James Parton, a hospitable collection that includes Fanny Fern (Mrs. James Parton) and Elizabeth Cady Stanton, themselves contributors to the volume. Florence Nightingale adorns the title page and leads the way in an untitled first section, whereas Victoria's biography is set alone in its own category, between "The Woman's Rights Movement and Its Champions in the United States," and "Eminent Women of the Drama." Parton quotes uncritically the popular imagery of Nightingale as heroine and saint of the Crimean War. He mentions Queen Victoria's gift to her of a cross, and the visit Nightingale paid to Balmoral, "receiving the homage of the royal family." Homage is due from the Queen to this practical world leader, an effective model for the American women who nursed soldiers during the Civil War (Parton 1869: 29–37). Parton's portrayal of Victoria is considerably less devout, mixed with satire of the historical fiction of monarchy and with novelistic insights into the emotions of the bride and wife (Parton 1869: 422–23). Like Carey, Thornton-Cook, and other biographers, Parton offers glimpses of the woman beneath the surface by strategically excerpting the "trifles" of her own memoirs. "Her Highland Diary . . . exhibits to us the picture of a happy family, always delighted to escape from the trammeling etiquette and absurd splendors of their rank" to find "pleasures which are accessible to most of mankind" (Parton 1869: 436–37). Whatever else Nightingale's story may be, it is not cozy; the royal family's escape from court to hearth is a small venture compared to Nightingale's campaigns to reorganize the apparatus of the empire. Victoria as both Nightingale's peer and a simple woman pleased with "trifles" might seem to cancel herself out, yet this discrepancy lies at the heart of representations of Victoria in a middle-class cohort.

In each of the biographies I have discussed, Victoria is one in a series of women chosen to represent that curious contradiction, a woman so unlike other women that it is remarkable that she is just like other women. With repetition, the measures of eminence appear to wear away, but the demand for such role models requires an unstable blend of intimacy and distance, likeness and singularity. Queen Victoria perfected an image of herself as middle-class and regal, alone yet containing multitudes. Collective biographies often recruit her into service because of this representative versatility, for different ends. In general, alongside contemporary commoners, Victoria is used more to encourage aspiration; her own qualities blend into the background of the age, allowing leaders such as Florence Nightingale to shine forth more brightly. Among famous women of all ages, she stands out for the simplicity of her quest, the refined compass of her actions and principles. As the culmination of a series of queens, she is most certain of pre-eminence by every standard except the demands of historical romance; here she may solicit in the audience a self-congratulatory fantasy of high hereditary rank and nationhood. As good queen or spirit of the age, as a woman unstained by an episodic quest, Victoria might seem the perfect model of historical womanhood. Yet she is by no means omnipresent in collective biographies of women from the 1840s to 1940s. Her virtues and her good fortune may detract from her narratability, just as the nation's and world's collaboration in recognizing her public role may prevent any of the declared individual initiative that traditionally elicits biography. Victoria, painfully, is never alone, in spite of her experience of the isolation of her position. Always, she must keep company in the categories of historical womanhood. Victorian middle-class models have the advantage of earning their own place in the ranks through efforts that might be replicated; there are far more openings for writers and nurses than for queens. In short, Victoria may underwrite the project of role model biography, and her exceptionally good life may serve to anchor or dignify volumes, but she is often outranked by more compelling representations.

The same-sex collection of role models tends to reproduce a normative womanhood, in spite or because of the comparative distinctions among the subjects included. As many feminist theorists now recognize, however, not all universalizing moves are alike; some are the precondition for social transformation on behalf of the posited category (Bordo 1993: 222–25). At the margins of these Anglo-American female role model anthologies one always detects a vast archive, the annals of European men's history compelled to ingest more representatives of the category of womanhood. Victoria assists the genre in chipping away at the undervaluation of such women's contribution to history, at the supposition that fame and virtue, history and happiness, are incompatible or unattainable for women, even at the shibboleths of race and nation, of birth and rank, of identity as isolated self-determination. It is collective, even collaborative biographical history, and it has been one strategy for empowering the women who could obtain but not get *in* such books.

1 Pioneering examples are *The Book of the Ladies* (Brantôme 1902), first published in 1665, representing recent European queens and noblewomen, and the 1752 anthology of women of arts and letters, *Memoirs of Several Ladies of Great Britain* (Ballard 1775). Ezell counts twenty-five "biographical encyclopedias and anthologies" of "literary Englishwomen" between 1675 and 1875, alongside specialized collections such as *Memoirs of Queens* (Hays 1821; Ezell 1993: 68, v–vi). Scarcely a year of Victoria's reign passed without publication in Britain and the US of collective biographies of women, with as many as ten or twelve a year in the 1850s or 1870s; often reprinted or repackaged, some specialized by religion, nation, region, or epoch, juvenile or prurient interest, or other categories. Thanks to Christopher Newton for a selective bibliography.

2 Recently Elizabeth Langland and Deirdre David read Victoria as the epitome of the queenliness urged upon Englishwomen as agents of the middle classes and British Empire. Nina Auerbach brought these same tropes of queenliness to the forefront of feminist Victorian studies back in 1982 (Langland 1995: 68–79; David 1995: 6, 117; Auerbach 1982: 58–61, 64–67). See Munich 1996.

3 A typical list appears in Mary Cowden Clarke's *World-Noted Women* (1858): Sappho, Aspasia, Cleopatra, St. Cecilia, Héloïse, Laura, Valentine de Milan, Joan of Arc, Margaret of Anjou, Isabella of Castille, Lady Jane Grey, Pocahontas, La Vallière, Maria Theresa, Catherine II of Russia, and Florence Nightingale. *Great Women Paper Dolls* (1994) offers Sappho, Cleopatra, Queen Boudicca, Theodora, Lady Murasaki, Eleanor of Aquitaine, Joan of Arc, Vittoria Colonna, Pocahontas, Madame de Pompadour, Amelia Earhart, Queen Victoria, Susan B. Anthony, Florence Nightingale, Sarah Bernhardt, Beatrix Potter, Madame Curie, Anna Pavlova, Bessie Smith, and Golda Meir.

4 A contemporary fixation on role modeling (see Comer 1990; Edwards 1994; Seligman 1991) assumes that such narrative models (e.g. the career of an African–American athlete) show others the way to transform marginalization (e.g. racial and class disadvantage) into success.

5 Victoria exposes, like Elizabeth I, an inherent "plasticity of gender in the field of sovereignty," which according to Louise Fradenburg is due to sovereignty's drive toward both "exemplarity" and exclusive "difference" from the common body (Fradenburg 1992: 1–3).

6 *Queens of England* concludes, "GOD SAVE OUR GRACIOUS QUEEN!" (Strickland 1851: 341). The specter of a debauched and bedecked Elizabeth I or of other transgressive queens helps construct Victoria's thorough goodness. The scandal of her attachment to her Scottish servant John Brown

does not appear on Howitt's soft-focus screen in 1868, though journals had blown it up in 1866/67 (St. Aubyn 1991: 360–62); if collective biographies mention Brown at all, they present Victoria's benign condescension to a faithful servant (Thornton-Cook 1927: 370–71). This was the closest glimpse of the flip side of a queen's card: the class-crossing "quean," in Howitt's punning term for Elizabeth (Howitt 1868: 404).

7  Abbot details Albert and Victoria's softening of Lord Palmerston's ultimatum concerning the incident on the British steamer *Trent*: "the influence of the royal couple undoubtedly averted British war with the Union in 1861" (Abbot 1913: 205).

# CHAPTER 5

# Gloriana Victoriana: Victoria and the cultural memory of Elizabeth I

## Nicola J. Watson

On June 20, 1837, when Victoria ascended the British throne, the reputation of the monarchy as an institution was arguably at an all-time low,
the Princess herself was virtually an unknown, and queens regnant had
been few and far between. In this atmosphere it was inevitable that the
new Queen would be assimilated to her most illustrious predecessor as
a Virgin Queen, Gloriana herself, and this despite Victoria's own thoroughly conventional condemnation of that lady as immodest (Longford
1964: 31). In 1831, for example, two members of parliament were already
arguing that on accession the Princess should assume the title Queen
Elizabeth II, a title altogether more Britishly auspicious than her own
promised to be (Gernsheim and Gernsheim 1959: 2); J. S. Mill, being
surly about the newly crowned monarch in his capacity as editor of the
*Westminster Review*, growled scathingly that "unless she has the qualities
of Elizabeth she will be nothing" (quoted in Stein 1987: 62); Lord
Holland, writing to the British ambassador in Paris, reported that he had
been to court to see "our Virgin Queen" and returned "quite a courtier
& a bit of a lover" (quoted in Woodham-Smith 1972: 1, 140); and both
Lord John Russell on her accession, and *The Times*, reporting the birth
of her eldest son in 1841, compared Victoria "with the two previous
queens regnant, Elizabeth and Anne."[1] Most strikingly, Victoria was
conflated with Elizabeth in an extraordinary painting by Charles Robert
Leslie (1794–1859), who had already made something of a reputation by
painting *May Day Revels in the Time of Queen Elizabeth* (1821) and who had
been commissioned by Victoria to paint *The Queen Receiving the Sacrament
at her Coronation* in 1838. *Lord William Cecil Giving News of her Accession to
Princess Elizabeth in the Garden of Hatfield House* depicts an Elizabeth-as-
Victoria.[2] The picture mendaciously translates Tudor court politics into
the romantically sexy language of the sort of genre painting which took
as its subject the courtship of pretty girls in vaguely historical fancy dress
in sunny gardens. This work could best be glossed, not by Holinshed's

account of Elizabeth's accession, but by the delectable chivalry with which the scene of the young Victoria receiving the news of hers at Kensington Palace three centuries later was regularly invested. Like H. T. Wells's painting *Queen Victoria Receiving the News of her Accession* and Mary Gow's watercolor *Princess Victoria Receiving News of her Accession*, Leslie's piece breathes the selfsame sentimental fervor that the future premier, Disraeli, conjured in his novel *Sybil* (1845):

> In a palace in a garden – not in a haughty keep, proud with the fame but dark with the violence of ages; not in a regal pile, bright with the splendor, but soiled with the intrigues, of courts and factions – in a palace in a garden, meet scene for youth, and innocence, and beauty – came the voice that told the maiden that she "must ascend her throne." (Disraeli [1845] 1895: 47)[3]

The fact that Leslie's painting exists at all points to the ways in which a nineteenth-century Elizabeth might be hypothesized as a useful alter ego for the young Victoria; the nagging incredulity that this picture raises in the mind of the viewer, however, points to the ways in which, as a modern monarch, Victoria could not in the end be poured into the mold of an Elizabeth, or Elizabeth into that of Victoria. In what follows, I shall be describing some of the occasionally contradictory ways in which the myths of these two queens nevertheless mutually constituted each other from Victoria's installation as heir-presumptive in 1830 until her posthumous apotheosis in the early years of the new century.

## TWO QUEENS IN ONE ISLE

At its most euphoric, the nation over which Victoria ruled raised Elizabeth I to dizzy heights of veneration, characteristically celebrating her as the "Good Queen Bess" who had ruled over that never-never land of Merrie England, complete with its maypoles, morris dancing and stout yeomen, Yule logs, mince pies and plum puddings, hey-nonny-nonny, jesters and picturesque hostelries, and an altogether remarkable amount of harmless rollicking and roistering. She featured equally, of course, as the ageless Faerie Queene of the golden age of romance and chivalric feeling, supposedly embodied in the great literature of the day, most especially within the writings of William Shakespeare, Philip Sidney, and Edmund Spenser. As the "Elizabethan" also became, in the wake of the Catholic Emancipation Act of 1822 and in the context of the Oxford Movement, the crucial founding moment when an England torn by religious faction was reunited as one nation, Elizabeth was increasingly lauded as a passionately populist and nonsectarian queen,

one who had ruled through the love of the people rather than primarily
through the exercise of divinely sanctioned despotism. At home, she was
supposed to have promoted an era of manly and Ruskinesque chivalry,
while in her foreign policy she was held to have presided over the founding of the British Empire, via her courageous and romantically reckless
patronage of that curious species, the sea dog, exemplified by Drake and
Raleigh. Finally, and most oddly, she was thought to have sponsored the
development of almost any sort of modernity associated with the greatness of Victorian Britain, spanning the emergence of high-tech science
and the invention of domestic conveniences, both, of course, major features of the royal-sponsored Great Exhibition of 1851.[4] This heavily
modernized notion of the nature of Elizabeth's power was reinforced
and perhaps even necessitated by Victoria's presence on the throne, suc-
cessively imagined as romantic young Queen, "the rose of England",
patron of Charles Kean's Shakespeare and the Great Exhibition,
Disraeli's Fairy Queen and the future Empress of India, for the most
part politically powerless but increasingly the repository of a tremen-
dous emotional investment on the part of her subjects. Vice versa,
Victoria's queenship could be legitimated and elaborated by this powerful fantasy of Gloriana. (In 1843, for example, the mayor and aldermen
of Southampton threw down their cloaks in the style of Raleigh to cover
puddles in the path of the young Queen, an incident considered worthy
of illustration in at least one contemporary periodical.[5]) It is, therefore,
rather startling to discover that, despite Gloriana's usefully inflated
iconic status, by mid-century depictions of the private woman behind
the national myth were for the most part unprecedentedly hostile, and
would remain so until about the 1870s.

   The nineteenth-century split between the national icon and the
private woman was fostered by the growth of a strain of popular biography of queens and courts, often explicitly encouraged by the presence
of Victoria on the throne, together with the huge popularity of this
genre's close cousin, early Victorian history painting. Both genres were
fascinated alike by the feminine, domestic, anecdotal and biographical
as the underside of the more officially historical. Both genres were interested, too, in the potential of this feminized history as morally exemplary
narrative directed at girls and young women.[6] The effect was to fracture
Elizabeth I decisively into two opposing incarnations – national and
sexual – which became increasingly difficult to fit together. This problem
is vividly displayed by William Cooke Taylor's *Romantic Biography of the
Age of Elizabeth* (1842), which includes a plate of Elizabeth (based upon

an authentic portrait) reverently captioned "The Founder of our Colonial Empire" opposite a satirically journalistic account of the way "her passion for flirtations continually interrupted state affairs" (Taylor 1842: vol. 1 facing 90).

Cooke's stated ambition was "to substitute Daguerrotypes for Fancy portraits" (Taylor 1842: 1, 4); in other words, to supersede the sort of portrait favored by the wealthier (including on more than one occasion Victoria herself) who regularly chose to have themselves painted in romantically historicized fancy dress. Instead, Cooke offered as a mode of history the aggressively modern form of domestic middle-class portraiture which Victoria herself came to favor from about 1847 onwards.[7] Viewed through this lens of modern, middle-class sexual morality, the modern-dress Elizabeth turned out to be anything but the prevailing ideal of Victorian womanhood. Accordingly, from the 1820s onward, she elicited a "singular mixture of admiration and contempt" (Abbott 1849: 207), supposed as she was to unite undoubted political and intellectual abilities with "the most craving vanity, the most irritable jealousy, the meanest duplicity, and the most capricious and unrelenting spite, that ever degraded the silliest and most hateful of her sex" (*Quarterly Review* 26 [1822], 143).

All too feminine in her vices, Elizabeth was nevertheless culpably unwomanly because, instead of refusing political power in favor of exerting an uplifting, softening influence, she had retained absolute executive authority. Her celebrated chastity, having guaranteed and maintained that authority, thus came to be construed not as virtuous but as aggressive, humiliating, hypocritical, mean, and vicious. For the deliberately iconoclastic Byron in 1821, for example, "our own half-chaste Elizabeth" displayed her lack of proper royal womanhood most clearly by her sexual parsimony, a parsimony expressed by the crime of her old age in putting her young favorite, the Earl of Essex, to death (Byron [1986] 1980–93: v, 433). Paradoxically, because Elizabeth's virginity was seen to be illicitly exploitative, it was possible simply to convert it into its equally antidomestic shadow, a latent, frustrated or actual promiscuity. So in 1825 Hugh Campbell's immodest, wanton and licentious Elizabeth was not only denied all moral credit for her actual chastity, but made a monster of perpetual lust by it, suffering from "some obstructions from nature, which disabled her from the offices of a wife, precluded her from the pleasures of a prostitute, and, contending with her strong desires, raised such a ferment and fire within her, as she was ever endeavouring, and never able, to extinguish" (Campbell 1825: 289). Nor was Campbell alone in brooding over this imputed aspect of Elizabeth's private character. By 1853 there was a lively public debate in progress over Gloriana's "morals": *Fraser's Magazine*, for example, ran a lengthy two-part article in October and November of that year attempting to vindicate her from suggestions of wantonness put about by, amongst others, John Lingard, Sir James Mackintosh, and Lord John Campbell.[8] But nineteenth-century writers on any side of this question, whether they believed Elizabeth promiscuous, chaste, or ambiguously one or the other, emphatically agreed that above all she had willfully and irresponsibly refused to be domesticated:

there are very few traits of her character which represent her clothed in any of the gentle proprieties of womanly beauty and grace; the dignity she had was of the throne, not of the sex, and her appearance and demeanour were only not coarse, because she was a queen . . .; she would not have been a desirable wife for any of us. (Abbott 1850: 69)

Elizabeth's newly discovered womanly shortcomings were rendered especially spectacular in the context of the royal personae constructed around her young successor on the throne of England. At her accession in 1837, for example, Victoria found herself depicted as only incidentally and even reluctantly queen. Elizabeth Barrett's early poem "Victoria's Tears" (published June 8, 1837), characteristically, constitutes the princess as a victim child-queen, another Jane Grey: "while the heralds played their part / For million shouts to drown – /'God Save the Queen' from hill to mart – / She heard through all, her beating heart, / And turned and wept! / She wept, to wear a crown" (quoted in Stein 1987: 74). Between 1840 and 1861, the years of Victoria's marriage to Albert and the births of their nine children, the Queen presented herself and was represented as elaborately wifely, maternal and domestic, a persona depicted most memorably and enchantingly by Winterhalter in 1846.[9] In May 1842 the *Illustrated London News* was celebrating a spectacle of state power discovered to be the practice of domesticity:

Queen Victoria will never appear more exalted in the world's opinion than when each side of the picture is thus revealed – the great Queen and states-woman in the gorgeous palace – the young, lovely, and virtuous mother amidst the pure joys of sylvan retreat and domestic relaxation. Our artist has chosen for illustration one of those happy moments of maternal life when the magnificence and etiquette of the Queen are put aside by womanly tenderness for the expression of a mother's love. (*Illustrated London News* 1842: 1, 40)

This royal domesticity was in fact explicitly premised upon the monarchy's loss of direct political power – witness the contemporary fascination with the doomed absolutist Charles I as the ideal family man, surrounded by his children[10]. Increasingly a politically impotent institution with only residual constitutional powers, responsible instead for "inspiring" and "influencing" the nation as its symbolic wife, the monarchy found its perfect representation in, as Margaret Homans has remarked, "the spectacle of royal domestic privacy, a privacy that centered on the ever-plumper figure of [the] Queen as wife and mother" (Homans 1993: 4). In the 1880s, twenty unpopular years of mourning Albert later, Victoria's renovated persona still relied upon a certain domesticity, though it was finally translated in portraits and in panoramic family photographs alike into an extraordinary amalgamation of her monolithic endured widowhood and her vast grandmotherhood of European monarchies.[11]

Despite the precedent set by Elizabeth for a rhetorical self-imaging as wife and mother to her nation (entirely familiar to Victorian historians), to envisage her within the terms of this romance of vulnerable, morally influential and domesticized queenship proved virtually impossible. To represent Elizabeth as a reluctant queen in the style of Barrett, despite Leslie's valiant attempt, generally seemed implausible. Representing her as morally influential, the guardian of the soul of the nation, was very nearly as difficult; in 1859, for example, against the trend of popular opinion, Charles Kingsley endeavored to argue for the private Elizabeth as having, in fact, been the properly Victorian governing inspiration of her age, in terms which sound less convinced the further they run into conventional Burkean hyperbole: "there was, in plain palpable fact, something about the Queen, her history, her policy, the times, the glorious part which England, and she as the incarnation of the then English spirit, were playing upon earth, which raised imaginative and heroical souls into a permanent exaltation" (Kingsley 1873: 123). Much more characteristic of prevailing opinion was the enormously influential historian J. R. Green's verdict that all the "moral aspects" of Elizabeth's England "were simply dead to her" (Green 1875: 381). Representing Gloriana as exerting appropriate forms of female power proved similarly impossible; as Anna Jameson would remark in 1834, "she never forgot the sovereign in the woman," for "when," asked Jameson indignantly, "did she comfort or help the weak-hearted? or raise up the fallen? or exalt humble merit? or cherish unobtrusive genius? or spare the offending? or pardon the guilty?"; instead, she had ruled by the obtrusive exercise of "acts of capricious power" (Jameson 1834: 11, 322; vol. 1, 298, 284). Elizabeth's politically obsolete absolutism is diminished in the modern context into a simple rage for engrossing illegitimate personal power – hence her representation as avaricious, jealous, envious, vain, and selfish. If, "by presenting herself as a wife, Queen Victoria offered the perfect solution to Britain's fears of female rule and of excessive monarchic power," as Homans has argued, her avatar Elizabeth raised these fears in their most virulent form (Homans 1993: 4).

During the 1840s and 1850s, years which, suggestively, coincided with Victoria's childbearing years, this anxiety over Elizabeth's political power – perhaps a surrogate for the cultural anxiety over Victoria's – crystallized into a series of remarkable paintings set in Elizabeth's private apartments in which Elizabeth's ageing body was for the first time revealed. So obsessed did mid-Victorian culture become with the figure of the old queen, indeed, that Kingsley could observe ruefully in 1855 that "it is much now-a-days to find anyone who believes that Queen Elizabeth was ever young, or who does not talk of her as if she was born about seventy years of age covered with rouge and wrinkles" (Kingsley 1873: 123). For the first time since her death, Queen Elizabeth was regularly pursued into the privacy of her bedchamber, to be triumphantly discovered in unflattering undress, all wrinkles and no rouge.

### THE CROOKED CARCASS

Her conditions are as crooked as her carcass. (The Earl of Essex on Elizabeth)

There are few sovereigns that make a more splendid and imposing state-figure in the regal statue-gallery of England than Queen Elizabeth; and as few, in sooth, that can less afford to be faithfully limned and displayed *en déshabille*. (William Russell 1857: 82)

Prior to 1848 Gloriana appeared in disarray or *en déshabille* only on one occasion, the unheralded return of the Earl of Essex from Ireland in 1599. (Essex returned against express royal orders, in an attempt to preempt his enemies at court from making disastrous political capital from his ignominious truce with the Irish leader Tyrone, whom he had originally been despatched to subdue.) In the original accounts of the incident, Essex forced his way into the Queen's bedchamber, found her not yet dressed, and was received "kindly." This sweetness had worn off, for whatever reason, when Essex came before her in the presence chamber some hours later, only to be summarily placed under house arrest. For the eighteenth century, the episode had neatly dramatized the separation between personal sentiment and state policy, conveniently and economically figured as the double location, or dislocation, of the Queen's private and public bodies: it is this division that structures two immensely popular she-tragedies on the subject, John Banks's *The Unhappy Favorite* (1682) and Henry Jones's *The Earl of Essex* (1753), and several more derived from them. The earliest of such depictions in a visual medium is probably Richard Westall's *The Earl of Essex's First Interview with Queen Elizabeth After his Return from Ireland* (1789), which shows a fully dressed Elizabeth as Gothic heroine taken by surprise and transfers all the historic detail of "her hair about her face" to a maid in the foreground, thus doubling private and public bodies (reprinted in Strong 1978: 27). The same disjunction is more revealingly dramatized in plate 5.1, an engraving by J. Rogers (after a painting by Robert Smirke) dating from 1806 but here reproduced with a new border from about the 1820s. The picture shows a young and pneumatic Elizabeth discovered in charming disarray, one slipper on, the other lying disregarded in the foreground, one hand protecting her loosely covered breast, the other lifting away her long and luxuriant hair. This sentimental and eroticized version of the private woman dominates the two added vignettes below of the beruffed and crowned public monarch in action, one of which shows Elizabeth administering the notorious box on the ear to her unruly favorite in Privy Council, the other of which depicts her signing his death warrant. The montage invites the viewer to emulate Essex in his eroticized worship of the vulnerable and quintessentially feminine Queen. Most importantly, it insists that her relationship with her favorite is essentially personal rather than political, and that therefore its severance on the block is heartbreakingly tragic rather than cold-bloodedly politic. The erotics of this bedroom encounter may be usefully glossed by the gaspingly indiscreet parallel scene in William-Henry Ireland's highly-colored fantasy *Effusions of Love* (1805), in which the doomed Essex-like favorite Chatelard witnesses the undressing of the Queen of Scots and fatally betrays his infatuated presence:

Upon your table stood the blazing tapers, whose light beamed full upon you: forth from the bandeau that enchained your hair I saw your flowing ringlets, of all art divested, hang loosely o'er your falling shoulders . . . What a profusion of enchanting tresses wanton'd o'er your heaving bosom, seeming to kiss the thrones of bliss divested of all covering . . . A torrent of luscious joy rush'd on my senses! – . . . I could no longer curb my raging transports – I rushed forth; then uttering thy dear name, my queen, sunk o'ercome with – * * * * * * * * * * * * * * * * * * * * * * * * * * * * * * * * * * * * * * * * * * * * * * * * * * * (Ireland 1805: 121)[12]

In 1875 David Wilkie Wynfield returned to the subject of Essex's return from Ireland in his *Incident in the Life of Elizabeth* (plate 5.2), which

Plate 5.1 Rogers after Robert Smirke, *Interview Between Queen Elizabeth and the Earl of Essex*, 1806, with a new border from *c.* 1820.

Plate 5.2 David Wilkie Wynfield, *Incident in the Life of Elizabeth*, 1875.

provides a dramatic contrast with the earlier visualization. Gone are the lusciously heaving bosom and the luxuriantly disarranged hair, in their place a nearly bald and diminutive Queen, shorn of ruff, jewels, wig, far-thingale, and robe, all of which are prominently scattered around the focal point of the picture. Clearly the meaning of this scene had changed dramatically over the intervening years.

Why? The historical record, of course, contained a good deal to embarrass an Ireland-style *mise-en-scène* of Elizabeth in her bedroom, not least the hard fact that when Essex went to his death on Tower Green aged thirty-five, Elizabeth was sixty-eight. But despite a thriving indus-try from the 1790s onwards in depictions of the Queen's death, it would not be until the second quarter of the nineteenth century that Elizabeth would actually be discovered as a ridiculous, if dangerous, old fraud. In

1822, Mary Roberts's companion poem to her sentimental set piece on the Queen of Scots, "Elizabeth," contents itself with describing her grandeur, her jewels, her throne, etc., before pointing out gleefully that the "Dreadful and dreaded Elizabeth" is nonetheless subject to time and death (Roberts 1822: 1, 171). But by 1824 this conventional suggestion is being amplified by Walter Savage Landor into a commentary fixated on Elizabeth's sexual obsolescence. Imagining the conversation between Elizabeth and her last suitor the Duc d'Anjou, brokered by their advisers Cecil and Fénelon, Landor unmasks the courtly language of sentimental passion as used to the Queen by the continual asides of all the players, concentrating particularly on the forty-year-old Queen's unwarranted personal vanity. We are left with Anjou's pen portrait of a sexually voracious old maid well past her sell-by date as a woman, if not as a political *parti*:

those long narrow ferret's teeth, intersecting a face of such proportions, that it is like a pared cucumber set on end. And then those foxy eyelashes and eyebrows! And those wildfire eyes, equal in volubility to her tongue and her affections, and leering like a panther's when it yawns . . . Sacré! the skinny old goshawk, all talon and plumage. (Landor 1846: 1, 177)

Landor's satirized Queen is not aware of the yawning gulf between her market value as political asset and as woman, but she would not be allowed to preserve this particular vanity very much longer. The most important visual depiction of the old Queen was certainly that of Augustus Leopold Egg, who, in 1848, exhibited his canvas *Queen Elizabeth Discovers she is no Longer Young* (plate 5.3) at the Royal Academy, a painting which met with such approval that it earned the artist his associateship.

Egg's ambitious painting penetrated the royal bedroom to discover, shockingly, not Gloriana but an old woman amidst her courtiers and ladies, forced into full realization of mortality by the mirror held up by her truly youthful lady-in-waiting, struck into an immobile trance of humiliated vanity. Around her suddenly shrunken and petulant form the gaudily stiff skirts have crumpled and collapsed, and her haggard face stares straight out at the viewer. This complicated picture insists not merely (like Landor) that the Virgin Queen is old, but that she herself, caught out, should recognize the fact in full pitiless conclave. This *lèse-majesté* achieves its impact by disestablishing Elizabeth's official portraits' mendacious claims to timelessness; as every Victorian child knew, these had been rigidly controlled by Elizabeth to save her personal vanity. (See, for example, the magazine *Bow Bells*, aimed at a mainly female readership, which in the 1860s offered this *aperçu*: "When Queen Elizabeth sat

Plate 5.3 Augustus Leopold Egg, *Queen Elizabeth Discovers She Is No Longer Young*, 1848.

for her picture in her old age, she ordered the artist to paint her portrait without any shadows, for shadows she knew would reveal the marks of age in her queenly countenance; and, with all her courage, 'Good Queen Bess' had not strength of mind to look her wrinkles in the face. She could defy the Spanish Armada, but she was afraid of her own infirmities."[13]) The painting itself thus aspired to act as a true looking glass; Egg's authenticity (praised lavishly by the critics) was guaranteed by his bypassing of such "inauthentic" and fraudulent contemporary portraits as sources in favor of Elizabeth's actual death mask. Refuting the iconography of Elizabethan absolutism, the canvas unmasks the ageless Gloriana as a uselessly bedecked harridan.

According to the catalog's explanatory quotation, the picture illustrates an episode supposed to have occurred during the Queen's last illness, following the death of Essex: "In the melancholy of her sickness she desired to see a true looking glass, into which she had not looked for twenty years" (quoted in Faberman 1983: 1, 151).[14] (Although this episode is almost certainly apocryphal, there was a well-established tradition of stories about mirrors and Elizabeth, in particular a strain of anecdote that dealt with Elizabeth's dislike of mirrors after a certain age, already familiar when Ben Jonson retailed it in his cups to Drummond of Hawthornden in 1619: "Queen Elizabeth never saw her self after she became old in a true glass" ([*Notes of Ben Jonson's Conversations* 1842: 23].) The Queen's self-discovery in Egg's picture, therefore, is brought on by her melancholy after Essex's execution; her guilt seems to be realized as a sudden, catastrophic ageing. In other words, this painting tells another in the long tradition of stories that describe Elizabeth's death (alluded to explicitly by the heap of cushions in the foreground, recognizably those onto which the Queen has collapsed in Paul Delaroche's much-reproduced *The Death of Queen Elizabeth* [1828]) as hastened by melancholy over the execution of her favorite, albeit one inflected by an unprecedented hostility.

The picture thus sets up at least two political arguments for visitors to the Royal Academy viewing in 1848, that turbulent year of European revolutions and of domestic unrest (including an abortive Chartist riot outside Buckingham Palace itself and a reputed Chartist march on Osborne; Longford 1964: 195–97). The first was to do with whether the monarchy itself, regarded by many as paralyzingly expensive, was, for all its display of hereditary power, actually as obsolete as the post-menopausal woman supposed to have been the most glorious of all English sovereigns. The second was specifically to do with revolution, for by the mid-nineteenth century the death of Essex as popular hero and spirit of chivalric Elizabethanism at the hands of a merciless and despotic old woman could point to a moral about arbitrary power both at home and abroad. (This is, for example, the burden of the historical novel by "Thomas of Swarraton, Armiger," *The Noble Traytour* [1857], which casts Essex, friend of Raleigh, Shakespeare, and the virtuous English squire Sir William Cheney, as the true – if spoiled and undisciplined – child of the age, snuffed out by the tyranny of the old queen.) Above all, *Queen Elizabeth Discovers She Is No Longer Young*, by destroying Elizabeth's magical agelessness, a central component of contemporary nationalist Elizabethan nostalgia, lays claim to being a political essay on the current state of England.[15] Returning to Wynfield's vision of the old Elizabeth stripped of her sexual glamor along with her wig and gorgeous clothes, we can see it similarly as an essay on whether Elizabeth's state power – used in its most extreme form against the most manly man of her age – is adequately legitimated by the femininity of her private body, or whether her political conditions are indeed as crooked as her carcass. Anodyne though it is, Wynfield's treatment nonetheless suggests that the disastrously superannuated Queen has, as it were, cheated both the hitherto infatuated Essex and, by extension, those moderns who have bought into the myth of Gloriana.

In 1849, the year after Egg's picture was shown, the Christmas pantomime presented at Drury Lane was entitled *Harlequin and Good Queen Bess, or, Merrie England in the Olden Time. A Grand Historical! Metaphorical!! Allegorical!!! and Diabolical!!!! PANTOMIME*, a text no less illuminating about the relation between this newly-hostile view of Elizabeth and contemporary strategies for celebrating Victoria. Collapsing together Elizabeth's courtships, the Kenilworth festivities, and Walter Scott's account in *Kenilworth* of Elizabeth's dealings with Leicester and Amy Robsart, the pantomime sets out to "make the town confess / The funniest figure of fun was GOOD QUEEN BESS" (*Harlequin and Good Queen Bess* 1849: 9). Elizabeth, in keeping with the cross-dressing traditions of the genre, here becomes Drag Queen Bess, her mock-heroic splendor entirely a matter of intimate items of costume:

Grand *entrée* of her Majesty, GOOD QUEEN BESS, attended by her Nobles and Dames of Honour, bearing the various parts of her Dress. LORD BURLEIGH carries the Royal Red Wig and Golden Crown – SIR WALTER RALEIGH the Royal Petticoat – the EARL OF ESSEX, attends with Royal Blushes, in the shape of a Rouge Pot – LORD BACON carries the Royal Ruff – Good Queen Bess is attired in a morning wrapper, and cap. (*Harlequin and Good Queen Bess* 1849: 12)

Once the Queen has put on the full royal panoply, the rest of the pantomime gives a lightning tour of the Queen's coquetry with her various foreign and domestic suitors before exhorting her to abandon this form of political courtship in favor of an altogether more Victorian version of affective monarchy: "Instead of dreaming more of Cupid's darts, / Dream of a throne built on your people's hearts." Her implied conversion is rewarded with "A Pantomime Vision of the Destruction of the Spanish Armada," moralized in terms as much to do with Palmerstonian gun-boat diplomacy as with the days of Drake:

> Henceforth is England mistress of the seas!
> Her flag "shall brave the battle and the breeze."
> In triumph now – in ages yet to come,
> And still the sea shall guard each English home.
> While then, as now, with pride 'twill be confess'd,
> A fair hand wields Old England's sceptre best.
> (*Harlequin and Good Queen Bess* 1849: 20)

Victoria – as implied passenger on a property ship, at least – finally arrives herself during the show's naval and wholly un-Elizabethan finale, in which contemporary events and the "fair hand" on today's scepter supersede the representation of Elizabeth altogether: this takes the form of a "Grand moving diorama,"

Illustrative of Her Most Gracious Majesty's Visit to Ireland; shewing the following points of interest; – Departure from Osborne – Passing Cowes; and approaching the Needles – the Royal Yacht passing through the Fleet, off Portsmouth – The Edystone [*sic*] Lighthouse – Passing the Land's End at Sunset – The Royal Squadron, by Moonlight – and Arrival at Queenstown. (*Harlequin and Good Queen Bess* 1849: 20)

This pantomime farcically restates Egg's view of the old Elizabeth's royal authority as a sexiness fraudulently constructed out of paint and farthingale by showing Elizabeth to be a man under the petticoats; the maneuver clears away Elizabeth's worryingly free-floating sexuality before summoning up a vision of a more suitable female embodiment of the nation, Victoria herself. In 1858, making a similar sideslip in conclusion to the first ever hostile account of Elizabeth's girlhood imbroglio with Admiral Seymour, William Russell wrote:

A few more chequered years of patient wariness, and the great prize was gained – Elizabeth was in her true place on the throne, the visible embodiment and illustration of national independence . . . and therefore clothed with a personal lustre in her people's eyes which the disenchanting breath of Time has indeed dissipated, but not happily till the crown of these realms had descended upon

the brow of a royal lady whose virtues shed a higher, purer lustre upon the imperial diadem than it confers. Mr. Macaulay, in one of his public addresses, eulogized Queen Victoria as "a milder, better Elizabeth"; a compliment which, at
all events, will not render the celebrated historian obnoxious to the charge of
flattery or servilism. (Russell 1857: 91)

Both Russell and the anonymous author of *Harlequin and Good Queen Bess*
suggest, finally, that the "answer" to Egg's problem picture might well
have been Victoria for many of its viewers.


### THE CHILD OF DESTINY

Mid-nineteenth-century narratives of Elizabeth's private life were thus
dominated by a vision of her post-menopausal body. Some thirty years
later, however, with the ageing and increasingly unpopular Queen
Victoria still secluded in heavy mourning for an Albert dead since 1861,
campaigns for the rehabilitation of both queens were afoot, the first in
the shape of efforts to force Victoria into public appearance to stave off
calls for her abdication that had started in about 1870, the second, almost
directly contemporary, in the shape of a series of representations of the
Virgin Queen as a child (Longford 1964: 380).

Why did Elizabeth so suddenly appear as a child? Part of the answer
must be that portrayals of Elizabeth as an old woman would, increasingly, have had a largely undesirable topical application to Victoria.
Part must also be, of course, the rapid development of histories and
historical fiction for children, and especially girls, offering usefully
English role models plus a dose of English history in palatable form.
That said, in order to render Elizabeth a suitable example for
Victorian girlhood, authors were obliged to go in for a good deal of
doctoring of the historical record. Simplest and most effective was to
rethink the Virgin Queen in terms of the newfound interest in painting historical characters as children or of the sort of juvenile historical fiction pioneered by Charlotte M. Yonge, or of that interesting
genre characteristic of girls' reading in the later nineteenth century,
"The Girlhood of Exemplary Women".[16] Such representations
abstract historical or fictional characters out of their known and often
compromising actual circumstances, projecting them back into infancy
and childhood in order at once to engage the sympathetic attention of
the child-audience but also, more importantly, to try to convey the
essence of the feminine character before it was overtaken by political
or historical contingency.

Both the attractiveness and the trickiness of these strategies are demonstrated by the earliest example of this genre as applied to Elizabeth – William Russell's *Extraordinary Women: Their Girlhood and Early Life* (1857). Russell's vignette of young Bess is, in fact, anything but sympathetic to the teenaged princess – at once overwanton and overprudent – although the accompanying illustration shows her, wishfully, as a pretty and domesticated three-year-old within an idyllic family setting, apparently in happily ecumenical religious harmony with her elder sister Bloody Mary (plate 5.4). Later portrayals of Elizabeth-as-child, however, attempt to realize the message of the picture rather than the text, countering hostile representations of Elizabeth as unwomanly – coded as post-menopausally infertile – by showing her as an acceptably infertile and unwomanly preadolescent child princess. This strategy offered the additional advantage of representing Elizabeth as enclosed within the domestic before her dubious entry into public life, as well as presenting her as entire potential, prenarrative, prehistory. The presexual childish body, in fact, becomes safely iconic, and can be returned to its function of representing national progress and triumph. Hence the child princess, the proto-Freudian expression of the private woman, can finally be conflated not only with the Protestant icon but with the Armada icon, as in Marcus C. Stone's (1840–1921) *The Royal Nursery* (1871, plate 5.5).[17] This painting, which surely owes something to paintings by Winterhalter and Landseer of Victoria and her family, effectively leapfrogs the whole vexed question of Elizabeth's sexed body to concentrate prophetically on the disinherited and neglected little girl's future role as the Protestant heroine of Tilbury, flanked by the Bible she has been studying diligently and the toy warship that the doting father has brought for his frail and doomed son Edward. Stone cunningly invests the child princess with a useful pathos that neither cancels nor is canceled by the intimation of future glory.

A late example of this strain, Harriet Comstock's *The Girlhood of Elizabeth: a Romance of English History* (1914) (probably prompted by the publication of Frank Mumby's compilation of letters under the title *The Girlhood of Elizabeth* in 1909), displays very clearly what was at stake in representing Elizabeth as a child:

I would have you know and love her, not as the great queen who ruled so mightily – not always wisely or gently – but as the little English maid of royal Tudor stock, who strove to learn that she might overcome error, and who, through much injustice to herself, was ever true and affectionate to those who served her well; and to the end was loyal to her name and country. (Comstock 1914: 2)

Plate 5.4 *Elizabeth Aged Three*, from William Russell's *Extraordinary Women* (1857).

Diligent, well-meaning, oppressed, loyal, affectionate, and patriotic, this princess is not yet corrupted by her questionable power. What Comstock offers us is an improbably "simple maid" (v), cloyingly pathetic, depressingly hard-working, who conducts Pollyanna-style government in the bosom of her family. This winsome five-year-old, for example, scolds her father for his treatment of her elder sister Mary ("had I more like you, little maid, surrounding my throne, I might have been a better king" is the unlikely response; 56), appears "ever wondrously tender towards children" (153), is best friends with her brother Edward, her cousin Lady Jane Grey, and her projected match Courtenay, and is absolutely nothing more than a favorite niece to her ambitious uncle, Seymour. But the familiar difficulty surfaces once again as she is crowned: "perchance we might not love her so well as Queen Elizabeth, and so, as the diadem presses her golden curls, let us bid her farewell" (286). The good-as-gold princess might not translate unscathed into the Queen of the Golden Age.

One of the effects of restating Elizabeth as child was to bring her back in a controllable form within the sphere of Victoria's monarchy. (It is a curiosity that Victoria herself was to be subjected to metamorphosis into the ideal Victorian girl in Sara Lippincott's probably unauthorized *Queen Victoria. Her Girlhood and Womanhood*, 1883, and then in the more reputable *The Girlhood of Queen Victoria: a Selection from Her Majesty's Diaries Between the Years 1832 and 1840*, *circa* 1900, both of which seem to have been designed to redomesticate the evermore formidable Empress of India.) This reimagining of the Armada icon as exemplary Victorian child perhaps received its definitive incarnation at the Mansion House juvenile fancy-dress ball held in January 1887 expressly to mark the now hugely popular and public old Queen's Golden Jubilee. The occasion began with a procession of 150 children dressed as British sovereigns and their most notable subjects since the Conquest; the star part was Elizabeth I, played by the nine-year-old daughter of the Lord Mayor (plate 5.6) in a costume clearly adapted from the Ditchley portrait (by then a public possession in the National Portrait Gallery) that shows Elizabeth standing on a map of England. The *Illustrated London News* reported that

Queen Elizabeth herself could not have wished for a more dignified representative than the great Monarch had in Violet Hanson on her ninth birthday . . . The train of the Queen of the evening was carried by a page yet smaller than herself . . . and in her Majesty's train were Shakespeare, Raleigh, Amy Robsart, and two other Maids-of-Honour, and a small edition of the Lord Mayor of London . . . (*Illustrated London News* 90 [1887], 117–18)

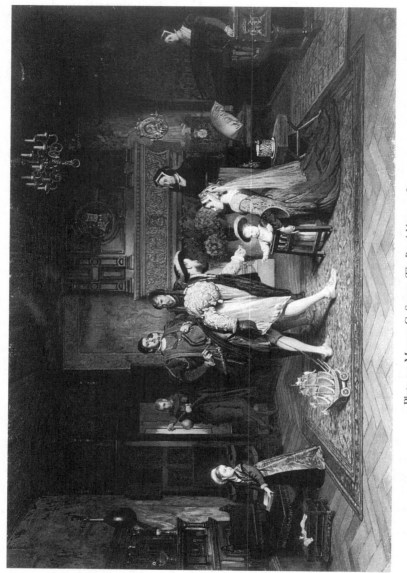

Plate 5-5 Marcus C. Stone, *The Royal Nursery*, 1871.

Plate 5.6 *Violet Hanson as Elizabeth I*, from the *Illustrated London News* (January 1887).

This diminutive and decorative Elizabeth could pay her court so suitably
to the Queen of Great Britain and Empress of India because she had
been reduced so spectacularly to a mere icon of the Elizabethan. The
Virgin Queen's real power and unscrupulous courtships, both unsuited
to Victorian notions, survive only in the Amy Robsart who appears in
the little girl's train. Moreover, it seems likely that the delight in the

piquant miniaturization of the Virgin Queen was underpinned by something rather more serious; it was, after all, not unreasonable to suppose
that the body within that particular farthingale was indeed virginally
domestic, still safely subject to her father, even if he was himself mini-
aturized in her train. Only infantilized in this way could the Virgin
Queen pay decorous homage to Queen Victoria, and the inheritance of
her political acumen be superseded by Victoria's decorative constitutional and domestic virtues.

POSTSCRIPT

These two Elizabeths, the barren old maid and the virgin child, illustrate
in the extreme how hard the Victorians found it to provide Elizabeth
with an acceptable feminine private self, let alone one that would seem
congruent with her other more public careers as national symbol in the
mode of the current Queen, raised by her Golden and Diamond Jubilees
to equally mythic status. So powerfully had Victoria's image conditioned
that of Elizabeth that it would only be after Victoria's death in the
opening years of the twentieth century that a way of rethinking the
female body into royal power began to develop. Nine years after
Victoria's state funeral in 1901, writing a sequel to the nationalistic set of
historical miniromances for children that makes up *Puck of Pook's Hill*,
Rudyard Kipling entitled one story "Gloriana" and added as a pendant
a poem called "The Looking-Glass." In the space of some twenty pages
he both recapitulated and entirely reconstellated the Victorian figures of
the child Queen and the old Queen with Elizabeth's other
contemporaneous incarnations as the ageless Good Queen Bess and
Gloriana, ruling a Merrie England, presiding over daring colonial
exploits, the figure romanced by Shakespeare and Spenser, the heroine
of the Armada. In Kipling's story, the immortal apparition of the ageing
Queen is conjured by Puck for the instruction of the child Una and her
brother Dan in their private hideout, "the Kingdom," where they are
proposing to roast that most famous of all Elizabethan imports, potatoes. The masked Queen replays compulsively a dance during which she
decided to outface Philip of Spain over the seemingly unauthorized
marauding of her adventurers and effectively seduced two young men
to future acts of covert patriotic piracy off the coast of Virginia, an
enterprise from which they would never return. As she dramatizes
herself – splitting herself into the one narrating and the object of
her story as her mirror does ("I've seen her walk to her own mirror by

bye-ends" [Kipling 1910: 48]) – it becomes clear that in this long-dead past, at the very moment she was persuading them to go, she was over-taken by a compassion that made her beg them to stay, and that she haunts because she is haunted by guilt. Retold, her story inevitably seduces the modern empire builder in the making, the boy Dan, while making Una profoundly uneasy and anxious by her usurpation of power over her brother and coruler of the "Kingdom." The question of the Queen's guilt is also at the center of the appended poem, which pursues a narrative logic whereby Elizabeth's sins against womanliness – exe-cuting the quintessentially feminine Queen of Scots, denying the love of Lord Leicester – are embodied not only as ghosts that rack her old age but are registered, Dorian Gray-like, upon her mirrored face as age; but Kipling goes one step further than, say, Egg some sixty-odd years earlier in showing a queen in part exonerated by her courage in facing down – literally – the price that queenliness has exacted from the woman. Her womanly stoicism would seem to atone, at any rate in part, for the per-sonal guilt the story obliges her to bear as the embodiment of England for the death of its young men on her behalf. To put it another way, when this Elizabeth looks into her glass, she doesn't see the accusing ghost of the young Victoria, the domestic womanliness she has rejected. At the same time, however, it does not seem too fanciful to suggest that in some ways Kipling's story of the deadly Gloriana manages remaining anxi-eties about the cost of the imperial adventure, anxieties that he initially formulated in "The Widow at Windsor" (from *Barrack-Room Ballads*) in 1898, in which the old Victoria figures as the Queen of Spades and a dreadful devouring mother to "Missis Victorier's sons" (Kipling 1940: 411; see Bredesen, this volume). It is a measure of the extent to which both the power of Elizabeth and the sexuality that figured it had been absorbed within a passionate but entirely respectable relationship between nation and female sovereign that by 1911, in a poem entitled "The Bells and Queen Victoria", Kipling was explicitly casting the Empress of India as heir to the Faerie Queene – but not so much to Elizabeth's power, domestic or imperial, but simply to the power of Britons' love. Victoria's apotheosis as the darling of a national love affair finally completes, even as its contours are defined by, that of Elizabeth.

> THE BELLS
> Here is more gain than Gloriana guessed –
> Than Gloriana guessed or Indies bring –
> Than golden Indies bring. A Queen confessed –
> A Queen confessed that crowned her people King.

Her people King, and crowned all Kings above,
Above all Kings have crowned their Queen their love –
Have crowned their love their Queen, their Queen their love.
                                                    (Kipling 1940: 734)

NOTES

1  See Ormond 1987: 30.
2  This painting does not seem to have been exhibited at the Royal Academy,
   and is not dated on the canvas. (I have been unable to trace any mention of
   it in any of the many contemporary biographical notices of its artist: it last
   surfaced when sold at auction by Phillips of London in 1978). It seems likely,
   however, that it dates from the early 1840s.
3  Wells's painting may be found reproduced in Gernsheim and Gernsheim
   1959: 28; a version of Gow's watercolor may be found in Longford 1964,
   facing page 160. Gow's picture clearly derives directly from Wells's depiction in its portrayal of Lord Conyngham and the Archbishop of
   Canterbury, who announced the news to the young queen, but the background has been much abstracted, and Victoria herself idealized even more
   thoroughly as a young and vulnerable girl.
4  See, for example, the remarkable Victorian print of Elizabeth supervising
   Royal Society-style scientific experiments, reproduced in Bush 1985: 103. It
   cannot have escaped the Victorians' notice, surely, that, thanks to Sir John
   Harington, Elizabeth was the first English monarch to possess a water
   closet.
5  See Gernsheim and Gernsheim 1959: 82.
6  Lucy Aikin published her *Memoirs of the Court of Queen Elizabeth* in 1818;
   Anna Jameson her *Memoirs of Celebrated Female Sovereigns* in 1832; Hannah
   Lawrence her *Historical Memoirs of the Queens of England* in 1839; Agnes
   Strickland her enormously popular *Lives of the Queens of England* between
   1840 and 1849 (and in many editions thereafter, including an abridgment
   for schools in 1867) and her *Tudor Princesses* in 1868; Mrs. Matthew Hall her
   twelve-volume *History of the Queens of England*, (1854–59); Mary Cowden
   Clarke her *World-Noted Women* in 1858; Lydia Hoyt Farmer her *Girls' Book of
   Famous Queens* in 1887. Of these writers on English queenship the most
   influential was certainly Agnes Strickland. Friend of both Sir Walter Scott
   and Jane Porter, guest at Victoria's coronation in 1838, presented at court
   in 1840, author of *Queen Victoria from Birth to Bridal* (1840), and dedicator of
   *The Lives of the Queens of England* to Victoria, Strickland persistently relates
   Victoria to her female predecessors, most especially Elizabeth. Under the
   conjoined influence of these women's histories and the vast success of the
   new historical fiction sponsored by Scott, Porter and others, the new
   generation of future academicians (Augustus Leopold Egg, E. M. Ward,
   William Powell Frith, Goodall, C. Landseer) similarly turned from grand
   historical panorama to, in Carlyle's words, "a history composed of small

dramatic incidents of the everyday lives of England's great men" (quoted in Faberman 1983: 1, 142).

7  On "fancy portraits" see Stevenson and Bennett 1978: 1–3. For photography and Victoria, see Gernsheim and Gernsheim 1959: 257–58, 261.

8  See, respectively, John Lingard, *History of the Reformation* (London, 1819–30); James Mackintosh in *Cabinet Cyclopedia*; Lord John Campbell, *The Lives of the Chief Justices of England* (1849). *Fraser's Magazine for Town and Country* 48 (October 1853), 376.

9  For the portrait of Victoria and Albert in their costumes for the Plantagenet ball in 1842, see Gernsheim and Gernsheim 1959: 75; for the Winterhalter, see Longford 1964: facing 193. For a discussion of Winterhalter's iconography of royal power in this painting, see Nadel 1987: 171. For the unfocused and anxious efforts to think Victoria as queen, see Stein 1987: 60–62. For some examples of hostile cartoons of the fertile Queen, see Gernsheim and Gernsheim 1959: 72, 73, 77.

10  See Strong 1978: 96–97.

11  See Nadel 1987 and Gernsheim and Gernsheim 1959.

12  Ireland is, of course, best known for his youthful forgeries of the mid-1790s, which famously included a letter from Elizabeth to Shakespeare.

13  I am indebted to Dr. Paul Barlow of the University of Northumbria at Newcastle for this reference.

14  In 1916 Beatrice Marshall relates exactly such an episode as taking place immediately after Essex's execution: "And it was now that the Queen asked to be shown her image in a 'true mirror' without powder or paint, and started at the sight of herself as she really was, shriveled and wrinkled by the hand of time" (Marshall 1916: 183).

15  It is instructive here to return to Kingsley's attempt to rescue the timeless Elizabeth from her embarrassingly temporal body; writing of her youthful beauty he remarks:

> it had been an important element in her great success; men had accepted it as what beauty of form and expression generally is, an outward and visible sign of the inward and spiritual grace; and while the inward was unchanged, what wonder if she tried to preserve the outward? If she was the same, why should she not try to look the same? And what blame to those who worshipped her, if, knowing that she was the same, they too should fancy that she looked the same, the Elizabeth of their youth, and should talk as if the fair flesh, as well as the fair spirit, was immortal? Does not every loving husband do so, when he forgets the grey hair and the sunken cheek and all the wastes of time; and sees the partner of many joys and sorrows not as she has become, but as she was, ay, and is to him, and will be to him, he trusts, through all eternity? (Kingsley 1873: 124–25)

Inverting Egg's proposition – that the national icon merely expressed the Queen's overweening and unfounded personal vanity – Kingsley argues, instead, that Elizabeth's deeply national femininity (characteristically imagined in marital terms, despite Elizabeth's awkward status as spinster) was best expressed by her painted face.

16  The most famous example of the "girlhood" genre is Mary Cowden
    Clarke's *The Girlhood of Shakespeare's Heroines* (London: 1850–52). Other
    examples would include Thomas Trollope's *The Girlhood of Catherine d'Medici*
    (London, 1856); William Adams's *Child-life and Girlhood of Remarkable Women*
    (London, 1883); Jane Stoddart's *The Girlhood of Mary Queen of Scots* (1900);
    Katherine Cather, *Childhood Stories of Famous Women* (New York and London,
    1924). These supplement innumerable examples of juvenile fiction.
    Paintings of childhood by Dante Gabriel Rossetti (*The Girlhood of Mary*,
    1848) and Millais (most pertinently the famous *Boyhood of Raleigh*) also clearly
    participate in this mode.
17  This picture was accompanied in the Royal Academy catalog by the fol-
    lowing quotation: "The king's grace was well pleased to see his heir so
    goodly a child of his age; although the little Lady Elizabeth was considered
    worthy of the honour of being admitted to keep company with the young
    Prince Edward, her brother, her father took but little note of her."

# CHAPTER 6

# "Be no more housewives, but queens": Queen Victoria and Ruskin's domestic mythology

### Sharon Aronofsky Weltman

In "Of Queens' Gardens" (1865), John Ruskin creates a notion of queenship that offers women under the reign of Queen Victoria a powerful political and mythological model for the broadening of their scope of action, thereby redefining the traditionally domestic arena to include a broad range of philanthropy and social activism. While vigorously supporting Victorian culture's strict separation of spheres for the sexes, Ruskin nevertheless encourages women to do things that other suffocating "woman worshippers" with whom he is normally conflated, such as Coventry Patmore, oppose. As a political entity with constitutionally defined powers, Queen Victoria seems far removed from Ruskin's mythmaking. But for Ruskin nothing is too real, historical, or ordinary to be mythologized and imbued with metaphorical significance. The *idea* of Queen Victoria as England's ruler stands always in the background of Ruskin's essay: when he defines queenliness, Victoria-as-symbol both participates in his idealization and provides a figure of such moral and political authority that his exhortation of average women to become mythological goddess-queens takes on a seductive aura of possibility. While ostensible opposites, both mythic and political images of queenship add agency to his conception of nineteenth-century women. By aligning mythic and political queenship in the age of Queen Victoria herself, he elevates politically powerless housewives to rhetorically empowered queens. He uses the category of "queen" in "Of Queens' Gardens" and *The Queen of the Air* to stretch the boundaries of domestic ideology and to explore newly defined possibilities for women within Victorian culture.

Queen Victoria is an unlikely analog to Athena, Ruskin's air deity and the subject of his 1869 mythological study *The Queen of the Air*. Indeed, Victoria may seem the antithesis of airy: short, dumpy, maternal, astonishingly fertile, sensible, and (while no fool) never celebrated for intellect, she hardly resembles the virginal goddess of wisdom and war. But although the Athena that Ruskin creates in *The Queen of the Air* represents Ruskin's feminine ideal and although he metaphorically offers women her mythic powers, the practical powers Ruskin describes in 1865 for the housewife queens of *Sesame and Lilies*[1] ultimately correspond to Queen Victoria's more than to any goddess's. In fact, the middle-aged sovereign appeared so familiar that middle-class women – who had already appropriated the title of Lady, as Ruskin sharply reminds them (Ruskin [1909] 1903–12: XVIII, 138) – might readily assume the title of queen as well. By mid-century Victoria had erased the image of profligacy and aristocratic decay that had been associated with royalty because of her predecessors' notorious behaviors: throughout her reign, she projected herself and her family as approachably domestic, wholesome, and even bourgeois.[2] But this cultivated familiarity cut both ways; what Victoria gained in respectability and affection, she lost in awe. For Ruskin to promote an ideal of *noblesse obligé* attractive to the middle class, he must offer his queens mythic power to glorify the prosaic political power associated with the Victorian monarchy; through myth he restores to queenship a divine potency.

Ruskin makes remarkably few references to Queen Victoria in his vast *œuvre*, especially given the significance of queens as icons in his thinking and writing. Their importance in the two famous works from the 1860s discussed here is obvious just from their titles, "Of Queens' Gardens" and *The Queen of the Air*, but Queen Victoria never explicitly appears in these texts, and only the most fleeting references show up in his other formal publications. A very few of his letters contain short anecdotes regarding the Queen, which will be examined here. While the dearth of references to his sovereign might suggest that she does not figure whatsoever in his idealized notion of what housewife-queens are; in fact, the opposite is true. The allusions, though few, reinforce the practical aspects of what Ruskin wants from middle-class women, aspects which might otherwise get lost in the rhapsodic mythopoeisis of his prose.

The oddest part of Ruskin's references to Victoria is their tone: Ruskin speaks of her utterly without reverence, invoking neither mythological nor even feudal paradigms in the kind of respect he offers his liege, which is surprising given his use of both models in so many other, less obviously applicable, circumstances.[3] The fondness and familiarity of his regard resembles his patronizing affection for most other women and girls that he likes and knows personally. It is tempting from a feminist perspective to read such a response to his real Queen as dismissive, but that would lose sight of Ruskin's entirely royalist psychology. An affectionate condescension to the Queen is as close as Ruskin the loyal subject could ever get to a relationship with Victoria, positioned immeasurably above him in social, political, economic, and even – whether or not he used such language directly about her or not – feudal terms. Neither Ruskin's brilliance nor fortune nor even his sex could ever give him sufficient advantage over the monarch to make his words mean other than a commoner's attempt to construct a connection with the Queen. Nevertheless, the ambiguity of such familiar homage suggests that in order to exalt a practical queenship based on the powerful but plain Victoria, Ruskin must mythologize her and her middle-class imitators.[4]

Ruskin's most extended reference to Queen Victoria lasts only half a paragraph in a letter to his father from the progressive Winnington school, where Ruskin taught girls art and geology, among other subjects. In "Of Queens' Gardens" and *The Ethics of the Dust*, Ruskin's 1866 textbook for girls on mineralogy and myth based on his experiences at Winnington, he expands upon the importance of solid philanthropic work that will genuinely benefit the poor. One of his chief examples is that when girls learn to sew, they should make garments to clothe the needy, rather than wasting their talent and industry producing unused altar cloths that serve nothing but the vanity of a preacher. He cites Victoria as instilling similarly sensible habits in her own daughters:

I hear . . . about the simplicity and good housewifery of the Queen at Balmoral; . . . some time ago, one of the little princesses having in too rough play torn the frock of one of her companions (a private gentleman's daughter), the Queen did not present the young lady with a new frock, but made the princess darn the torn one. I would not at first believe that the princesses had learned to "darn"; but Miss Bell was able at once to refer me to a notice of one of their exclamations at the great Exhibition about the sewing machine, which showed – being an expression of an earnest wish to have one, "for it would save so much trouble" – that they had real experience of what sewing meant. (Ruskin [1909] 1903–12: XXXVI, 453)

While this quotation says nothing outright of the princesses making clothes for the needy, they in fact did. Victoria and all the ladies of her household also knitted mittens and scarves for the soldiers in the Crimea (Longford 1964a: 248); by engaging in these homey demonstrations of charity and patriotism, Victoria consciously presented examples for behavior she wanted to encourage in her people while weaving links of comforting similarity between herself and average women. Remembering that the point of Ruskin's essays is that housewifery has symbolic significance beyond keeping house for one family, we must note that, for him, raising princesses with practical skills and social conscience carries political ramifications beyond the private good sense and courtesy Victoria might hope to inculcate in her daughters. Every sock the Queen knitted would be multiplied indefinitely. A princess or queen aware of her royal obligations to her people has a huge range of influence, even without the clout of Victoria; an average Victorian girl who sees herself in queenly terms can define the scope of her developing powers in the same way.

In "Of Queens' Gardens" Ruskin argues that average middle-class women should act with the same kind of social responsibility that we see Victoria cultivating in her children, performing duties of regal stewardship outside the home. The essay has already received ample analysis as the quintessential statement of Victorian glorification of women, both a description of what the Victorians believed and a prescription for what Victorian women should be.[5] Some critics have demonstrated Ruskin's extraordinary claims for queenship to be political compensation for women's practical powerlessness;[6] others have defended Ruskin from charges of misogyny.[7] The fact that Ruskin's famous description of the home and its queen in "Of Queens' Gardens" can be read as either misogynist or feminist indicates the complexity of his thinking on the "woman question," and shows how his ideas on the subject proliferate beyond the capacity of his own philosophical categories – or those of Victorian culture – to contain them.[8]

Even more famous than Ruskin's queen is the Angel in the House, the virtuous woman like Charles Dickens's Agnes Wickfield or Esther Summerson, who carries her household keys as a proud badge of office, bringing harmony and happiness to her domestic retreat. Although Dickens's characters most prominently figure in discussions of the type, the phrase "the Angel in the House" comes from Coventry Patmore's poem of that name, "whose title is so much more resonant than its content" (Auerbach 1982: 66). Following Virginia Woolf's lead, feminist critics have particular reason to point out how suffocating such an image of womanhood can be. Although often conflated with Patmore, Ruskin offers an alternative ideal for women in "Of Queens' Gardens," the second lecture in his most popular book, *Sesame and Lilies*.[9] Ruskin's queen is still "decidedly Victorian," (Hewison 1976: 154), but she takes on more power and greater responsibility than Patmore could imagine for his angel, whose significance derives from a very patriarchal view of Christianity rather than from political or mythological sources.

A book-length narrative poem, Coventry Patmore's *The Angel in the House* (1854–56) recounts a young man's courtship of, engagement to, and wedding with his angelic bride. The paragon this poem presented to the Victorians is all that Kate Millett abhors famously (in *Sexual Politics*) about the woman portrayed by Ruskin's essay; Honoria epitomizes the unspeakably passive and domestic girl, devoid of any will beyond her husband's, irreproachably pure, childlike, and innocent. The poem gives its heroine no public power whatsoever in her own right, and her only connection to the world outside the home is through inspiration of her husband to protect her and to achieve great things for her sake. In its time, *The Angel in the House* was a popular poem. Rarely read now, it often serves as an example of what is most repressive about idealizing an image of femininity.

The list of critics who conflate Ruskin's queen and Patmore's angel is a long one.[10] It is no wonder that scholars connect the two works: Ruskin himself quotes from *The Angel in the House* in "Of Queens' Gardens" to support his argument concerning the potential influence women have on men. And a glance at Virginia Woolf's passionate renunciation of the angel in "Professions for Women" illustrates why such an identification of the two works poses problems for any feminist attempt to recuperate Ruskin:

In those days – the last of Queen Victoria – every house had its Angel. And when I came to write I encountered her with the very first words. The shadow of her wings fell upon my page; I heard the rustling of her skirts in the room. Directly, that is to say, I took my pen in hand to review that novel by a famous man, she slipped behind me and whispered: "My dear, you are a young woman. You are writing about a book that has been written by a man. Be sympathetic; be tender; flatter; deceive; use all the arts and wiles of our sex. Never let anybody guess that you have a mind of your own. Above all, be pure." And she made as if to guide my pen. . . . I turned upon her and caught her by the throat. I did my best to kill her. My excuse, if I were to be held up in a court of law, would be that I acted in self defence. Had I not killed her she would have killed me. She would have plucked the heart out of my writing. For, as I found, directly I put pen to paper, you cannot review even a novel without having a mind of your own, without expressing what you think to be the truth about human relations, morality, sex. And all these questions, according to the Angel in the House, cannot be dealt with freely and openly by women; they must charm, they must conciliate, they must – to put it bluntly – tell lies if they are to succeed. Killing the Angel in the House was part of the occupation of a woman writer. (Woolf 1942: 237–38)

Since Ruskin's ideal is so closely associated with Patmore's, and with it participates in a larger cult of the domestic woman so problematic for twentieth-century critics, it is hardly surprising that it has come under attack. But Ruskin's queen differs significantly from Patmore's angel. As Woolf sees it, the Angel in the House cannot honestly criticize men's work, either in books or in life. But to get women to criticize men is precisely the point of Ruskin's essay. While Woolf must kill the Angel in the House to enable herself to write, she need not dethrone Ruskin's queen because, far from its being the queen's job to flatter men, it is her job to criticize them.

Elizabeth Helsinger has distinguished between two visions of Victorian womanhood as the Angel in the House and the Angel *out* of the House, selecting Ruskin's "Of Queens' Gardens" to define the outside angel. Her phrase underscores how Ruskin's text broadens women's dominion beyond the contracted domestic heaven provided by Patmore. But Helsinger's play on the Angel in/out of the House obscures the very real difference in Ruskin's choice of the word "queen" over "angel." The word "queen" grants a more immediately present and political power in the age of Victoria than does the word "angel" – a distant, ethereal wisp. While an angel might sound more potent than a queen, it is not the empirically verifiable, proven entity that is a queen. A metaphorical queen occupies a more real imaginative space for subjects of Victoria than the equally metaphorical but avowedly supernatural angel. Those historically specific Manchester housewives alive and listening in the Town Hall, King Street on December 14, 1864, whom Ruskin addressed in the original lecture itself, would recognize in an analogy to their sovereign more immediate significance for them than a comparison, even by the religious Patmore, to an angel.

We might expect Ruskin's ideal woman most closely to resemble Patmore's in Ruskin's renowned glorification of the Home, a passage that even Millett has to admit is a prose "classic of its kind" (Millett 1970: 72). But here – where the queen is "in the House" along with the angel – instead of Christian imagery we find pagan imagery, which mythically elevates woman into a colossal nature goddess, holding dominion over flora and fauna, controlling darkness and light:

This is the true nature of home – it is the place of Peace; the shelter, not only from all injury, but from all terror, doubt, and division. Insofar as it is not this, it is not home; . . . it is then only a part of that outer world which you have roofed over, and lighted a fire in. But so far as it is a sacred place, a vestal temple, a temple of the hearth, . . . so far it vindicates the name, and fulfils the praise, of Home.

And wherever a true wife comes, this home is always round her. The stars only may be over her head; the glowworm in the night-cold grass may be the only fire at her foot; but home is yet wherever she is; and for a noble woman it stretches far round her, better than ceiled with cedar, or painted with vermilion, shedding its quiet light far, for those who else were homeless. (Ruskin [1909] 1903–12: XVIII, 122–23)

In the very image that might make Ruskin seem most like Patmore, we see that for Ruskin home is portable. Far from enclosing this queen, Home opens up around her, obliterating the inside/outside dichotomy which forms the basic division of Victorian sex roles and the premise of *The Angel in the House.*

The titanic woman of Ruskin's vision yokes nature to her train, commands the stars for her canopy, and stands in the "night-cold grass" impervious and warm. She bids the "glow worms at her feet" to build her a hearth in the wilderness in an image that is simultaneously whimsical and diabolic.[11] Ruskin invents a queen of the night who does not just symbolize home but encompasses it, or as Nina Auerbach puts it, "casts off four walls for a nocturnal landscape with the contours of a grand woman" (Auerbach 1982: 60). By mythologizing his queen in such elevated and magical terms, Ruskin creates an image of ideal womanhood whose very existence eradicates the distinction between public and private. But this is precisely what the solidly unmythical Victoria already does. Adrienne Munich points out the Victorian age's difficulty in conceptualizing "the apparent contradiction of a devoted wife, prolific mother, and extravagant widow who is also Queen of an Empire upon which the sun never sets," exemplified in the joke that Victoria "ruled her nation as a mother and her household as a monarch" (Munich 1987: 265). Ruskin's radicalism is that, because he views the world through a mythic lens, he sees no contradiction in these roles, for Victoria or for any woman. When, in his first publication as poet laureate, Alfred Tennyson voices popular sentiment by calling Victoria "Mother, Wife, Queen" in that order, he domesticates the sovereign by subordinating her public to her private self and unwittingly contributes to the atmosphere for the snide remark Munich quotes.[12] In contrast, Ruskin aggrandizes housewives by urging them to reject a false loyalty to the private and to don symbolically the mantle of public queenship. He does so by demonstrating that the public and the private are the same.[13]

Ruskin champions the Queen as both ruler and (grieving) wife in a letter to his father just after the death of the Prince Consort: "The Queen, by first accounts in the paper, seems behaving very well.

Widowed Queens generally get on pretty well – if you look to history; – it is odd how a woman seems to take to the notion of government, considering that they are not supposed to be intended for it" (Ruskin [1909] 1903–12: XXXVI, 397). Not just Victoria, but all women could "take to the notion of government": when they are all symbolically queens and when queenship is conceived as housewifery on an Olympian scale.

After Prince Albert's death, in 1861, Victoria closeted herself with her private affliction. For ten years she frustrated her people with too few public appearances, with barely an attempt to fulfill any duties that would force her outside her palatial homes and royal gardens. Although she never stopped signing papers or meeting with ministers, in the early 1860s Victoria refused personally to open Parliament, to make speeches, to engage in virtually any public ceremonies other than those commemorating Albert or connected with her internationally important private family. Popular displeasure with the Queen's behavior found expression in the famous *Punch* cartoon of 1865 urging Victoria to satisfy her public responsibilities by showing her as Hermione from *Winter's Tale* up on a pedestal, with Britannia as Pauline commanding the "Widow of Windsor": "'Tis time! Descend, Be Stone no more" (Fredeman 1987: 51). One way in which the housewives that Ruskin constructs in "Of Queens' Gardens" most resemble their queen in 1864 and 1865, when all of England called for her to come back into view, is in what Ruskin depicts as their obsession with their private concerns to the detriment of their public duties. Against the backdrop of Victoria's widowed retirement and presumed selfishness in despair, Ruskin's urging the women in "Of Queens' Gardens" to relinquish the pull of the private for public action carries special resonance. His message is for them to be queens like Victoria, not as she is but as she should be; in fact, he implicitly addresses Victoria as well, admonishing her to get out of her garden of grief and back into the public action he knows she can do well.[14]

Regardless of the degree to which Ruskin consciously evokes Queen Victoria in *Sesame and Lilies*, his message to middle-class women is very unlike Patmore's, whose Honoria remains firmly on her pedestal, with no one begging her to get down. The passage of *The Angel in the House* that Ruskin quotes in "Of Queens' Gardens" demonstrates the difference between the two men's idealizations:

> Ah, wasteful woman, she who may
> On her sweet self set her own price,
> Knowing he cannot choose but pay,
> How has she cheapn'd Paradise;

How given for nought her priceless gift,
  How spoiled the bread and spill'd the wine,
Which, spent with due, respective thrift,
  Had made brutes men, and men divine!
              ("The Prodigal," also called "Unthrift")

In Patmore's poem this passage castigates women who marry for money rather than love, making a common point about the Victorian marriage market. It may also allude to prostitution, not that different, after all, from marrying for money. Most critics emphasize the corrupt nature of the passion, either monetary or carnal, that prompts the unthrifty, prodigal woman to spill her wine for nought – or at least the wrong kind of payment. However, surprisingly, Ruskin's use of the passage does not support any of these interpretations. He quotes it to illustrate something entirely different: the wasted energy of a woman who could persuade her husband to social justice but instead moves him merely to "play at precedence with her nextdoor neighbour" (Ruskin [1909]1903–12: xviii, 141). While Ruskin saddles women with a prodigious burden of guilt for failure to manipulate events not directly under their control, his exhortation to them to use their influence in economic and political matters recognizes their abilities to understand these subjects and invites women into discussion about them.

Patmore's *Religio Poetae* (1893) echoes *Sesame and Lilies* (1865) in a way that could easily damn the earlier work, if it were not that the very similarity of word choice underscores the contrast in meaning. A glance at passages from the two books reveals how far apart the men really are in their definition of female ability. Patmore says:

To maintain that man and woman are equals in intelligent action is just as absurd as it would be to maintain that the hand that throws a ball and the wall that casts it back are equal. The woman has an exquisite perception and power of admiring all the man can be or do. She is the glory of his prowess and nobility in war, statesmanship, arts, invention, and manners; and she is able to fulfil this, her necessary and delightful function, just because she is herself nothing in battle, policy, poetry, discovery, original intellectual or moral force of any kind.

  The true happiness and dignity of woman are to be sought, not in her exaltation to the level of man, but in a full appreciation of her inferiority and in the voluntary honour which every manly nature instinctively pays to the weaker vessel. (Patmore 1893: 162–63)

Compare that to Ruskin's much quoted passage from "Of Queens' Gardens" concerning the difference between the sexes:

We are foolish, and without excuse foolish, in speaking of the "superiority" of one sex to the other. . . . The man's power is active, progressive, defensive. He is eminently the doer, the creator, the discoverer, the defender. His intellect is for speculation and invention; his energy is for adventure, for war, and for conquest, wherever war is just, wherever conquest necessary. But the woman's power is for rule, not for battle – and her intellect is not for invention or creation, but for sweet ordering, arrangement, and decision. She sees the qualities of things, their claims, and their places. Her great function is Praise; she enters into no contest, but infallibly adjudges the crown of the contest. (Ruskin [1909] 1903–12: XVIII, 121–22)

The two passages show similarities disturbing for anyone defending Ruskin, and certainly his prescription of complementary roles according to gender stifles individual choices and abilities. But Ruskin finds it distasteful to claim women "inferior," unlike Patmore, who does so quite unabashedly. Patmore's comment that "woman has an exquisite perception and power of admiring all the man can be or do" and Ruskin's that woman's "great function is Praise" sound a lot alike, but the resemblance is illusory. Patmore has women admiring *all* that men can be or do, an activity which no doubt is pleasant for the men in question, but can hardly – as we have seen is Woolf's point – comprise adequate criticism. Ruskin, on the other hand, states that woman's intellect is for "decision," that "she sees the qualities of things, their claims, and their places." More problematic is Ruskin's statement that "her great function is Praise; she enters into no contest, but infallibly adjudges the crown of the contest." While Ruskin bars his queen from the contest and makes her judge "infallibly," she does not merely admire; she discriminates, judges, and praises only when appropriate. For Ruskin the function of the critic, the woman, and the queen are the same: analysis and due praise, but also due blame. Indeed Dinah Birch has pointed out, in her article "Ruskin's 'Womanly Mind,'" that Ruskin defines women's role of praise and judgment precisely as his own profession of art and social critic; far from calling women "nothing in original intellectual or moral force of any kind," Ruskin gives women the same job that he gives himself.[15] This role also resembles Queen Victoria's function, at least in Walter Bagehot's famous 1867 statement of a constitutional monarch's legal powers: "the right to be consulted, the right to encourage, and the right to warn" (Bagehot [1867] 1966: 111).

In an example of the social criticism Ruskin wants women to perform, he specifically enjoins them to prevent men from waging war if the purpose is unjust: "Men, by their nature, are prone to fight; they will fight for any cause, or for none. It is for you to choose their cause for them, and to forbid them when there is no cause" (Ruskin [1903] 1903–12: XVIII, 140). We may shiver at so convenient a method of leaving the blame of war to women, but it remains a clear call for women to speak out for or against public policy. For Patmore, for whom women have no place in statesmanship, for whom women are a blank wall to cast back the ball, to assign women such a role would be ludicrous and irresponsible.

Queen Victoria's opportunity for statesmanship was assured by her official position, but not all British monarchs took their role as seriously or worked as doggedly as she. As queen, she often used her rank to press her opinion about Britain's military conflicts. She engaged in considerable maneuvering to achieve her goals, although ineffectually in the case of the Crimean War, which she at first deplored (Longford 1964a: 237–42; Weintraub 1987: 235).[16] As a constitutional monarch, she did not have the power to prevent war, even when its declaration demanded her signature; however, she strongly voiced her concerns about performing the official role required of her in conflicts of which she disapproved, using her considerable political and popular influence to deflect parliamentary action away from foreign policy she considered wrong-headed.

Ruskin's suggestion that women stay out of the contest in order to judge it sounds like the laudatory perception of the aged Victoria late in her reign as above politics, representative of imperial Britain as a whole, despite her impact on government. John Lucas suggests that she cultivated this image strategically; in a century of revolutions and republicanism, she had reason to fear dissolution of the monarchy, to make every effort to avoid becoming "a plain Miss Guelph" (Lucas 1987–88: 65). Too publicly partisan a position could jeopardize her crown (Bagehot [1867] 1966: 90, 100). But earlier in her tenure she entered the political game head on, the most colorful example being how as a very young monarch she caused a constitutional crisis by successfully refusing a Tory government when it meant giving up her Whig-appointed ladies of the bedchamber. However, when Ruskin invokes the image of queen in 1864, between these two extremes of Victoria's career, her unpopular retirement from public view would make her seem not only above the fray, but even apathetic to it. If that is what his readers imagine when they think of queenship, Ruskin aims to change the picture.

Very much to the point of this chapter, another parliamentary issue Victoria spoke vehemently about was women's rights: her influential voice in this matter connects directly to Ruskin's. In "Of Queens'

Gardens," Ruskin positions himself between the proponents of women's rights, like Mill, who was after all very radical for his time, and people like Patmore, whose reactionary brand of "woman worship" we have just seen. From the beginning of his 1865 essay, Ruskin makes clear that it represents his contribution to the Victorian debate over the "woman question":

> There never was a time when wilder words were spoken, or more vain imagina-
> tion permitted, respecting this question – quite vital to all social happiness. . . .
> We hear of the "mission" and of the "rights" of Woman, as if these could ever
> be separate from the mission and the rights of Man – as if she and her lord were
> creatures of independent kind, and of irreconcilable claim. This, at least, is
> wrong. And not less wrong – perhaps even more foolishly wrong . . . – is the idea
> that woman is only the shadow and attendant image of her lord, owing him a
> thoughtless and servile obedience, and supported altogether in her weakness by
> the pre-eminence of his fortitude. (Ruskin [1909]1903–12: XVIII, 111)

The rhetorical strategy here is to assume that the lecture audience, middle-class women and men of Manchester and, after publication, of the rest of England and the English-speaking world, would already agree with him that radical feminism advocating women's rights (to vote, to enter professions) is wild and vain.[17] He assumes that his audience agrees with their queen's famous statement of distrust of "this mad wicked folly of 'Women's Rights' with all its attendant horrors, on which her poor sex is bent, forgetting every sense of womanly feeling and pro-priety" (Longford 1981: 9). He makes no attempt to preach to the con-verted on that question, as he could have; he makes no effort to convince this audience, as he does the working class women he addresses in *Fors Clavigera* 29, that it is better to tend babies or sew than to work in a tele-graph office. He certainly expects no one to shudder at the phrase "she and her lord." He enters "Of Queens' Gardens" into the "woman ques-tion" debate in argument not against a more liberal, but against an even more conservative position than his own. Dismissing radical feminism, he reforms women's status by arguing against the "even more foolishly wrong" notions we have seen expressed later by Patmore.

While Patmore restricts women to admiring men, Ruskin requires men to obey women, whose queenly authority gives them the right to direct the opposite sex.

> In all Christian ages which have been remarkable for their purity or progress,
> there has been absolute yielding of obedient devotion, by the lover, to his mis-
> tress. I say *obedient;* – not merely enthusiastic and worshipping in imagination,
> but entirely subject, receiving from the beloved woman, however young, not

only the encouragement, the praise, and the reward of all toil, but, so far as any choice is open, or any question of decision, the *direction* of all toil. (Ruskin [1909]1903–12: XVIII, 119)

Ruskin's difficulty fitting a vision of sovereign women with a belief in complementary spheres shows up when he tries to reconcile the male lover's absolute obedience to the beloved woman with her "true wifely subjection." His method of doing so is to designate women's mandate for "*direction*" as "a *guiding*, not a determining, function" (Ruskin [1909] 1903–12: XVIII, 121), the sort of power which, as we all know from our history lessons on The Articles of Confederation, is really no power at all. Again the implicit analogy to Queen Victoria helps Ruskin out here: in a constitutional monarchy, the queen's legal powers are sharply restricted, but remain symbolically and politically significant. Victoria used her position to affect domestic affairs and foreign policy all the time. She impressed the public by voluntarily paying her seven-per-cent income tax; she infuriated them by her sympathies with Prussia and active politicking against Denmark, effectively keeping England out of at least one armed conflict.[18] In social matters her guidance certainly prevailed.[19] Her court set the tone for society: unlike her uncles and grandfathers, she resisted the presentation of women whose past included annulments or other questionable experiences.[20] While she by no means invented the Victorian cult of mourning, she was its most prominent practitioner. Her taste in art and clothing, both infamously middle-class, made middle-class tastes fashionable. Her use of anesthesia for childbirth brought acceptance for a treatment many doctors would have otherwise scrupled against as unnatural or ungodly.[21] Her aesthetic, literary, and even medical choices had far-reaching effect.[22]

In all of these cases her acknowledged influence operated without legal leverage; like other British women, she was subordinate to law and convention. David Sonstroem attempts to show how woman's "subservience" in Ruskin differs from Mill's "Subjection," but in this regard Ruskin's sense of women's importance does not overcome his finally patriarchal definition of sex roles. More surprising than the fact that John Ruskin, Victorian sage, had patriarchal notions about women's subservience to men is the fact that he had such peculiar notions about men's subservience to women. It is because he has just granted ordinary women the extraordinary power of their sovereign that he qualifies it, and he does so in precisely the same terms that he uses to describe men's curtailment of power, that men are "entirely subject" to women, as free men are loyal subjects of Queen Victoria.

Ruskin says that a man must receive "from the beloved woman, however young, . . . the *direction* of all toil." What is peculiar here is that the "however young" woman should be "the superior in knowledge and discretion" to the however old man. By attributing such prudent understanding to young girls Ruskin sacrifices some credibility, and critics rush to remind us of his private purpose in writing this essay in part to teach and woo the very young Rose La Touche. However, ascribing this kind of discretion even to adolescent girls seems to me more than a biographical quirk. That knowledge and discretion are the property of all women, however young, is impossible; obviously, immaturity and maturity are incompatible characteristics. But the contradiction evaporates when we realize that Ruskin mythologizes women; in addition to being ordinary (perhaps childish) mortals, they are the human incarnations of Wisdom, Athena on earth, queens of the air. Thus, a man's obedience to a "beloved woman, however young" is not "merely enthusiastic and worshipping in imagination," but genuine service to an ideal element of moral, compassionate, life-giving intelligence described in *The Queen of the Air* that for Ruskin real women both embody and represent.

One of the most favorable contemporary reviews of "Of Queens' Gardens" is from Emily Faithful's magazine *Victoria*, run entirely by women, including all female compositors. The feminist journal, whose very title suggests the Queen's political significance for Victorian women, critiques some of the conservative aspects of Ruskin's position on women's role, but praises Ruskin's ideas about women's power foolishly squandered. *Victoria* gives the example of how bored girls flirt to control men. The reviewer abhors the waste of energy that could be better invested and applauds Ruskin's shrewd psychology.[23] In the following passage from "Of Queens' Gardens," Ruskin himself compares the power instinct with the sexual instinct, suggesting that both can be either triumphantly channeled into human happiness or disastrously perverted.[24]

Deep rooted in the innermost life of the heart of man, and of the heart of woman, God set it there, and God keeps it there. – Vainly, as falsely, you blame or rebuke the desire of power! – For heaven's sake, and for Man's sake, desire it all you can. But *what* power? That is all the question. Power to destroy? the lion's limb, and the dragon's breath? Not so. Power to heal, to redeem, to guide, and to guard. Power of the sceptre and shield; the power of the royal hand that heals in touching – that binds the fiend, and looses the captive; the throne that is founded on the rock of Justice, and descended from only by steps of Mercy. Will you not covet such power as this, and seek such throne as this, and be no more housewives, but queens? (Ruskin [1909] 1903–12: XVIII, 137)

Such a passage confirms Auerbach in emphasizing the demonic power of woman in Victorian imagination, as here Ruskin evokes the king of the animals (straight from England's seal) and the fire-breathing worm to lend their potency – masculine, animal, political, and mythological – to his human queen. But the powers he lists ("to heal, to redeem, to guide, and to guard. Power of the sceptre and the shield") are traditional to royalty, Victoria's as much as that of any earlier rulers. Still traditional, although no longer simply political in definition, is the idea of the laying on of hands, which Ruskin proceeds to dwell upon a moment longer, "the power of the royal hand that heals in touching," a power that I doubt many Victorians attached to their respectable real-life queen. With the healing touch Ruskin begins to elevate his ideal beyond even the exaltation of merely prosaically political leader.

Ruskin injects into his ideal the prerogatives of a male Christian God, with thrones of justice and mercy and with power to bind the fiend.[25] When Ruskin says that "they who govern verily 'Dei Gratiâ' are all princes, yes, or princesses of Peace," he invokes the divine right of kings and queens that Victoria claimed as based on their traditionally direct link to God: *Regina Dei Gratiâ*, queen by the grace of God (Ruskin [1909] 1903–12: XVIII, 139–40). He even lends them Christ's title, carefully including both sexes. Although this connection to God may remind us of Patmore, the relationship is quite different. For Patmore, women's job is to inspire because they reflect God's light (Patmore 1949: 63), not to rule because they have God's say-so.[26]

While a queen's garden may sound fenced in, the point of Ruskin's essay is to open it up: he urges women not to immure themselves behind their garden walls, but rather to redefine those gardens to include all of England, Victoria's demiparadise and sceptered isle. For those to whom the radical possibilities proffered by women's rights were out of the question, the offer of an acceptable urge for power and a wide venue in which to apply it must have been intoxicating. Ruskin's queen-making is a heady rhetorical tool, and the popularity of *Sesame and Lilies* testifies to its effect to the end of the nineteenth century.

Examining "Of Queens' Gardens" with Ruskin's real-life Queen in mind helps explain why twentieth-century readers, for most of whom Queen Victoria has become a faded caricature of prudery, would overlook the essay's feminist appeal in its own day. In many ways Victoria really is Ruskin's queen and her presence inflects his text whether he meant her to or not. Ruskin superimposes a mythological conception of queenship onto a political one, offering his audience a much richer and much more enticing role than either model would allow by itself in historical context. Victoria grants his use of the word "queen" palpable authenticity; Ruskin's mythopoesis takes the housewife-queens and makes their rule seem glorious and magical beyond the respectable possibilities Victoria alone could muster. By merging political and mythic images of queenship, he transforms the patronizing ideal of "woman worship" into an empowering model for material action.

NOTES

1 "Of Queens' Gardens" is the second lecture of the book *Sesame and Lilies*.
2 See Nadel's study of Victoria's portraiture, images whose purpose is to "reflect the ideals of the crown for public consumption and influence" (Nadel 1987: 175). Nadel comments that "the promotion of this public display of private life had political dimension in its effort to encourage the values of hearth and home in Victorian society"; Victoria commissioned official portraits that linked her "domestic happiness to public stability" (ibid.: 185).
3 Victoria's own preferred method of idealizing herself in iconography is feudal rather than mythological. Consider for instance the 1842 Landseer portrait *Victoria and Albert as Queen Phillipa and Edward III* (Nadel 1987: 187) or the frontispiece to Nicholas's *The Orders of Knighthood*, 1842 (Lucas 1987–88: 64). See Shuman for discussion of Ruskin's use of a feudal fantasy of queenship (Shuman 1994).
4 I am indebted to Margaret Homans for suggesting that while Ruskin uses Victoria to construct housewife queens, he also uses mythical queenship to construct Victoria herself (Homans 1995).
5 For a good example of its use in this fashion, see David 1987.
6 See Sawyer 1990: 140.
7 For the most significant contributions to this debate, see Millett, Sonstroem, Gilbert and Gubar, Auerbach, Helsinger *et al.*, Birch's "Ruskin's 'Womanly Mind'," and Nord. For more recent and analyses of Ruskin's approach to gender, see Sawyer 1990, Dellamora 1990: 116–29, Emerson 1994: 207–28, and Munich 1989: 179–86.
8 Helsinger's formulation of the "angel out of the house" to describe Ruskin's queenly housewife and her task of helping the poor shows how he uses the domestic ideal to campaign for women's efforts outside the home.
9 *Sesame and Lilies* sold over 160,000 copies by 1905 (Ruskin 1903: 5). It was Ruskin's most popular work in America, where it was commonly taught in high school well into the twentieth century (Helsinger 1982: 96).
10 To mention just a few, Walter Houghton brings *Sesame and Lilies* and *The Angel in the House* together in his chapter on love in *The Victorian Frame of Mind*, where both fall under the rubric of the 1860s expression "woman worship" (Houghton 1957: 377n). In *Sexual Politics*, Kate Millett sums up her

indictment of Ruskin's ideal by defining it as "the very stuff of the era's pet sentimental vapors enshrined in notions such as 'the angel in the house'" (Millett 1970: 80). Although Auerbach's grand mythic conception of Ruskin's queen is very close to my own, she also subsumes the woman of *Sesame and Lilies* under her wide-ranging analysis of the Angel in the House, whose pervasive power her book *Woman and the Demon* demonstrates. See also Harrison 1977: 46–47, Christ 1977: 147, Gilbert and Gubar 1979: 24, Nord 1988: 79, and Swindells 1985: 98.

11 See Arrowsmith 1982.

12 References to Victoria fulfilling her multiple roles are common throughout her reign. In just 1842 the *Illustrated London News* repeatedly presents her as "Queen," "woman," "wife," "mother," "mother of her people"; simultaneously as "The great Queen and stateswoman in the gorgeous palace – the young, lovely, and virtuous mother amidst the pure joys of sylvan retreat and domestic relaxation" (quoted in Nadel 1987: 189). Her jubilees spawned many odes on the topic, not least of which is Swinburne's 1887 "The Jubilee," which lauds "Thee, mother, thee, our queen" for fifty stanzas (Swinburne 1987: 106).

13 Victoria's record of political agitation in international affairs offers another example of how her position as monarch conflates public and private spheres. Her friendly delight with Louis Napoleon of France provides an instance of a personal relationship that historians see as having affected her opinions about appropriate foreign policy. Scholars usually interpret her acknowledged bias toward Germany, with enormously important consequences for domestic and European politics, as personal. Historians have good reason to see her favoritism as privately motivated: her mother and husband were German; many of her children married Germans; she had particularly strong family ties to Prussia; she was related by marriage to Bismarck. Of course, for a sovereign who marries children off to foreign rulers to achieve national security, the personal really is political.

14 The only direct allusion to Victoria's retirement in Ruskin's *Works* comes a decade later in a letter to one of his May Queens. Ruskin instituted a tradition in which schoolgirls would choose one of their classmates as May Queen to receive Ruskin's books; the queen in turn distributes the books to others of her own choosing in the school. Maintaining that she must rule actively, Ruskin advised one May Queen in 1876, "You don't intend to let yourself be put on the shelf out of the way, like poor Queen Victoria, I hope?" (Ruskin [1907] 1903–12: XXX, 343).

15 Also, both Rosenberg (1963: 8), and Birch (Birch 1988b: 312) mention that for Ruskin the purpose of "all great art is praise," as he wrote on the headnote to *The Laws of Fésole*. So not only is woman's duty explicitly for criticism in Ruskin's paradigm, but implicitly it is for creation after all. Sheila Emerson comments on the gender implications of this in *John Ruskin: the Genesis of Invention* (1994: 218).

16 While all of the comprehensive biographies deal with Victoria's political
   influence, the most thorough – though dated – treatment is Hardie's. He
   provides a useful, brief summary (Hardie 1935: 240–41).

17 Non-English-speaking as well: no less than Proust translated *Sesame and Lilies*
   for the French edition.

18 See Hardie for a detailed discussion of Queen Victoria's vast political influence, especially in foreign policy (Hardie 1935). The Schleswig-Holstein
   question is one in which Ruskin disagreed with Victoria, although he never
   mentions her in context of his concern over it. He does, however, mention
   the Princess of Wales as his future queen, and how terrible it would be to
   desert her country in need.

19 Hardie also provides some less satisfactory discussion of Victoria's influence
   on social matters (ibid.: 137–41). For a contemporary analysis, see Bagehot
   [1867] 1966: 90–99.

20 One relevant example: as Mrs. Ruskin, Effie was presented at court. As Mrs.
   Millais, she was snubbed, and "the more conventional among the aristocracy followed the Queen's example" (Lutyens 1967: 265).

21 See Poovey 1988: 24–50 for discussion of the controversy over anesthesia.

22 See Rowell 1978 for the importance of Victoria's love of the theater and
   patronage of the opera.

23 See Helsinger *et al.* 1983: 1, 98–101. I am indebted to them for reprinting so
   large a section of this hard-to-locate article.

24 This is yet another way in which Ruskin's queen differs from the Angel in
   the House, who must scrupulously avoid seeming to want power over men,
   although as Woolf points out, she may well flatter in underhanded
   manipulation of them.

25 This invocation of Christianity does not resolve what seems suddenly an
   anomalous female Christian God into that other Queen of Heaven, the
   Virgin Mary, whose intercessory influence comprises not both justice and
   mercy, but mercy alone. Ruskin quickly abandons the image of godhead,
   however, and other religious references in the lecture compare the ideal
   woman not to God himself, but more orthodoxly to Mary Magdalene, in
   urging the queens beyond their garden walls (as Magdalene to her garden
   gate) into the wider garden of England, there to feed the hungry and house
   the poor. Also, the reference to the purity of the title lilies and the many
   roses in the essay evokes association with the Virgin Mary.

26 However, Ruskin describes women's authority as influence over men rather
   than as direct control over political machinery. When Ruskin grants women
   a power which they hold "straight in a gift from the Prince of all Peace"
   (Ruskin [1909] 1903–12: xviii, 139), it is merely over her husband, son, or
   lover: "the tender and delicate woman among you, with her child at her
   breast" has "a power, if she would wield it, over it, and over its father, purer
   than the air of heaven, and stronger than the seas of earth" (Ruskin [1909]
   1903–12: xviii, 140–41).

# CHAPTER 7

# How we lost the empire: retelling the stories of the Rani of Jhansi and Queen Victoria

*Maria Jerinic*

I

Queen Victoria may have never gone to India, but her strong affection for her Indian protégés did manage to raise more than a few eyebrows. Victoria's notorious appreciation of "male beauty" as well as her fascination with the exotic side of India encouraged her patronage of Duleep Singh, whose debauched lifestyle eventually caused her court great embarrassment (Weintraub 1987: 13 and 238). Her patronage of the promiscuous "Munshi" (Abdul Karim), another "good looking young man," was also deeply resented by the royal household. Victoria refused to believe any of the numerous accusations aimed at the Munshi, who was suspected of leaking confidential government information in India (St. Aubyn 1991: 502–4). Her willful blindness encouraged speculations by "people in high places" that she was "'mad on this point'" (St. Aubyn 1991: 504). Was her supposed madness motivated by maternal concern for her protégés or by a darker, sexual desire?

While history may only continue to speculate upon the nature of these "royal relations," fiction has allowed a number of Victoria's British subjects to express the licentious side of Indo-British relations. George MacDonald Fraser's 1975 novel *Flashman in the Great Game* contains one such expression. In the novel, Flashman, the irreverent Victorian British antihero, is sent to India prior to the "Mutiny," or Uprising, in order to investigate the rumblings of native discontent.[1] While there, however, he manages temporarily to set aside his royal responsibilities in order to engage in a particularly provocative sexual encounter with the Indian Rani of Jhansi, the woman whom the British initially considered responsible for the June 1857 Jhansi massacre, and whom they still consider a primary insurgent of the Indian Uprising.[2]

Responding to the summons of a perfumed handkerchief, Flashman hurries off to a secret rendezvous in an isolated pavilion:

She turned her head, and then in one movement raised the net and slipped out, standing motionless by the couch, like a bronzed statue. She was wearing bangles, all right, and a little gold girdle round her hips, and some kind of metal headdress from which a flimsy veil descended from just beneath her eyes to her chin – not another stitch. I let out an astonishing noise, and was trying to steady myself for a plunge, but she checked me with a lifted hand, slid one foot forward, crooked her arms like a nautch-dancer, and came gliding slowly towards me, swaying that splendid golden nakedness in time to the throbbing of the music beneath our feet. (Fraser [1975] 1989: 98)

In this scene, the Rani, the contested ruler of the central Indian state of Jhansi, presents herself as a seductive dancing girl, exuding a sexuality which draws upon the most extreme orientalist stereotypes.[3] Her animalistic passion incites her to thrust "up and down like a demented monkey on a stick," and her insatiable sex drive exhausts even the lecherous Flashman. Drained by this encounter, he is unprepared for the attack on his life which follows shortly after the Rani has slipped out of the love nest.

To read this interlude merely for its titillating effects ignores a series of provocative political questions about the linking of the wild sexual encounter with a "rebel" female leader and nineteenth-century British imperial relations. Is the novel making any connection between Flashman's sexual possession of the Rani and Queen Victoria's eventual assumption of the title "Empress of India" after the Uprising?[4] What is the relationship, in the novel and in history, between the Rani, "that gorgeous, wicked witch" (Fraser 1989: 11), and the British queen, or, as Flashman calls her, "little Vicky" (Fraser 1989: 320)? And why, at the end of the twentieth century, does Fraser, as well as a host of other English-language writers, choose to retell a story of the Rani of Jhansi and the Queen of England? By examining a series of texts spanning over a century – primarily histories and dramas – this chapter will argue that the Rani has been the subject of so many twentieth-century Western representations because of the position of conflict Queen Victoria occupies in the British cultural imaginary.

The Indian Uprising began on May 10, 1857, when sepoys in Meerut mutinied against their British officers. According to Patrick Brantlinger, the "immediate" cause of the Uprising was the sepoys' suspicion that the cartridges for their new Enfield rifles had been "greased with cow and pig fat" (Brantlinger 1988: 200). Since the cartridges had to be bitten before use, both Hindu and Muslim sepoys would violate their religious convictions if their suspicions were true. After Meerut, the fighting spread on to Delhi, Cawnpore, and eventually Jhansi. In the massacre at Jhansi on June 8, 1857, all the Europeans residing at Jhansi were reportedly murdered by the indigenous residents.

There is still a debate among British and Indian historians on whether the "uprising was only an army 'mutiny,' or a 'civil rebellion' as well" (Brantlinger 1988: 201). Jenny Sharpe argues that the "Indian Mutiny or Sepoy Rebellion was not quite the military insubordination that its name suggests but rather a wave of uprisings in which Indian soldiers, princes, religious leaders, and peasants all played a role" (Sharpe 1993: 57). Sharpe, however, does argue that even if it was not such an extensive "insubordination," the Uprising did bring about a crisis in representation for the British, who could no longer rely on "the racial typing of the 'mild Hindoo'": "the absence of consent that the anticolonial uprisings represented could not be understood according to the racial stereotype of Hindu passivity or logic of British rule by native consent. A new racial typing was required . . ." (Sharpe 1993: 58). Drawing upon one aspect of this new "racial typing," Fraser's novel relies on an established tradition of representations of the Rani of Jhansi, who appears in almost every Western account of the Jhansi massacre since the actual event. The pre-Uprising stereotype of Indian women as particularly passive and oppressed was replaced, and the Rani becomes one of the infamous women "behind the barbaric acts of rape and mutilation" in the Uprising, both admired for her bravery and despised for her treachery (Sharpe 1993: 74).[5]

Historical controversy surrounds the Rani's biography. Although her eventual correspondence with the British authorities documents the later part of her life, the would-be biographer is hard pressed to separate fact from fiction.[6] Born, as many Indian sources agree, in 1835, she was married to the Maharajah Gangadhar Rao Newalkar of Jhansi, a much older, childless widower in need of an heir. The Rani gave birth to a son in 1851, who died within three months, once again leaving the kingdom without a natural heir. This became a truly pressing problem with the death of Gangadhar on November 21, 1853. Governor-General Dalhousie's "Doctrine of Lapse" dictated that states in which the rulers died without a natural heir lapsed automatically to the British. On his deathbed, Gangadhar adopted a five-year-old relative, Damodar Rao, but the British government did not recognize the adoption.

Following her husband's death, the British offered the Rani a life pension of 60,000 rupees, with the expectation that she discharge her troops and quietly surrender her position. Not waiting for the official declaration of lapse, the Rani, enlisting the help of a sympathetic Major Ellis, the Jhansi Political Assistant, and the British barrister John Lang, immediately began a letter campaign barraging Dalhousie with claims of her legitimacy to rule. Her series of letters were either ignored or received sharp refusals; the state of Jhansi lapsed to the British in May of 1854.[7]

Although it is hardly surprising that she would harbor hostility towards the British, there is no proof that on June 15, 1857, the outbreak of the Jhansi rebellion, the Rani had completely severed her ties of loyalty. Besieged within the fort walls, the European residents of the city pleaded for the Rani's assistance, but it is not clear whether she was unable or merely unwilling to assist them. Following the massacre of these Europeans, an outraged Rani still appeared eager to cooperate with the British who, at least for the moment, seemed to believe her protestations of innocence. They gave her temporary control of Jhansi, but withheld crucial support to ward off invading principalities eager to take advantage of a "helpless" widow. Forced to fight independently, she joined the insurgent forces on March 15, 1858, and by the 23rd the Central India Field Force besieged Jhansi, finally overrunning her on April 3, 1858. Eluding British soldiers, the Rani managed to escape to Kalpi, where she formed an important segment of the rebel command in conjunction with Rao Sahib and Tantya Tope, two prominent Indian male rebels. Once Kalpi fell, the rebel army drew back to Gwalior, and according to many reports it was here on the battlefield that the Rani was killed on June 17, 1858.

In India, the Rani is a celebrated national icon, while British reaction to her remains ambivalent. The British both despise her as a female harridan and admire her as an extraordinarily brave soldier. From historical tracts to imaginative literature, a large body of nineteenth- and twentieth-century texts written in English have repeatedly attempted to reimagine and reposition her role in the Jhansi massacre, trying to ascertain her complicity or innocence.

The manner in which the British repeatedly expressed their interest in the Rani was shaped by Victoria's presence on the throne of Britain. Any ruling woman disturbs a perceived natural order and upsets ideas, particularly Victorian ones, of normalcy. As the stunned British try to understand the phenomenon of their "rebelling" native troops, they employ the image of their queen in order to understand the phenomenon of the Rani. Victoria may pose as a model of queenhood for the Rani, who needs to be tamed and pacified. Forging into battle, leading her warriors, actually fighting British soldiers, the Rani has overstepped the boundaries that ideologically surround her as a woman and as a native. She is too violent, too active in the wrong arena, a far cry from Victoria's domestic model. Yet the figure of the Rani seems, simultaneously, to pose a warning that any queen may become unruly. The Rani's status, in

British eyes, as a primary insurgent indicates a British discomfort with ruling women and consequently with their own queen. This interest in the Rani is tied to an imperialist vision, one that looks with suspicion on *all* female political involvement, British as well as Indian.

In the twentieth century images of both the Rani and Victoria provided a means for understanding why the British were losing, and ultimately lost, in 1947, their Indian empire. According to Margaret Strobel, as late as 1985 Sir David Lean, the director of the 1984 film *A Passage to India*, claimed that "'It's a well-known saying that women lost us the Empire'" (Strobel 1991: 1–2). Twentieth-century interest in the Rani is linked to this prejudice. But it is not the Rani who is solely blamed for this loss. Victoria is also implicated. In the days of imperial collapse, the Rani's story is reimagined in texts that celebrate the inevitability of British imperialism. It is, however, a decidedly male imperialism that allots no space to female leadership. Instead, female leaders, Western as well as Eastern, are presented in these works as undermining Britain. The Rani then, in these English-language texts, becomes a signifier for the assertion of British male power at the very historical moments when that power is threatened.

## II

This chapter considers how images of the Rani and her rule are juxtaposed to those of Victoria and her queenship in Western English language texts. Because of Victoria, the term "queen" carries a particular and powerful cultural resonance for a British nineteenth-century audience (a resonance that still manages to pervade twentieth-century anglophone culture). The manner in which the term "queen" is manipulated throughout this anglophone writing on the Rani demonstrates that just as Victoria's presence was constantly felt in India as a "mother-deity," she appears in the numerous English retellings of the Rani's story even when she is not directly mentioned (Worsick and Embree 1976: 1).

In two histories that appeared immediately following the Uprising, the Rani appears with no obvious connection to Victoria; in fact Victoria is not mentioned at all. Walter Coningsey Erskine in *A Chapter of the Bengal Mutiny as Seen in Central India by One Who Was There in 1857–8* (1861) accuses the Rani of promising protection to the Jhansi Europeans who were then "most basely and treacherously murdered" by her orders (Erskine 1861: 5). It was after the murders, then, according to Erskine, that the Rani "took possession of Jhansee district . . . and proclaimed herself queen; but ever writing (through secret messengers) to the Commissioner that she was his friend, and doing all for him" (Erskine 1861: 5). Erskine's Rani is duplicitous and cruel, and her queenship is presumed; she is an imposter. Erskine does not call her a queen, yet the Rani calls or proclaims herself one, and Erskine implies that she does so in order to assume enough iconographic power to rule Jhansi in the British absence. Because it is necessary to call herself "queen" once she takes "possession" of Jhansi, the Rani is presented in this account as understanding the amount of power inherent in this label; Erskine projects onto the Rani a sensibility that could only come from her own knowledge of Victoria's status. Erskine does not then deny the Rani the title of "queen" because of any sensitivity to cultural particularities (i.e. an English queen is not the Western version of an Indian rani) but because he wishes to invalidate the Rani's position as ruler. Just as the indigenous races are not capable of ruling themselves, an Indian woman is not capable of ruling at all.

Early accounts condemning the Rani largely perceive her, in the words of Sharpe, as a "hag" or a "she-fiend" (Sharpe 1993: 74). But this is *not* the only reaction. In his *History of the Indian Mutiny* (1858–59), Charles Ball struggles with his ambivalent feelings towards the Rani. While he does not identify her as a queen, he does call her a "princess," a label which ascribes to her some royal status while denying her the importance of being a queen. Unlike Erskine, Ball does not wholeheartedly condemn the Rani; she is at once an "extraordinary woman . . . who appears to have united the martial spirit of her race with extraordinary ability and aptitude for command" and a "cruel," "treacherous," "artful woman" (Ball [1858–59]1981: II, 289), a "tiger-hearted woman" (Ball [1858–59] 1981: II, 291) whose "indomitable spirit" was accompanied by "extreme cunning" (Ball [1858–59] 1981: II, 289).

Ball's identification of the Rani as a "princess" and not as a queen accounts for both her power and her powerlessness; she was a native woman who may have had enough power to destroy the inhabitants of the European fort, but also not enough power to save them. Furthermore, for both Ball and Erskine, to call the Rani a queen would be to make her, on one level, Victoria's peer. It would also allow her the power she attempts to claim for herself. In refusing to call her queen, both men make clear that the Rani has overstepped her boundaries as a native woman. Only Victoria, a white woman sovereign, has the right to use this appellation.

While Erskine and Ball do not specifically mention Victoria, nor do they seem to critique her position, authors such as John Lang, Philip Cox, and Henry Scholberg – whom I will discuss shortly – explicitly compare Victoria to the Rani. In these latter Rani texts, however, Victoria does not have a stable identity; her function in each text differs and she is treated with a great deal of ambivalence. As a queen, Victoria has the potential to become like the Rani, leaving behind her pacific domesticity, fighting British men. Just as the Rani sided with Indian men against British men in an attempt to pull the empire apart, so might a British queen try to destroy what it means to be British. Written by a Western pen, the Rani's story is, then, not about India but about Britain.[8] Western fascination for the Rani is so strong because Britain, ruled by a woman, becomes the subject of the Rani's story.

Through their treatment of Victoria and the Rani, the authors of these texts exhibit a commitment to a male imperial project and subsequent distrust of any female leadership. This male vision is an extension of the misogynistic sentiment which, according to Jenny Sharpe, dominated post-"Mutiny" India: "In the jingoistic discourse of the Mutiny, English women were represented as abused victims so that English men could be their heroic avengers. During a post-Mutiny era of reform, the women themselves were held responsible for the aggressiveness of the military action" (Sharpe 1993: 91). At some point in the latter half of the nineteenth century there is a representational shift; white women, who were at one point seen as the victims of the "Mutiny," are now blamed for it. White women become sexual temptresses who arouse "the sexual appetites of indigenous men, . . . women had then to be protected from the latter" (Strobel 1991: 6). White men, however, do not only believe that white women are desired by Indian men. White women also are accused of feeling desire, as when Victoria's subjects questioned her relationships with her Indian protégés.

John Lang's *Wanderings in India and Other Sketches of Life in Hindostan*, which appeared in 1861 with a chapter devoted to his interaction with the "Ranee" of Jhansi, ultimately attempts to undermine the credibility of female leadership. While in Agra, Lang (a barrister) was invited by the Rani to Jhansi to oversee her attempts to annul the annexation of Jhansi. The Rani believed that British justice would prevail and revoke the doctrine of lapse. According to Lang, many "officials of rank in India" regarded this annexation as "unjust." Although he ultimately condemns her for her participation in the Jhansi massacre, Lang himself "sympathized with the woman" (Lang 1861: 85–86) and the loss of her kingdom, particularly since she was the widow of a ruler who "had been . . . faithful to the British Government" (Lang 1861: 85). It is only as a woman, as a private individual and not as a ruler, that he is concerned for her. As far as he is concerned, she is the wronged wife of a loyal British subject.

Lang's refusal to acknowledge the Rani's position as the legitimate regent ruler of "the little native state of Jhansi" is emphasized by his indignant response to the Jhansi finance minister's "repugnant" request that he "consent to leave [his] shoes at the door when [he] entered the Ranee's apartment" (Lang 1861: 89). Lang asks the minister "whether he would attend a levee at the palace of the Queen of England, if informed that he must enter her Majesty's presence with his head uncovered, as did all her subjects, from the lowest to the highest" (Lang 1861: 89). What follows is a wrangling conversation of compromise in which the minister suggests

"You may wear your hat, Sahib; the Ranee will not mind that. On the contrary, she will regard it as an additional mark of respect towards her." Now this was what I did not want. My desire was, that she should consider the wearing of my hat, supposing I consented to take off my shoes, as a species of compromise on her part as well as on my part. But I was so amused with this bargaining as it were, that I consented; giving them distinctly to understand, however, that it was to be considered not as a compliment to her rank and dignity, but to her sex, and her sex alone. (Lang 1861: 90)

Lang's chivalry to the female sex, not respect for the Rani's rank, governs his behavior. He, in fact, suggests that through her womanliness the Rani may be able to recapture her kingdom: "'if the Governor-General could only be as fortunate as I have been, and for even so brief a while [to have caught a glimpse of her voluptuous body from behind the purdah curtain]' I feel quite sure that he would at once give Jhansi back again to be ruled over by its beautiful Queen" (Lang 1861: 94). The Rani's body, not her right to rule, will regain her kingdom.

While neither Erskine's nor Ball's report seems critical of Victoria's position, Lang seems to question her authority as well as the Rani's. If Lang believes that this Jhansi minister would be equally hesitant to appear with a bare head in front of the British queen, is it implied that the minister should also compromise because of Victoria's sex? One might quickly assume that native obedience of and respect for Victoria would be automatically expected, but if Lang believes that the Rani's rank does not guarantee her "an additional mark of respect," what does he think of Victoria's?

According to Lang's account, Victoria's and the Rani's rule are both illegitimate. They are women who are allowed to rule because of the chivalrous impulses of British men. Yet even a native male has the power to stand up to Victoria and decide not to bare his head. Ultimately Lang's text asks: If the Rani cannot hold onto her kingdom, can Victoria hold onto hers?

III

Twentieth-century texts tend to vindicate the Rani from the taint of the massacre, and it is as a vindication, as well as part of an effort "to 'sell' Indian personalities to the Western reader" (Tahmankar 1958: 6), that D.V. Tahmankar presents his biography *The Ranee of Jhansi* (1958). Although he chooses to describe her as India's Joan of Arc, Tahmankar actually equates the Rani with Victoria: "Her [the Rani's] disappearance from the scene, therefore, is rightly regarded as a significant landmark in Indian history and the beginning of a new phase in Indo-British relations. It was in 1858 that by a Royal Proclamation Queen Victoria formally took over the Indian administration of the East India Company" (Tahmankar 1958: 5). The syntax of these two sentences forges a connection between the Indian rani and the British queen. The Uprising threatens to become a war between matriarchs. The Rani's involvement in the Jhansi massacre and subsequent Uprising activities justifies a switch in monarchs from the Rani to Victoria.

That Tahmankar is also writing in the reign of a new queen, Elizabeth II (who ascended to the throne in 1952), may elucidate why there is a fresh need to "understand" the Rani in terms of Victoria. In fact, according to Dorothy Thompson, Elizabeth II "continued and reinforced the trends" of Victoria's reign, rescuing the country from "a half-century of war, depression, and scandal" witnessed by the intervening male monarchs (Thompson 1990: xiv). Comparing the Rani to Victoria, in Tahmankar's text, provides the means to vindicate and forgive the native woman who has turned on the British. The Rani's involvement in the Jhansi massacre and subsequent Uprising activities was part of a historical determinism that allowed for a switch in monarchs, from the Rani to Victoria. Victoria's eventual takeover is part of a linear natural progression of imperial rule and Indian independence. Tahmankar presents these two women rulers as working towards a common goal. They are not really enemies, and the current "new phase in Indo-British relations" mentioned above, a relationship between two independent countries, is only possible because of the Rani's rebellion and Victoria's imperialism.

Sir John Smyth's *Rebellious Rani* (1966), however, is not so enamored of Indian independence; ultimately his text suggests a nostalgia for former imperial glory. Smyth's text, however, compares the Rani not to Victoria but to Elizabeth I: "Was she ruthless, cruel and insensitive? Or was she rather like our own Elizabeth I, a woman conscious of female weaknesses, encircled by danger and trying to steer a diplomatic and skillful course to safeguard her throne and succession. I think this latter picture is nearer to the truth" (Smyth 1966: 17). While Tahmankar celebrates the power of queenship – female rule has encouraged the "new phase in Indo-British relations" – Smyth chooses to focus, instead, on the limitations inherent in female rule. A queen's power is inhibited by her femininity. Because of her "female weaknesses" she must exert much of her energy facing challenges that a *male* ruler would not encounter. Consequently, she would pose a danger to her country because of her vulnerability.

Yet while a Western queen is *in* danger, an Eastern "queen" like the Rani is dangerous. Smyth draws upon the Rani's appearance in defending her innocence regarding the massacre, but the way she looks also presents a subtle threat. While defending her innocence, Smyth bases his defense largely on a group of portraits of the Rani in which the common feature is "the magnificent eyes, dark, lustrous and full of character" (Smyth 1966: 14–15). These eyes, which are also "warm, generous, and open," demonstrate her "natural character" and thus prove her innocence. With eyes like these, Smyth argues, how could she be guilty of the cruel Jhansi massacre? In his vague reference to a description "we have" of the Rani, by contrast, Smyth draws his readers' eyes down to her low-cut bodice, which displayed "a well-developed bust" and was then "drawn in tightly at the waist with a belt embroidered with gold into which was stuck two carved silver mounted pistols and a small dagger" (Smyth 1966: 15). By presenting her as armed in such a way, he emphasizes her dangerous and threatening sexuality.

The Rani, however, also possesses masculine qualities that act as purifying agents. Her "masculine spirit and great resolution" (Smyth 1966: 15) redeem her from an insidious oriental femininity: "Her tomboyish qualities, her ability to get on with boys, her intelligence and generous spirit, seem to show an antithesis to the ultra-feminine, sometimes secretive love of intrigue and acceptance of whatever came along, which marked the character of many Indian women – often from force of circumstances and upbringing" (Smyth 1996: 19). Smyth ostensibly attacks the Rani's femininity because it is an oriental one, but his celebration of masculinity, which he links with intelligence and a "generous spirit," asks if this negativity does not apply to all femininity, Western as well as Eastern. A queen's power, as we have seen in the case of Elizabeth I, is contested because she is female. Western female leadership, personified by Elizabeth, is hampered by an inability to navigate "danger" successfully. In Smyth's eyes, Western women are unable to manipulate threatening political situations, while Eastern women are able to do so only too well. While Western femininity is ineffective, Eastern femininity is dangerous.

According to Tahmankar, the Rani is replaced by Victoria, but for Smyth it is Sir Hugh Rose, the commander of the Central India Field Force, who ultimately vanquishes the Rani. Smyth's text presents the Rani and Sir Hugh Rose as the "two brilliant and forceful personalities" who emerge from the "story of the Rani and the Central India Field Force" (Smyth 1966: 13). Just as the Rani is purified by her masculine qualities, Rose, a man, triumphs over her because Smyth, unlike Tahmankar, finds all feminine power suspect. Smyth's history, unlike Tahmankar's, does not celebrate the "new phase in Indo-British relations" or independent India. Rather, Smyth's triumph revolves around male conquering female, the British domination of India.

IV

Like Smyth's text, three plays written about the Rani also condemn female power. Alexander Rogers's 1895 play *The Rani of Jhansi or the Widowed Queen: a Drama of the Indian Mutiny* is still, technically, a nineteenth-century work, but it is the product of a historical moment when the inevitability of empire was being questioned. The late nineteenth century was an uncomfortable period for the British government in India. On the one hand "India had become the greatest, most durable, and most profitable of all British, perhaps even European, colonial possessions" (Said 1993: 133). Yet, particularly after 1870, British control of the territory was threatened by foreign encroachment and the rise in, and increasing support for, Indian nationalism. Legislation such as the Ilbert Bill of 1883 and the formation of the Indian National Congress in 1885 threatened British imperial control (Paxton 1992: 123). Furthermore, after 1890 there was a marked shift in Indian opinion toward viewing the Uprising as the first war of Indian independence (Lebra-Chapman 1986: 147).

Rogers's play does not openly articulate this threat to imperial power. Rather, it dramatizes an uneasiness surrounding an alliance between authority and femininity. In the beginning of the play, the Rani is a vindictive warrior woman. She draws upon her supposed defenselessness as a "widowed queen" (Rogers 1895: 27) – drawing also upon images of a mourning Victoria – in order to manipulate the British political agent's belief in her compassionate, pitying "woman's heart" (Rogers 1895: 26). The Rani's queenship seals her guilt in the massacre because queenship is inextricably linked to an unreliable femininity: "Oh beware! She was a pensioner, and is a Queen; / And women's fancies are like butterflies, /

That flit from flower to flower without a cause" (Rogers 1895: 35). This warning from the mouth of a British woman in the play does not deny the Rani's queenship but instead indicts all queens, Western as well as Eastern, for a queen rules by her "fancies" and not by rational judgment. For Rogers, femininity is unreliable. The play only vindicates the Rani when she finally abandons her aspirations to power; she acts like the proper Indian widow and dies so that she can join her husband in the afterlife.

While the Rani has been properly pacified in the manner of her race, it seems that Ellen, the British woman, has "gone native" and denied her Englishness. When she is threatened with rape, Ellen's speech is elucidated in terms of sati: "And as the sati mounts the funeral pyre . . . So can the Christian woman also die." The Indian woman becomes a role model for the British woman. In attempting to act as the "pure" British woman, Ellen undermines her national identity. According to this play, not only are queens untrustworthy, but even British women can easily deny their national allegiances. This skepticism regarding the loyalties of British women is not surprising when one considers the above discussed misogynistic climate introduced after the Uprising. What is somewhat surprising is that Victoria should be targeted in an era when her reign was generally celebrated by her subjects.[9] Rogers never specifically mentions Victoria, but this play cannot openly dramatize an uneasiness with her rule because of government restrictions on dramatic representations.[10] Instead, by describing the Rani as an Eastern Boadicea, Sir Edwin Arnold's preface to this play reinforces its Western orientation. Victoria enjoyed presenting herself as Boadicea (Weintraub 1987: 426). Consequently, identifying the Rani as Boadicea places the Rani in a frame of reference comfortable to a Western audience and alerts this audience that Britain and Britain's female ruler is the real subject of this play.

This silence regarding Victoria becomes less necessary in the early twentieth century, when there is no longer a queen on the throne. In Philip Cox's *The Rani of Jhansi* (1933), the Rani is a democratic and just ruler who claims Victoria as her role model; much of her behavior is directed by a consideration of what "the Great White Queen" would have done. The Rani barrages a visiting Major Ellis with questions about Queen Victoria. While Victoria is not yet a widow, the Rani is, and she is interested in knowing how Victoria would act if Albert were to die. The Rani's mourning, however, will be quite different from Victoria's, for the Rani was not in love with her husband. The Maharajah's age and his physical infirmities denied the Rani what she most wanted from life, not power and a kingdom but the goals of the ideal Western Victorian woman, "children," "love," and "a husband's society" (Cox 1933: 45). Consequently, the Rani then identifies her desire to rule as a product of her widowed state: "Now that sati has been denied to her [the Hindu widow], she is compelled to search for other ways of expressing her fidelity to her dead lord" (Cox 1933: 47). Bereft of a husband, even one she did not love, she feels obligated to pour her energies into her late husband's state. Victoria's influence encourages the Rani to manage state affairs, a job traditionally allotted to men. Frustrated by the Rani's independence and sense of justice, her duplicitous and self-interested native courtiers (including her father) blame the influence of Queen Victoria for her behavior.

The portrayal of the Rani as a widowed ruler draws upon the powerful image of the ever-mourning Victoria that dominated the latter half of nineteenth-century England. Victoria's mourning serves to validate the rule of both women in this play. Victoria and the Rani are not autonomous females but loyal wives celebrating their dead husbands.

While Victoria and the Rani authorize each other's reigns in this play, Cox ultimately draws upon the authority of Queen Victoria to discredit the Rani as an Indian nationalist icon. For the first three decades of the twentieth century the Rani was employed as a metaphor for resistance to the British that could not be voiced openly.[11] But in Cox's text the Rani is a ruler because she admires the British queen and not because of Indian nationalist sentiment. Written during a time when the demands for Indian independence were rising, this play presents the Rani not as a rebel but as one whose true sympathies are with the British.[12] Although the British are trying to annex her land, eventually they are presented as sympathetic and understanding; the Rani has much more in common with the forthright British than with her deceitful countrymen, who accuse her of siding with the British at the beginning of the Uprising. The Rani's actions in this play only seem to support Indian suspicions. Enraged by the slaughter of the Europeans at the Jhansi fort, the Rani *only* joins the rebellion so that she can prevent the murder of more innocents by exercising control over the unruly forces.

Ultimately, it is not the British who really thwart the Rani, but Indian men, who one minute plot with the British, the next with the mutineers, all to fulfill their own nefarious plans. Many of the British agents she encounters express their kinship. Governor-General Dalhousie himself explains that he is a Scot and Colonel Low is Irish; their ancestors, like the Rani, fought against English annexation. Dalhousie clarifies that when his ancestors finally "realised that it was much more profitable to work for the English king than to fight against him, we took service wholesale

under the English flag – determined to get the best out of the bargain"
(Cox 1933: 71). Now it is an honor for him to serve "my King and to be his
loyal subject" (Cox 1933: 73). But what about his queen? Dalhousie's
neglect to mention Victoria, the Rani's inspiration, is a glaring historical
omission. Is Cox rewriting history so that English rule and imperialism
become ultimately male? India, like queens, the Scottish, and the Irish,
must surrender to the eventual domination of British men.

In his forward to the play, Cox claims to resist the temptation to use
the image of Joan of Arc as a way of understanding the Rani. To employ
Western metaphors seems inappropriate because of the Rani's "racial
background and social setting." Despite this apparent sensitivity to racial
particularities, however, the Rani's story, for Cox, is still very much about
Britain in India. Even the story of Joan of Arc has some autonomy since
she was the precursor, according to Cox, of the French national state,
while the Rani was the precursor to "the consolidation of the Indo-
British connection." The Rani's story here is one about the inevitability
and appropriateness of British rule in India.

*Lakshmibai and the Captain* (1985) by Henry Scholberg (the son of
American missionaries) was written during the "reign" of another
British woman, Prime Minister Margaret Thatcher. In this play, the
Rani identifies herself "As a queen of a small but important kingdom"
(Scholberg 1985: 15) to the Englishman Captain Ford, assigned as the
new resident to Jhansi. She uses this identity to demand that he describe
to her how he won the Victoria Cross in the Crimea: "Your queen is
ordering you to tell her. Would your Disraeli disobey a command of
Queen Victoria?" (Scholberg 1985: 16). Not only does she perceive
herself as queen, she is Captain Ford's, an Englishman's queen; the two
of them replicate the relationship of Victoria and her prime minister.
Like Cox's Rani, this Rani ultimately identifies with the British. Even her
fellow rebels understand this as they accuse her of admiring the English
too much because she studies their military tactics (Scholberg 1985: 73).

While the Rani admires Ford, he is in love with her. Ford's romantic
feelings persuade him that the Rani has been forced into her position as
rebel because the British unfairly held her responsible for the Jhansi massacre. In addition Ford, with a strong instinct for justice, is sympathetic
to Indian reaction to British policy particularly regarding the infamous
cartridges, ostensibly greased with cow and pig fat. He does not,
however, sympathize with the rebel cause. He never questions that the
British should dominate and sternly reprimands the mutinous Rao: "We
are not plunderers. We have given you schools and universities, roads

and canals and bridges, a civil service and postal system; and now we're trying to give you telegraph and railways. The plunderer does not pay for his plunder" (Scholberg 1985: 55).

The relationship between the Rani and Ford differs from earlier representations, for in the Rogers and Cox dramas the Rani offers her body to sympathetic Englishmen. Rogers's Rani is motivated by physical attraction and a wish to spare the attractive Lieutenant Purcell from the mutineers. Cox's Rani offers herself to Major Ellis in a desperate attempt to gain complete control over her Jhansi. Although both Englishmen manfully resist an encounter, they are severely tempted. In the Scholberg play the Rani attempts no such seduction and it is she who chastely insists that the only relationship she and Ford can ever maintain is a "friendship" (Scholberg 1985: 33). While Scholberg presents a contrasting view of the Rani's sexuality, his play does not challenge the imperial visions of Rogers and Cox. These three plays still work towards a similar outcome by pushing the Rani into one of the two familiar categories for women: lascivious seductress or domestic angel. In Scholberg's play, the Rani becomes the latter as she is the object of Ford's chivalry; ultimately he dies trying to save her. The love Ford bears for the Rani represents a necessary bond between the two countries. England as the male provider and protector is willing and able to sacrifice for female India, who demands guidance yet admires and emulates her male partner. But this paradigm undermines the royal hierarchy that the Rani at first attempts to establish when she demands that Ford treat her as if she is his Queen Victoria. Ultimately the Rani is conquered by her subject, and ultimately the power of queens is proven to be virtually nonexistent in the face of British masculinity.

None of the British characters ever refer to the Rani as a queen. Rather she is called a "widow," a "young woman of rather dynamic qualities" (Scholberg 1985: 9), the "bravest and best they had. A truly noble lady" (Scholberg 1985: 79), as well as "one of these niggers" (Scholberg 1985: 12). Yet it is the name assigned by Lord Canning, the governor-general of India, that demonstrates the instability of female rule. Astonished "that the British Empire is being stopped in its course by a woman" (Scholberg 1985: 40), Canning can understand the phenomena of the Rani as an "Indian Boadicea," the woman England produced who "raised unmitigated hell with the Roman Empire" (Scholberg 1985: 40). Remember that from time to time Victoria considered herself a Boadicea, and it is as Boadicea that Sir Edwin Arnold can understand the Rani. V. G. Kiernan believes that Tennyson's poem

"Boadicea" (1859) is "very likely" about the Rani of Jhansi (Kiernan 1989: 141). But could Tennyson be referring to Victoria as well? As Boadicea was eventually vanquished by the Romans, so will the Rani be defeated by the British, who can then afford to remember her with ambivalent admiration. It is not only the Rani who will be conquered, however, but Victoria by her own country*men.*

Although this play allows a nostalgic indulgence for lost causes, it does not identify as nostalgia the phenomena of British imperialism. Instead, imperial domination is presented as inevitable. However, this belief in the inevitability of imperial Britain is a result of a nostalgic longing. According to Salman Rushdie, the 1980s was a period in which the "refurbishment of the Empire's tarnished image [was] under way," because the increasing poverty of Margaret Thatcher's Britain, combined with the "euphoria of the Falklands victory," "encourage[d] many Britons to turn their eyes nostalgically" to their perceived former glory (Rushdie 1991: 91–92). Under the strain of economic hardship, Britons try to reimagine and reunderstand the power they lost and why they lost it. Scholberg's play provides one answer; his imperialism is rewritten as the project of British men. Women, Eastern as well as Western, only threatened and ruined the empire.

All three plays argue for the inevitability of the British Empire, and a male imperialism, at three historical moments when that very inevitability is challenged. At the same time, these plays argue that it is female rule which threatens the nation. These plays want to discredit women as rulers and former imperial territories as autonomous nations. The Rani's defeat then becomes a symbol of the reassertion of British male power and the wresting away of power from Victoria as well as from the Rani. To tell the Rani's story, then, is not only to relate a gendered fable of British men and imperial domination in a political and historical climate that denies the very importance of an imperial male program, but it is also to express ambivalent feelings towards a British queen and subsequent female leaders who perpetuated Victoria's legacy and lost the British their empire.[13] In the wake of the collapse of imperial power, authors like Fraser and Scholberg can blame this collapse on women rulers, specifically Queen Victoria, who set dangerous precedents. These texts imply that if a king had sat on the throne instead, Britain might have maintained and strengthened its imperial control. As Fraser's Flashman demonstrates, the only place for a woman in the empire is as an object of fantasy and sexual exploration. As a ruler, a woman is a dangerous Rani or an ineffectual "little Vicky."

NOTES

1 After this reference I choose to use the term "Uprising" instead of "Mutiny." The latter term is the one used by imperial powers while Indian texts often choose to use the former. To use "Mutiny" without quotes would risk unconsciously replicating imperial ideologies.

2 Sir John Smyth argues that Lord Canning, the governor-general, and Lord Elphistone, the governor of the Bombay Presidency, "attached the very greatest importance to the defeat of the Rani and the capture of Jhansi, which they considered to be the main stronghold of rebel power in Central India." (Smyth 1966: 12–13). Joyce Lebra-Chapman provides a discussion of how the British admired the Rani as "undoubtedly one of the ablest of the rebel leaders" (Lebra-Chapman 1986: 178).

3 Edward Said's *Orientalism* (1978) provides a discussion of stereotypes revolving around the Eastern World. All other references to Said's work will be from his *Culture and Imperialism* (1993).

4 Although the Crown assumed control of India in 1858, Victoria received the title "Queen-Empress" on May 1, 1876.

5 Gayatri Spivak's "Can the Subaltern Speak" (1988) encourages one to consider how the Sati debates of the earlier part of the nineteenth century positioned British men as the saviors of Indian women.

6 Lebra-Chapman (1986) provides a wonderful account of the Rani's history. I am indebted to her text for most of the following biographical information.

7 The Rani's letters are now located in the Oriental and India Office Connections in London and the National Archives of India in New Delhi.

8 Dipesh Chakrabarty argues that Europe acts as the "silent referent in historical knowledge" (Chakrabarty 1992: 2). Much of his article is concerned with the manner in which Third World writers need to refer to European texts – this was very helpful to my thinking of the cultural violence enacted with the Western appropriation of the Rani's history.

9 St. Aubyn claims that the closing years of Victoria's reign were filled with protestations of loyalty. Earlier discontent had evaporated (St. Aubyn 1991: 493).

10 In his discussion of George Bernard Shaw's *Caesar and Cleopatra* (1898), Weintraub explains that the lord chamberlain's office "censored plays for their politics and their allusions to the sovereign" (Weintraub 1987: 105).

11 Lebra-Chapman provides an initial discussion of how the Rani was used as a symbol by Indian nationalists (Lebra-Chapman 1986: 142–44).

12 Sarkar provides a discussion of growing Indian national sentiment in the late twenties and early thirties (Sarkar 1995: 254–348).

13 Rushdie also points out that following the Falklands victory, Margaret Thatcher called for a return to "Victorian values" (Rushdie 1991: 92).

# CHAPTER 8

# "I know what is due to me": self-fashioning and legitimization in Queen Liliuokalani's Hawaii's Story by Hawaii's Queen

*Robin L. Bott*

> Our people feel that in honoring their chiefs, in respecting those who are legitimately their rulers, they are doing not only a duty, but a pleasure to themselves.
>
> (Queen Liliuokalani, 1898)

Originally published in 1898, *Hawaii's Story by Hawaii's Queen* is Liliuokalani's attempt at self-fashioning, in which she uses signs to construct herself as a legitimate and Westernized Hawaiian ruler. Liliuokalani succeeded her brother Kalakaua in 1891 and became Hawaii's first queen and last monarch. She came to the throne during a period of political and economic distress. Foreign interests in Hawaii were moving the nation towards annexation, while royalists fought to keep the monarchy intact and the islands independent. Amidst such opposition, Liliuokalani was a non-Western ruler who fashioned herself as a civilized Western queen in order to gain respect from her imperialist American neighbors. In Hawaii, many native Hawaiians did not believe that Kalakaua and Liliuokalani had a strong enough claim to the throne. To legitimize her right to the throne, Liliuokalani relies on her genealogy, representing herself as a legitimate descendant of the noblest ruling chiefs of Hawaii. At the same time, she employs the signs of Western elite society to mark herself worthy of the attention given to other Western monarchs. Vital to this effort is her emphasis on a close personal relationship and identification with Great Britain's Queen Victoria. In her autobiography, Liliuokalani models herself after the most famous Western monarch alive, Victoria, in order to construct for herself an identity of legitimacy and authority. She draws on the similarities between herself and Victoria, focusing on the signs of nobility – long-standing associations with Britain's royal family and material displays of power and culture – to mark herself as civilized and, therefore, deserving of the homage of the American people. However, her attempt is in vain because she does not fully

Plate 8.1 "Her Majesty Queen Liliuokalani."

understand her audience, the American public, and their animosity towards monarchy.

By 1891, when Liliuokalani ascended the throne, the monarchy of Hawaii was hanging by a thread. In 1887, while Liliuokalani was attending Queen Victoria's jubilee celebrations, the American business community revolted and her brother Kalakaua, then king, was forced at bayonet-point to sign a new constitution, known historically as the "Bayonet Constitution." This illegal document, never ratified by the people of Hawaii, "deprived the sovereign of all power," and "from that day the 'missionary party'[1] took the law into its own hands." (Liliuokalani [1898] 1991: 180–81). When Liliuokalani became queen she refused to take her brother's place as the missionary party's puppet. Fearing that Hawaii would be lost to the Hawaiian people if she did not reclaim control of the government, Liliuokalani gathered her cabinet on January 14, 1893 and told them that she planned to proclaim a new constitution that day and that they would all gather publicly to sign it.[2] At the public gathering, her ministers refused to sign the document and Liliuokalani was forced to back down in order to maintain a peaceful assembly. Three days later, with the aid of an American warship, the American business leaders, later known as the "annexationists," overthrew the monarchy and set up a provisional government with Sanford B. Dole as its president. In January 1895 royalists staged an unsuccessful rebellion that ended with the arrest of Liliuokalani and 200 supporters. Liliuokalani was put on trial, found guilty of conspiracy and sentenced to a fine of $5,000 and imprisonment with hard labor for five years. Never executed, the sentence was used to terrorize the native Hawaiians and humiliate Liliuokalani. In October 1896 Liliuokalani was fully pardoned and had her civil rights restored to her. Shortly after, she made a progress across the United States. In Boston she was met by an old friend, Julius A. Palmer, a Boston newspaper reporter, who persuaded her to write her own story of the overthrow.

Liliuokalani wrote *Hawaii's Story by Hawaii's Queen* to counter negative American journalistic representations that depicted her as a weak, self-serving, pagan queen ruling over a heathenish nation of barbarians (Blackman 1899: 90–91, 129–30; Musick 1898: 29–30, 348–49). Published in 1898, the book is just over 400 pages and fifty-seven chapters long; it includes genealogical trees, newspaper articles, excerpts from Liliuokalani's trial, and the text of the annexation treaty. The first part of the book covers Hawaii's history during Liliuokalani's childhood. She talks briefly about her upbringing, the lives of her royal relatives, and the kings who ruled before her. By chapter 8, she begins detailing the establishment of her family's dynasty with the popular election of her brother Kalakaua. Chapters 8 to 35 deal with Kalakaua's reign and Liliuokalani's adventures as heir apparent, sometime regent, and ambassador to Queen Victoria's 1887 jubilee. The account of the trip to and from the jubilee celebrations and the events of the jubilee itself cover ten chapters of this section; this narrative is the longest, most detailed event in the entire book. The remaining twenty-one chapters document Liliuokalani's short and troubled reign, the overthrow, her imprisonment and trial, her trip to the United States (at eight chapters, it is the second longest account next to the jubilee), and her plea to the American people for mercy towards the dispossessed Hawaiians.

As Queen of Hawaii, Liliuokalani was in a social and political trap: she wanted to keep her royal identity intact and rule her kingdom unimpeded by outside forces, but she acknowledged her dependence upon the protection of the United States. Consequently, she had to construct herself as more Westernized than her Western readers. The Hawaiian signs of status were not recognized as worthy of respect by the American businessmen who held the true power in Hawaii. Hence the markers of her Hawaiian status had to be normalized through a Western lens. She does this by emphasizing the similarities between her cultural beliefs and practices and those of the British and their monarch, Victoria. By identifying herself with Great Britain and its queen, Liliuokalani allies herself with America's former master, perhaps suggesting to her American audience that she is not a viceroy and her country is not a colony – as the US once was – but instead a peer to Victoria and her great empire.

Liliuokalani attempts to fashion herself as a civilized and powerful monarch by fostering relationships with other nobility from around the world. In particular, she continues the Hawaiian monarchy's tradition of friendship with and emulation of Great Britain's royalty. In 1794 Kamehameha I pledged allegiance to King George III through Captain George Vancouver, and asked the British king to watch over the Hawaiian kingdom and help defend it against other foreigners who might come to take possession (Tate 1962: 328). Thirty years later Kamehameha II and his favorite wife and half-sister Kamamalu traveled to England to visit George IV and died there in 1824 (Tate 1962: 327). While still Prince Alexander Liholiho, Kamehameha IV and his brother Prince Lot, later Kamehameha V, were received at the court of St. James in 1848 (Allen 1982: 97).

By the time Kamehameha IV became king, in 1854, there existed among the Hawaiian aristocracy "a preference for English institutions, a partiality for British aristocracy," and a desire "to make Queen Victoria a model in all official matters" (Tate 1965: 21). Kamehameha IV asked Queen Victoria to be godmother to his only son and she agreed. On August 25, 1862 the young prince was officially christened Albert Edward Kauikeaouli Leiopapa a Kamehameha (Tate 1965: 97). Unfortunately, the young Prince Albert, named after Victoria's deceased consort, died of brain fever two days later. His father, Kamehameha IV, blaming himself for his son's death, sank into depression and died two years after his son. After these tragedies, a sympathetic Queen Victoria is said to have called herself and the Hawaiian Queen Emma "'sisters in grief'" (Tate 1965: 195).

Further evidence of the Hawaiian monarchy's relationship with British royalty was Kalakaua's "cordial reception in England in 1881" (Tate 1965: 195). And in 1869 Prince Alfred, the duke of Edinburgh, visited Hawaii. At Kamehameha V's request, Liliuokalani put on a grand luau for him at her Waikiki residence (Liliuokalani [1898] 1991: 32–33). They did not meet again for many years, but Liliuokalani cherished her relationship with the Duke:

We have met once since those days, at the Queen's Jubilee, during my visit to London in 1887. Our past acquaintance was cordially recognized by the prince, who was then my escort on a state occasion, my nearest neighbor on the other hand being the present Emperor of Germany. (Liliuokalani [1898] 1991: 34)

Liliuokalani was proud of her continued relationship with Prince Alfred, although she was even prouder of her connection to his mother Queen Victoria. She demonstrates this pride in the longest and most detailed section of her autobiography, her attendance at Victoria's 1887 jubilee.

Liliuokalani's invitation to and account of the jubilee celebrations further constructs her identity as an internationally recognized sovereign. In 1887 she is only the heir apparent, or, as she is called in England, the Crown Princess of Hawaii attending upon the current queen, Kalakaua's wife Kapiolani (Liliuokalani [1898] 1991: 146).[3] But by relating in her book her experiences with European royalty and aristocrats at the jubilee, Liliuokalani constructs herself as a civilized Western monarch. From the moment she stepped down off the *City of Rome* at Liverpool Liliuokalani realized what it meant to be royal in Europe. She describes with great detail the welcoming party:

Amongst these were the Hon. Theodore H. Davies, the British Consul to Hawaii; Mr. R. H. Armstrong, the Hawaiian Consul at London; the Rt. Revd

Bishop Staley, formerly Anglican Bishop of Honolulu; Mr. Janion of the mercantile house of Janion, Greene & Co., long in mercantile relations with the Hawaiian Islands. These all bent the knee, kissed the hand of the queen, and saluted us with proper form. (Liliuokalani [1898] 1991: 136)

She is excited to be accorded the respect and deference she does not receive at home. It is almost as if she is instructing her audience through example on how they should treat royalty.

It is interesting to note, however, that even though Liliuokalani is socializing with Western aristocracy, she and the rest of the Hawaiian royal party are lodged apart from them:

Rooms were assigned to us at the Alexandra, where there were many other members of the royal families of the distant world. Amongst these were Prince Komatzu of Japan; the Siamese Prince, brother of the King of Siam; the Prince of India; and the Prince of Persia. At other leading public houses were quartered the princes and princesses of other nations of Europe. (Liliuokalani [1898] 1991: 141)

This hemispheric segregation does not seem to daunt Liliuokalani in the least.[4] It does not diminish the fact that she and her sister-in-law are the honored guests of one of the world's greatest living monarchs. European or not, Liliuokalani is still recognized as royalty, with the right to socialize and celebrate with other royalty from around the world.

Her descriptions of actual audiences with Victoria stress the kinship Liliuokalani feels with Great Britain's queen. She is careful to establish for her audience a preexisting relationship with Victoria by recounting the Queen's fond remembrance of Kalakaua and his "agreeable visit" (Liliuokalani [1898] 1991: 145). She uses familial terms to describe her initial meeting with Victoria: "Her majesty Victoria greeted her sister sovereign, Kapiolani, with a kiss on each cheek, and then, turning to me, she kissed me once on the forehead; we were asked to be seated, the two queens sitting together on the sofa and engaging in conversation" (Liliuokalani [1898] 1991: 144). The language Liliuokalani uses indicates that she sees the women as equals. But, of course, as Liliuokalani is proud to intimate, because she can speak English and Kapiolani cannot, she is able to get along better with Victoria and the other royals than Kapiolani. For instance, after the official meeting, Kapiolani leaves but Victoria holds Liliuokalani back and introduces her children to her other sister sovereign (Liliuokalani [1898] 1991: 145). Her Westernization, demonstrated by her ability to communicate with the Queen of England in her own language, gives her the social advantage over her sister-in-law, who can speak only Hawaiian. Liliuokalani is not just a Hawaiian aristocrat, but an international sovereign civilized enough to converse with the crowned heads of the world.

Not only does Victoria behave like a sister sovereign in conference, but she further favors the queen and crown princess of Hawaii by allowing them the use of her carriage and personal guard while they are in London. For the Westminster Abbey service, Kapiolani and Liliuokalani were "accorded the most unusual honor of an escort drawn from the Life Guards of Her Majesty Queen Victoria" (Liliuokalani [1898] 1991: 151). At the service itself the guests are seated according to their rank. Liliuokalani and Kapiolani are seated with the other kings, queens, princes, and princesses of the world. Being accorded places of honor at Westminster Abbey reinscribes Liliuokalani's importance for her readers.

Liliuokalani is amazed by all of the pomp and grandeur of the jubilee and recounts meticulously the company, the carriages, the costumes, and the conversations surrounding the events. She describes the finery she sees at a dinner party one night:

There were duchesses with shining tiaras, marchionesses with coronets of flashing stones, noble ladies with costly necklaces or emerald ear-drops, little women who seemed almost bowed down under lofty circlets of diamonds over their brows, tall women bearing proudly off their adornment of stones of priceless value. I have never seen such a grand display of valuable gems in my life. (Liliuokalani [1898] 1991: 148)

At the same dinner party she is careful to mention that her party is given "the position of honor in the very center of the room" by being seated beside Lord Salisbury at his table (Liliuokalani [1898] 1991: 149). This example of deference, as well as her recorded conversations with other international royalty present at the jubilee, marks Liliuokalani as part of a coterie of social elite.

After the jubilee Liliuokalani continued her friendship with Victoria until the Queen's death.[5] Her experiences in England, and the material displays of power she witnessed, made an impact upon her and reinforced her belief in the divine right of absolute monarchy. Upon her return to Hawaii, she justifies her numerous progresses and the extravagance and conspicuous waste of her reign and Kalakaua's as necessary marks of their royal status. This extravagance seems to be in line with the excess Liliuokalani witnessed during her attendance at the jubilee in England. Her demands upon her people's hospitality and their willing compliance are, for her, markers of her high rank. In July 1891 she makes "the usual royal tour of the islands" (Liliuokalani [1898] 1991: 220). She maintains that the expense of the progress to her people was a welcomed one because of the people's love for their rulers: "At all of these places the people who came to receive us were delighted to have the opportunity to show their loyalty and manifest their love" (Liliuokalani [1898] 1990: 223). Only through such conspicuous waste and displays of affection can the authority and legitimacy of the Queen of Hawaii be tangibly affirmed. After all, Liliuokalani had seen thousands of people turn out for Queen Victoria's jubilee celebration. As a sister sovereign, Liliuokalani expected the same enthusiasm in order to validate her status.

These material displays of power, however, were meant to do more for Kalakaua and Liliuokalani than reinscribe their status as the rightful rulers of Hawaii; they were needed to help place a difference between their family dynasty and that of the former ruling dynasty, the Kamehamehas. Hawaiians, like the British, were assigned a position in the social hierarchy based upon their ancestral lines. Rank was determined by "blood ancestry," and genealogy functioned as vital proof of high birth (Beckwith 1972: 11). Political power combined with a strong bloodline enabled Kamehameha I to establish his family dynasty in Hawaii. The Hawaiian islands prior to the reign of Kamehameha I were divided into a number of warring chiefdoms and principalities. Kamehameha, through brute strength, superior strategy, and physical conquest united the islands under one rule in 1795. He was the most powerful and feared chief at the time, and as king ruled the islands with Machiavellian ruthlessness. To insure the survival of his dynasty, Kamehameha took for his sacred wife Keopuolani, the highest ranking woman in Hawaii.[6] Five Kamehamehas reigned in Hawaii from 1795 to 1872.

When Kamehameha V died on December 11, 1872, unmarried and without an heir to succeed him, the direct line of authority was broken. Instead of naming a successor from among a number of eligible candidates, Kalakaua and Liliuokalani included, Kamehameha V refused, letting the Kamehameha dynasty die with him. By his royal decree, the problem of succession was instead solved through election. All interested and eligible claimants to the throne were invited to run for office, the winner being elected by the legislature. Kalakaua, not the popular favorite, lost the election to Lunalilo, first cousin to Kamehameha V. However, King Lunalilo died of tuberculosis, aggravated by his intemperate drinking, only a year and twenty-four days after coming to the throne. Like Kamehameha V before him, King Lunalilo, unmarried and childless, died refusing to name an heir on February 3, 1874. Another election was held and this time the legislature chose Kalakaua to become the next king of Hawaii. However, his election and the establishment of his dynasty did not come easily. Supporters of Kamehameha IV's widow, Queen Emma, Kalakaua's opponent in the race, rioted outside of the courthouse where the election was held and attacked members of the legislature. The mob destroyed property and assaulted those unlucky enough not to escape from the building (Liliuokalani [1898] 1991: 46). Clearly the Hawaiian people were somewhat divided over the question of succession.[7] They were not as united behind Kalakaua as Liliuokalani would have her readers believe.

While related to the Kamehamehas, Kalakaua and Liliuokalani were not direct descendants of Kamehameha I. The native Hawaiians did not recognize the Kalakaua family as having "true high-chief blood" (Tate 1965: 48). This matter was further complicated by the fact that Kalakaua "ran" for the office of king, losing the first time and winning the election the second time. Until the death of Kamehameha V, all of the kings of Hawaii had succeeded to the throne.[8] In addition, Queen Emma's popularity among the Hawaiians was another thorn in the side of the new dynasty. In order for Kalakaua and Liliuokalani to establish and maintain their family's dynasty, they had to distance themselves both from the former dynasty and from the seemingly Americanized form of succession, the election. Kalakaua's first act as king was to name a successor; after that, he worked on bolstering the public esteem of his family.

Kalakaua and Liliuokalani, whose Hawaiian claim to the throne was less than secure, moved towards Westernizing themselves and their court. Instead of eliding the difference between themselves and the Kamehamehas, they punctuated it by aligning themselves more explicitly with Great Britain. By adopting the signs and markers of a monarch greater than any of the Kamehamehas, Kalakaua and Liliuokalani in effect constructed themselves as superior to that family. However, this self-fashioning required money, and lots of it. Kalakaua's spending seemed to know no bounds. Liliuokalani justifies the extravagance of her brother's reign as the absolute right of a divinely appointed monarch. Kalakaua nearly bankrupted the country in order to build and furnish Iolani Palace in 1879. This was a necessary expense, according to Kalakaua and Liliuokalani; sovereigns from around the world lived in palaces, and the ruling family in Hawaii believed they needed to live in one too. The grand building was another marker of their royal status adopted from the British. Helena Allen explains that "Liliuokalani had read and learned from foreign visitors of these palaces and Kalakaua had seen them, been entertained in them, but the Americans felt the new palace was much too grand for the 'comic opera monarchy'" (Allen 1982: 162). Despite complaints from the foreign residents, the royal family was pleased with its material symbol of power. Later, the money spent on Kalakaua's coronation in 1883, and the festivals surrounding it, drew criticism from many people in Hawaii,[9] but Liliuokalani justifies the expenditure as "wise and patriotic"; in her view, the money spent on the coronation helped "to awaken in the people a national pride" in their monarch (Liliuokalani [1898] 1991: 105). By making this event a momentous occasion, Kalakaua's family was able to deflect attention from his election and place emphasis on his rank and importance through excessive financial displays of power. Besides, no one questioned the extravagance of Victoria's jubilee; certainly no one should have resented the money spent on the Hawaiian monarchy. Kalakaua and Liliuokalani further modeled themselves after Victoria by having their crowns, scepters, and coronation gowns made in England after the fashion of that country (Liliuokalani [1898] 1991: 100). In addition to these articles, Kalakaua had a special ring and coach made for his coronation. Like Victoria, Liliuokalani and Kalakaua felt entitled to a degree of respect made manifest through conspicuous waste.

By distancing themselves materially from the former rulers of Hawaii and marking themselves as Westernized, Kalakaua and Liliuokalani hoped to legitimize their dynasty. Their claim of legitimacy would not come from a strong bloodline, but from the appearance of culture and refinement. They would not be native chiefs of heathen descent ruling over a tiny island kingdom; rather, they would be internationally known sovereigns, dressing, speaking, and behaving like their powerful Western counterpart, Queen Victoria. Indeed, Merze Tate claims that before becoming king, Kalakaua was an "amiable prince of polished manners and bearing" who "spoke English well" and who studied international law in preparation for someday becoming king (Tate 1965: 34). Liliuokalani was even more educated and cultured than her brother; a social leader in the Hawaiian kingdom for many years, "she had a perfect command of English and had had good literary training" (Tate 1965: 112). When she succeeded to the throne as the Queen of Hawaii in 1891, "Liliuokalani was described by Hawaiian and American papers as 'well-educated,' 'tactful,' a woman of 'state craft,' and even 'handsome.' She was without doubt the best educated woman in Hawaii"

(Allen 1982: 341). She uses her education to mark herself as civilized for her American audience.

Liliuokalani further aligns herself with Victoria by showcasing her knowledge of and skill with the English language. Not only does she behave and dress like Victoria, but she shares Victoria's superior command of English. *Hawaii's Story by Hawaii's Queen* is entirely in English, written comfortably and well. Even the smallest details and nuances in her writing display her Western learning and literacy. For instance, in her last chapter entitled "Hawaiian Autonomy," Liliuokalani refers to the works of Western literary figures to support her argument against the annexation of the islands by the United States. She maintains eloquently that "Shakespeare has said it is excellent to have a giant's strength, but it is tyrannous to use it like a giant" (Liliuokalani [1898] 1991: 370). With this reference to *Measure for Measure*, Liliuokalani demonstrates not only that she can write like any other cultured Westerner, but also that she is familiar with even the lesser known works of literary icons. This high culture reference thus inscribes her as one of the educated Western elite.

A prolific writer and musician, Liliuokalani composed numerous musical and literary works in both Hawaiian and English that mark her as civilized and cultured. She composed the music and wrote the lyrics for over 200 songs. Many of her works were composed while she was in prison in 1895 after the overthrow. She is best known for "Aloha Oe" or "Farewell to Thee," which was published in Chicago and became a very popular song in the United States and later around the world (Allen 1982: 188). During her lifetime her compositions were in demand in the United States; people wanted samples of Hawaiian music and literature (Liliuokalani [1898] 1991: 351). In 1897, the year of Queen Victoria's diamond jubilee, two special volumes of Liliuokalani's compositions were printed. One was deposited in the Library of Congress and the other, Liliuokalani states, was "my contribution to the souvenirs of this Jubilee year of Her Majesty, the great and good Queen Victoria" (Liliuokalani [1898] 1991: 352).

Even Liliuokalani's policies mimicked Victoria's. Unlike Victoria, however, Liliuokalani made decisions that became nails in her own political coffin. For example, as a justification for their revolution, the American annexationists charged Liliuokalani with proposing to issue licenses for the "importation and sale of opium" (Liliuokalani [1898] 1991: 240). To her accusers this was a crime, but to Liliuokalani it was a means of controlling an unlawful trade which had, up until this time, been impossible to suppress. She defends her decision by looking to Great Britain:

The British government has long since adopted license instead of prohibition, and the statute proposed among my final acts of my government was drawn from one in use in the British colonies; yet I have still to learn that there has been any proposition on the part of the pious people of London to dethrone Her Majesty Queen Victoria for issuing such licenses. (Liliuokalani [1898] 1991: 214)

Modeling her political actions after those of Queen Victoria, Liliuokalani does not understand why she is deemed a criminal for doing the same thing that her sister sovereign has done in Great Britain.

Where Liliuokalani's self-fashioning failed her was in her misjudgment of the American attitude toward kings. To her American audience, monarchy equaled tyranny. Her association with Victoria may not have been as prestigious to her audience as she believed. Writing in 1898, John Musick questions Liliuokalani's political leanings when he states, "it is claimed by many that she was under English influence. While visiting in London, she was entertained by Queen Victoria" (Musick 1898: 348). Indeed, Liliuokalani's emulation of Victoria appeared successful; but instead of earning respect, she brought suspicion upon herself. Furthermore, Musick, influenced by his meritocratic cultural background, cannot understand how Liliuokalani could accept a salary and income from crown lands that totaled more than the salary of the President of the United States (Musick 1898: 349). What Musick does not understand is that the crown lands belong to the Hawaiian monarchs. Coming from a culture whose mind-set does not favor royal inheritance, Musick, speaking for the annexationists in Hawaii at the time, begrudged Liliuokalani monies that were due her by right of her royal status. Moreover, the American annexationists sought to limit Liliuokalani's monarchist politics. In 1893, when Liliuokalani was planning to bring out a new constitution, one that would give her more power, the American minority rebelled. Musick's comment on this event reflects American hostility towards monarchy of any kind:

That constitution was to be a return to absolute monarchy, a constitution that would deprive every white man, unless married to a Hawaiian woman, of the elective franchise, and which made the property of the whites alone assessable for taxation – a far more tyrannical measure than that which caused our forefathers to throw off the British yoke. (Musick 1898: 351)

Here Musick links Liliuokalani to the monarchs of Britain, but in a negative way. To the Americans, Liliuokalani is more dangerous than her

British models and needs to be checked. Perhaps this hostility, not quite understood by Liliuokalani, was one of the reasons why her petitions to the United States to restore her to the throne were unsuccessful.

By the nineteenth century the American people had evolved into a culture that had no use for monarchy or absolute rule. Indeed, William Adam Russ, Jr., writing in 1959 about the 1893 overthrow argues that:

There can be no doubt that Royal Government under Kalakaua and Liliuokalani was inefficient, corrupt, and undependable. That the powerful American minority disliked it is understandable, and that these same whites would wish to bring the islands under the control of the United States is equally understandable. After all, violent revolution against tyranny was the American birthright established in 1776. (Russ 1959: 349)

Russ's work demonstrates the American view that monarchy of any kind was synonymous with tyranny. As late as 1959, the year that Hawaii became the fiftieth state of the Union, there were arguments in print justifying the 1893 overthrow as necessary and correct.

Other less partial historians and scholars appear to have examined the larger picture and taken into account many of the issues surrounding the overthrow. Noel J. Kent claims that Liliuokalani always had her people's interests in mind: "A woman of strong character, acutely sensitive to the long traditions of *Hawaii nei* and the threat to the kingdom's independence, she was determined to preserve Hawaiian sovereignty from outside encroachment" (Kent 1983: 62). Part of the problem with Liliuokalani's reign was that, by 1891 when she became queen, her country was already in disarray. Ralph S. Kuykendall and A. Grove Day maintain that "Liliuokalani came to the throne at a difficult moment in the history of Hawaii and her whole reign was one of trouble. It was a time of great economic distress" (Kuykendall and Day 1961: 174). Historians seem to agree that Liliuokalani was ill-prepared to handle these crises. Kent argues that "She did not take into account that these were times of crisis, times when a monarch could no longer hope to maneuver at the top, alternately confronting and allying with the elite, especially in the absence of a solid base of support of her own" (Kent 1983: 62). Furthermore, the tensions between the natives and the foreigners divided the people's loyalty to her. Some of the native Hawaiians felt she was more concerned about courting foreign support than helping her own people (Tate 1965: 119). The foreign elite, by contrast, believed she posed a danger to their power and had to be constrained. Her attempt in 1893 to restore royal power by proclaiming a new constitution failed because the American businessmen, the only unified group in the islands, were not on her side.

Ironically, perhaps, the most disappointing actor in this tragedy was Queen Victoria herself. On January 31, 1893 Queen Liliuokalani wrote a letter to Queen Victoria seeking

the "friendly intercession and mediation" of the British monarch with the United States for the restoration of the Hawaiian sovereign or, if that was impossible, for the succession of her niece, then in England, who would be of age in October. Upon its receipt, Queen Victoria opened the Queen of Hawaii's letter and returned it to the foreign office without comment. (Tate 1962: 342)

Certainly this was not the reply Liliuokalani expected from her sister sovereign. The excuse her ministers gave for Victoria's inaction was that she did not want to interfere unless there was a real danger to British life or property, which she did not believe existed (Tate 1965: 192).

Victoria's response – or lack of one – to Liliuokalani's plea betrays Great Britain's attitude towards Hawaii and the question of annexation to the United States. According to Tate, the situation by and large "did not occupy the British mind at all" (Tate 1962: 345). Indeed, the Marquis of Salisbury, in a conversation with Count Herbert Bismarck in March, 1887, remarked that Hawaii was "'of no interest whatever to England'" (Tate 1962: 335). Viewing the overthrow and eventual annexation of Hawaii as inevitable, Great Britain's policy during the time was to allow the United States to do whatever it pleased.[10] Britain was much more interested in fostering a friendly relationship with a world power than in saving a doomed island province. The country's reaction to the Hawaiian annexation sent out a clear message that Anglo-American relations were of most importance.[11]

In *Hawaii's Story by Hawaii's Queen* Liliuokalani recognizes the United States' imperialist design and questions it. She realizes that "there is little question but that the United States could become a successful rival of the European nations in the race for conquest," but then asks "is such an ambition laudable?" (Liliuokalani [1898] 1991: 372). Almost as a last resort, she directly pleads with her readers, "Oh, honest Americans, as Christians hear me for my down-trodden people!" (Liliuokalani [1898] 1991: 373). But her efforts come too late and fall upon deaf ears. The political aims of the United States did not include preserving the Hawaiian monarchy. After all, the Queen was a controversial figure, both vilified and lauded by the American press as "the 'savage' or the 'gracious lady'; the 'beheader' or 'savior of Hawaii blood'; the 'primitive' or 'the woman who spoke impeccable English'; the 'pagan' or the 'lady who attended church every Sunday'" (Allen 1982: 356). The American people and their leaders found it difficult to sympathize with someone whose public image was so debatable, and whose plight was out of alignment with their own self-interest.

In an effort to counter current constructions of herself and to establish her authority as a ruler, Liliuokalani fashions herself as a legitimate descendant of the noblest ruling chiefs of Hawaii, distancing herself from the legislative ways and election processes of the foreign political powers that threaten to crush her; at the same time, she portrays herself to the Western world as a cultured Western monarch and not a paganistic heathen chief. She fights against the casual classification of her people as merely another aboriginal American group, contained and dispossessed, insisting on her nation's right to cultural uniqueness and dignity. In arguing for assimilation, not annihilation, she recognizes the necessity of her nation remaining a separate and distinct part of a larger whole.

As a book about Liliuokalani herself, *Hawaii's Story by Hawaii's Queen* reveals what interested its author and shows her priorities and expectations. The work is not so much a political or historical tract as it is a memoir and swan song of a deposed queen. The amount of time Liliuokalani spends discussing politics is brief and the details are vague. Conversely, the attention and detail given to her numerous progresses, parties, balls, trips overseas, and her social obligations is vast and, at times, tedious. The numerous descriptions of gowns, menus, entertainments, and guest lists suggest that Liliuokalani may have enjoyed, remembered, and possibly preferred the celebrity of being a queen over the political responsibility of governing a nation. She was born a high chiefess and raised to be at the head of her kingdom. She enjoyed pomp and circumstance and was aware, quite keenly, of her rank and the respect owed her. She was a queen, so she believed, who could claim sisterhood with a queen as powerful as Victoria. Her mistake was in believing that the style of monarchy that thrived in Great Britain could be transferred successfully to Hawaii. Right or wrong, Liliuokalani saw Victoria as a useful model, an influence, and a point of comparison for Hawaii's queen, who only wanted the respect and deference she was raised to expect. She wanted to be what she believed she was – a Hawaiian queen and a civilized Western monarch. Amidst overwhelming imperialist forces that would consume her identity, Liliuokalani uses *Hawaii's Story by Hawaii's Queen* to construct and legitimize her authority as a Hawaiian queen and a civilized Western sovereign in an attempt to regain respect for her birth, her station, and her heritage.

NOTES

1 This epithet disdainfully referred to the children of the original Protestant missionaries who left the ministry and went into business for themselves in Hawaii. Politically and economically powerful, this party for many years had control of the cabinets appointed by the previous kings. It is this group of businessmen who were responsible for the overthrow of the monarchy and the annexation of Hawaii to the United States.

2 The new constitution was to give the sovereign more power, the legislature less. It would also have given the vote to Hawaiian subjects only, not to temporary residents.

3 Liliuokalani is named heir apparent by her brother King Kalakaua. While she is in England she is referred to as the "Crown Princess of Hawaii," the European title for a female heir apparent. Like so many other markers of royalty adopted from the British, this title is familiar to Liliuokalani. When discussing her experiences with European royalty, she understands well the hierarchical differences between a king, a duke, a crown prince, and an emperor (Liliuokalani [1898] 1991: 146).

4 Archer (1888: 228) writes that "Queen Kapiolani and Princess Liliuokalani of Hawaii, and their suite, resided at the Alexandra." This is the only time Hawaii is mentioned in this account of the jubilee.

5 Victoria's account of her meeting with Kapiolani and Liliuokalani is much less detailed than Liliuokalani's. She writes in her journal, on June 20, 1887, that she first meets with all of the European royalty. "Afterwards I received the Queen of Hawaii, and then saw, in quick succession, the Japanese Prince Komatzu and the Siamese Prince, and finally the Persian Prince, who speaks no English." The only other reference to the Hawaiian party that Victoria makes is about the gift she receives: "The Queen of Hawaii gave me a present of very rare feathers, but very strangely arranged as a wreath round my monogram, also in black feathers on a black ground, framed." Interestingly, the only other gifts Victoria mentions in this entry are those given to her by her children and by Leopold and Marie and Philip and Marie of Flanders. See Victoria 1930: 321, 325.

6 Kamehameha had many wives. Keopuolani was his "sacred wife," and the children of her body were designated heirs to the throne. The reason Keopuolani's rank was so high was because she was *niaupi'o*, the child of a union between a brother and sister who were high chiefs. The child of such a union was a god, entitled to the highest degrees of veneration. Keopuolani's rank was higher than Kamehameha's. Even the king of the Hawaiian Islands was required to prostrate himself in her presence. For additional information on rank in Hawaii, see Beckwith 1972: 11–14.

7  Immediately after his coronation, Kalakaua was accused by the press of not having sufficient royal lineage to be eligible for the throne. His reaction to the accusation was to discredit his opponent, Queen Emma, the widow of Kamehameha IV and a popular favorite with the Hawaiian people. The fact that Kalakaua's grandfather had been hanged for poisoning his wife was also made public. The story was also later used against Liliuokalani. For further reading on this subject, see Allen 1982: 170ff.

8  The election decreed by Kamehameha V may suggest that he wanted to pattern the future government of Hawaii after the US model. However, I do not believe that Kamehameha V, whose sympathies were pro-English and anti-American, had any intention of adopting US customs when he declared that the next ruler be elected by the people. Rather, his inaction signified that he was not about to bastardize the pure bloodline of the Kamehamehas by appointing a successor not directly descended from his powerful ancestor, Kamehameha the Great.

9  Kalakaua actually became king in 1874. He waited until the completion of Iolani Palace to formally crown himself.

10  Tate maintains that "Correspondingly, British periodicals, while questioning the moral validity and wisdom of annexation, interposed little or no opposition to the proposed union, saw no reason why Great Britain should object, and recognized the imperial significance of the United States' drift outward from the American continent. One reemphasized the necessity of cultivating an identity of interests with America" (Tate 1965: 339).

11  Another example of Great Britain's Eurocentrism was the Anglo-Japanese alliance. Tate states that "In 1897, as in 1921, when the Anglo-Japanese alliance came up for renewal, Great Britain had no intentions of joining Japan in any arrangement which would antagonize the United States." According to Tate, the sympathy of the British people is clear. He quotes Rear Admiral Nathan Crook Twining, Jr., naval attaché to the American embassy in London, who said to the Director of Naval Intelligence in November 1921, "In case of a white race against a yellow race the English would side with the white race." Indeed, "the most pressing need of Britain at both periods was for 'close and most friendly relations with the United States'" (Tate 1965: 346).

# PART III

# Victoria's career, early and late

# CHAPTER 9

# Reading and writing Victoria: the conduct book and the legal constitution of female sovereignty

### Gail Turley Houston

> Reading the narrative ministories told in conventional jurispru-
> dence and legal opinions *as literature* . . . no less than reading litera-
> ture as legal criticism, might enrich our sense of who we
> are and what might be our relationship to the law and legal system
> that we make and that makes us.
>
> (West 1993: 11)

> [If a woman's role is submission] even when the submission is
> forced, there are a thousand ways in which resistance can and will
> take place.
>
> ("The Performance of Obvious Duties" 1867: 3)

In this chapter I argue that nineteenth-century conduct books acted as
primers explicating and inculcating the Victorian's legal definition of
gender, which I take from William Blackstone's *Commentaries on the Laws
of England*. Generically different documents, the conduct book and
Blackstone's treatise describe gender in essentialist terms, naturalizing
the female as a "failure of issue male" (Blackstone 1899: 1, 196). The
success of these inherently unstable regulatory texts is a consequence of
their failure. In other words, the conduct book and the legal treatise,
implicitly acknowledging their participation in the construction of
gender, trope the self as naturally formed by universal laws but also as
always in need of being informed of and inculcated with those laws –
hence the need for "texts of reform." As Lynne Vallone explains, in the
"text of reform" the child – "a potential revolutionary" – becomes "a
well-mannered and content subject" through repeated exposure to
didactic fictional representations of the socially and legally reformed self
(Vallone 1995: 70). Thus conduct books and legal codes end up representing the need for the continual engendering of the subject, for, as
these texts imply, instead of being natural, gender is something that constantly must be learned, memorized, and regulated.

Since the English rejection of Salic law is a pivotal site of the
instability of gender ideology, an examination of the conduct books
Princess Victoria read *vis-à-vis* Blackstone's *Commentaries* seems an
appropriate way to study the heterogeneity that is at the core of seemingly monolithic Victorian constructions of gender. Training the
Victorian Young Person for her ostensibly natural subordinate role as
domestic queen, the conduct book "point[ed] out the line of conduct,
which ought to regulate the actions of human beings" (Trimmer 1794:
advertisement page). That conduct was always clearly demarcated for
boys and girls. Explicitly instructed to give up her own desires in order
to serve her male betters, the female reader quickly learned of her inferiority when compared with her male counterpart. Queen Victoria's
own mother assumed her daughter's feminine inferiority when she
stated categorically that the Princess's education was tailored to her
gender: "Had the object, been a Prince," said the Duchess, "the case
would have been different, – as then, the established plan adopted in
such cases, would have been pursued" (Victoria, Duchess of Kent
1830: 5).

Yet, as I will show, these didactic texts include unexpected resistances to the patriarchal order, for both the conduct book and English
law also acknowledged that women were capable of ruling in the
public sphere. Indeed, the sexual "difference" the Duchess of Kent
found so crucial to her daughter's course of education had multiple
trajectories. For one thing, as Kate Flint notes, in the Victorian period
reading "was an activity through which a woman could become aware
of the simultaneity of the sensations of difference and of similarity"
(Flint 1993: 327). Just as texts have multiplicitous, contingent, and conflicted intentions whose meanings may change over time, so too is the
reader a dynamic subject-in-process whose "practice of reading"
results from "psychological and . . . sociocultural" forces (Flint 1993:
330). The self's interaction with a text, then, depends upon various
situational factors. These include but are not limited to the individual
reader's unique personal makeup, as well as her experience of race,
class, and gender categories, as they are understood and expressed by
the larger culture, which is itself dynamic and multitudinous. Though
it is impossible to elaborate fully the cause–effect relationship between
reading and behavior, an understanding of the "extreme heterogeneity of readers and their texts" (Flint 1993: 187) helps to account for the
seeming monolithic nature of dominant ideologies as well as the sometimes dramatic, usually incremental, changes that occur in a culture's

ideological systems as a result of reading, writing, and actions based upon those sedentary operations.

A dynamic subject who tracked her own reading habits, Victoria was also an author. Giles St. Aubyn points out that, between her personal and official correspondence, Victoria wrote on average 2,500 words daily, which comes to an astonishing total of sixty million words by the end of her reign. She was a best-selling author, who discretely excerpted idyllic domestic scenes from her journals to circulate amongst her adoring subjects. *Leaves from the Journal of Our Life in the Highlands,* for example, outsold other books that came out in 1868, including *The Moonstone, Ring and the Book,* and *Little Women.* The Queen enjoyed her success as an author, gleefully writing to her daughter Vicky that "Eighteen thousand copies were sold in a week" (St. Aubyn 1975: 127, 128–29).

Though it would be erroneous to designate Queen Victoria – or any female – as the Victorian Everywoman, focusing on her adolescent reading and her adult writing textualizes the complex dynamics of Victoria(n) subjectivity. As a female monarch, reader, and writer in a patriarchal society, Victoria must have simultaneously experienced her own sexual difference and similarity as well as authority and subordination. An author and authority figure whose "principal duty" as monarch was "to govern h[er] people according to law," (Blackstone 1899: 1, 205), she was also the failure of male issue that proved the rule of patriarchy. Tracking Victoria as reader and writer, I focus on how her concurrent experience of similarity and difference *vis-à-vis* the dominant gender ideologies found in the conduct books she read as a child appear in her adult writings about her marriage *vis-à-vis* her sovereignty. I see her conflicted statements about her right to rule as, in part, reformulations of the conduct books she read and the Victorian law they were based upon. Before looking at how Victoria processed her reading of these conflicted disciplinary texts through her writing, it is helpful to elaborate on the ways gender fails as a category and a categorical imperative in Blackstone's *Commentaries.* Asserting her own authoritative identity, Victoria provided in her journal a list of "Books Queen Victoria read from her sixth to thirteenth year," and her mother also documented the books her daughter read "in the lessons of 1826, 1827, 1828 and 1829."[1] In one form or another, these "texts of reform" constitute the social, legal, economic, and religious laws Victoria would embody as British sovereign and would undermine as a woman.

I

Erecting English law as universal and self-consistent because it is based upon divine, eternal law, Blackstone's *Commentaries* assert that the law is "a rule of action dictated by some superior being." That superior male being ostensibly gives universal law to man in an unmediated form. As Blackstone explains, the Creator established "certain immutable laws of human nature" that would "regulate and restrain" man's free will, and thus man "must necessarily be subject to the laws of his Creator" (Blackstone 1899: 1, 34, 35). But though natural laws were immutable they were not inscrutable, for men could discover their purpose through reason. According to Blackstone's purportedly objective narrative, the British male as the mirror image of God consequently had the most perfect understanding of God's designs and implemented them in the most consummate of man-made legal systems.

One of the problems with this legal narrative is that "man" is assumed to be both a generic- and gender-specific term, and thus, for all appearances, objectively disinterested, but in practice serving the interests of men. This bifurcated foundation allows for the law's blindness to and imposition of its own gender biases. Figuring the laws of England as "the birthright of the people," the *Commentaries* view the male sovereign as their incarnation (Blackstone 1899: 1, 205). Thomas More's statement equating the body politic and law with the male body typifies this reasoning: "A kingdom in all its parts is like a man . . . The king is the head; the people form the other parts. Every citizen the king has he considers a part of his own body" (quoted in Hale 1971: 49). Equating monarchy with the masculine position, this image of the social body designates man as the universal subject and the king as the embodiment of law. But in an incongruous lapse allowing for the distribution of special privileges, Blackstone explains that though "the principal duty of the king is, to govern his people according to law," the king "is not under the coercive power of the law"; the king legally cannot be held accountable for the conduct of public affairs – the "king can do no wrong" – and "no court can have jurisdiction over him" (Blackstone 1899: II, 1237; I, 205, 214, 212). Imaging the king as both above and below the law, the *Commentaries* incarnate a divinely based law that excludes its chief representative – and by association, his male subjects – from adherence.

The notion of the universality of man also undermines the *Commentaries'* implicit acknowledgment that the law is historically located and that gender is an arbitrary category. Blackstone intimates the root-lessness of selfhood when dividing "persons" into the natural and the artificial: "Natural persons are such as the God of nature formed us; artificial are such as are created and devised by human laws for the purposes of society and government, which are called corporations or bodies politic" (Blackstone 1899: I, 113). Though Blackstone refers to the artificial construction of groups as nations, the definition of artificial persons also suggests that the self is a fabrication. Thus the Constitution, which asserts its divine, unchanging foundation, also admits that the gendered self, rather than existing as a member of a fixed generic category, is, in fact, created by the institutions that impose those categories.

As a result of these inconsistencies, when the *Commentaries* define gender, Blackstone's compendium deconstructs its prescriptive pronouncements. For example, Blackstone proclaims that there are "three great" eternal, hierarchical, generic "relations in private life": "(1.) That of *master and servant*; . . . (2.) That of *husband and wife* . . . (3.) That of *parent and child.*" The legal authorization of the husband's mastery over the wife also ensures his legal identity (success) and her legal annihilation (failure) through coverture. As the *Commentaries* declare, "By marriage, the husband and wife are one person in law" with "the very being or legal existence of the woman . . . suspended during the marriage" (Blackstone 1899: I, 358, 387). In this binary narrative, the child is to the wife and servant what the parent is to the husband and master. But these analogs quickly break down because the traits associated with a particular category, and which make possible the power relations between categories, are unstable markers: the disempowered male child can look forward to an empowered status when he becomes a husband and father; meanwhile the female parent is simultaneously figured as a child and servant.

Blackstone's narrative becomes especially muddled when it defines female sovereignty. Indeed, Victoria's accession was a "glaring anomaly" pointing up the inconsistent nature of English law (Killham 1958: 104), for, if woman was generically categorized a slave and child, the rules of logic would suggest that she could not, as queen, temporarily dissolve the boundaries imposed by those categories without also destabilizing them. Queen Victoria's reign creates a breach in other narratives besides the *Commentaries*. In *The Queen: a Memorial of the Coronation*, the anonymous pamphleteer pledges obeisance to Victoria while pinpointing her as the exception to English law. To authorize Victoria's reign, the writer cites Blackstone's statement that "the supreme executive power is vested by

our laws in a single person, the *King* or *Queen*; for it matters not to which
sex the crown descends." The pamphleteer qualifies the lack of meaning
accorded to sexual difference when adding from Blackstone that "not till
the failure of the male issue is [sovereignty] allowed to be taken by the
female" (*The Queen* 1838: 7). Thus this memorial constructs a compliant
and resistant reader, for, despite its celebration of the Queen's accession,
it implies that when Victoria fulfills the law of royal succession she breaks
the unwritten English law that man is the generic prototype and primal
source of sovereignty.

II

The children's books Victoria read, including such titles as *Juvenile
Correspondence: or Letters, Designed as Examples of the Epistolary Style, for
Children of Both Sexes; Always Happy!!! or, Anecdotes of Felix and his Sister
Serena; Female Improvement; and Claudine: or, Humility the Basis of all Virtues*,
continually define the female reader in terms of her failure to be male.
The injunction that she sacrifice herself for the men in her life – a kind
of sibling coverture in which the brother succeeds as a result of his
sister's sacrifices – naturally follows. In this section I will examine Maria
Edgeworth's two children's books *Harry and Lucy* and *Frank* and the
anonymously written reform text *A Puzzle for a Curious Girl*, all of which
Princess Victoria read, as representative of those themes.

In the preface to *Harry and Lucy*, Edgeworth trains her youthful audience in the seemingly natural hierarchical relationship between men and
women. Extolling reason, analysis, and curiosity, Edgeworth claims that
children need access to some "*nonsense*" as "alloy" for "sense work"
(Edgeworth 1827: I, xii). She then equates the male protagonist, Harry,
with sense and reason and the female protagonist, Lucy, with nonsense.
At the same time that she naturalizes the sex roles, Edgeworth acknowledges the social construction of gender, for she focuses her narrative on
the onset of adolescence when Harry and Lucy must prove that they can
perform their gender roles. In the last book of the series on the intellectual adventures of the protagonists, Lucy learns that her place is in the
domestic sphere, where she will be separated – mind and body – from
Harry, who will go off to a public school, the "public" in the designation
indicating his future masculine role.

Lamenting that as she gets older she does not seem to have the same
relationship with Harry, Lucy receives instruction from her mother: "as
you grow older this must be; your different employments must separate
you during a great part of the day." Now adolescent, Lucy realizes that

she is not as fond of scientific investigations as she formerly was and that her brother now seems more capable of such pursuits than she. Lucy's mother explains this as a natural phenomenon, with the advice that "You have been learning other things, which it is more necessary for a girl to know." Increasingly more concerned with social relations than with scientific endeavors, Lucy admits that she only shows interest in her brother's scientific experiments because she wants to be a good companion to him. Reiterating the mastery of men legalized in the *Commentaries*, her mother then explains that "you must be content to go slowly, and you must submit to be inferior to your brother for some time. This may mortify you, my dear, but it cannot be avoided, you must bear it." Learning that it is her brother who must succeed at and receive the attention for scientific endeavors, Lucy fears being "abhorred" for being a "vain" scientific woman, abhorred because she would not accept coverture as the lawful norm (Edgeworth 1827: 1, 2, 3, 5–6, 9, 11).

*A Puzzle for a Curious Girl*, which Victoria also read in her youth, graphically displays the vanity of a girl's inquisitiveness. Viewing the adolescent protagonist's curiosity negatively not because it results in disastrous or even mildly mischievous results but rather because the inquisitor, Laura Belfast, is a girl, this text endeavors to correct feminine inquisitiveness regarding the laws of nature and the laws of men. Laura's father decides that she must learn a lesson and her mother carries it out. During a shopping trip Mrs. Belfast exits the carriage, leaving her daughter alone for a long period of time. When she finally returns she refuses to answer any of Laura's insistent questions about what she bought during her absence. Because of Mrs. Belfast's unresponsiveness, when a package is delivered to the house Laura takes advantage of her parents' absence to search the box; in the process of lifting the container, she breaks some of her mother's things.

Still her parents give no information about these mysteries, and Laura concludes that the secret her mother is hiding is that her family must move to the country because her father has had financial losses. Already well-trained in womanly self-sacrifice, Laura is determined to be a governess to help her family, but she leaks the secret to her neighbors, who then tell the community. In an act which implies that curiosity is always indiscreet in a little girl, Laura's mother accuses her of being "capable of meanness and treachery" and claims that in her desire for knowledge she has brought "a stain" upon the family name. Mrs. Belfast finally reveals the secret of the original shopping trip, having instructed Laura in her feminine failure: when she was away so long from the carriage she had merely purchased some ribbon. The moral is, perhaps, that once

Laura is cured of her curiosity she can achieve the appropriate educational objective for middle-class adolescent girls – learning how to use and become ornamental objects.

In stark contrast, in Edgeworth's *Frank* the narrator praises the male protagonist's inquisitiveness and his mother's patient responses to his incessant questions. The mother implicitly encourages the boy's explorations of his environment by always responding positively to his questions as though her whole purpose as a mother is to reward her son's incessant – frankly obnoxious – curiosity and his subsequent mastery of the world. Edgeworth's express purpose for writing *Frank* is to show parents that children naturally learn because they are inquisitive and that parents should respond positively to such childish inquiry. But then Edgeworth disrupts the text by asserting that this natural educational process leads to "manly" character:

if you would save your sons from destruction, moral and worldly, give them, before you send them to public school, just ideas of what is, or ought to be, meant by manly character . . . Teach your son the truth, that manly exercises are useful in themselves, as part of a manly character, but not the whole. Teach him that to be manly, strength of mind is still more essential than strength of body. (Edgeworth 1836: 157)

Thus, like the legal condition of coverture, the boy becomes the generic student as the girl is suddenly evacuated from the category of generic child. As a kind of gloss on the *Commentaries*, Edgeworth's text establishes man as both generic and gender-specific signifier, thus ostensibly representing while simultaneously erasing the female.

According to the *Commentaries*, the boy will eventually move out of the position of child into that of master and husband while the girl will remain essentially a child as a wife and servant. *Frank* explicitly narrates this future legal condition through the display of Frank's relationship with his cousin Mary. Because she is a few years younger, Mary is a perfect companion for her "manly" cousin, who plays amiably with her because he is obviously her superior in age, intellect, and physical strength. A pedagogue educated in the hierarchical relations between the sexes, Frank trains Mary to play by the culture's rules. Indeed, the children's play enacts their future sex roles, which will be based, respectively, on paid and unpaid economic labor. Frank explicitly establishes the gendered division of labor when, while they are building a playhouse together, he explains to Mary that it is not efficient for him to come down every time he needs straw to thatch the roof. He rebukes her, declaring that his job is to thatch the roof (design and construct the edifice), and her job is to bring the bundles of straw to him (provide menial, free labor). As becomes clear in this childish game, the economic efficiency of the division of labor is based upon the arbitrary but naturalized coverture of one sex by the other.

But the dominant gender ideology found in these conduct books based upon English law could not be monolithic because of the inconsistent definitions of gender and the resulting resistances to those inconsistencies. In particular, the possibility of female sovereignty dramatically disrupts the purportedly seamless account of the sexes found in Blackstone and the children's writers Victoria read. For instance, in *Fabulous Histories*, Mrs. Trimmer naturalizes gender roles by intertwining a story about the lives of a family of robins with that of a human family named the Bensons. This text, then, simulates the *Commentaries*' appeal to natural and divine law as the foundation for gender roles. Like Blackstone, assuming a privileged position as the authority who can transcend human fallibility and pronounce the immutable nature of law, the narrator of *Fabulous Histories* constructs the robins according to human notions of the natural and then uses the humanized, gendered robins as models for human behavior. For example, the male robin, presumably named "Robin" as a sign of its generic embodiment of the category of robin, is described as "a very strong robust bird." In contrast, the sister robin Flapsy is "distinguished for the elegance of her shape." Peksy, another sister, has "no outward charms to recommend her" but this is compensated for by the

sweetness of her disposition, which was amiable to the greatest degree. Her temper was constantly serene, she was ever attentive to the happiness of her parents, and would not have grieved them for the world, and her affection for her brothers and sister was so great, that she constantly preferred their interest to her own. (Trimmer 1794: 34)

Thus while master robin struts his successful masculinity, the bird-brained sister robins model the self-sacrificing essence of femininity, to be found, ostensibly, in all of nature's female entities.

However, when the narrator addresses the matter of sovereignty, the paradigm quickly breaks down. Telling her son that the bees' loyalty to their sovereign is a pattern that Englishmen should follow, Mrs. Benson exclaims, "I wish our good king could see all his subjects so closely united in his interest!" She concludes that "it is your duty to love your King, for he is to be considered as the father of his country." Mrs. Benson's son

Frederick rather gleefully responds, "But mamma, . . . it is the Queen that the Bees love, and we have a queen too." Caught by the inadequacy of the law's classification of male and female sovereignty (in nature there are always exceptions to biological grounds for gendered hierarchies), she explains, "I believe her majesty is as much honoured by her subjects as a queen bee in her hive, though she has not so full a command over them, for it is a king that governs England as your papa governs his family, and the queen is to be considered as the mother of the country" (Trimmer 1794: 147). Mrs. Benson's gloss on the English Constitution unravels because the sanctioning of masculine authority, both in the animal and human kingdoms, falls apart when a queen rules. A queen's very body – be it bee or human – upsets the purportedly unchanging masculine body politics manifest in English law.

This same anomaly occurs in another text Princess Victoria studied, the Reverend Edward Ward's *The Reciter*, which consisted of *"Pieces Moral, Religious, and Sacred, in Verse and Prose."* Containing an eclectic array of authors and excerpts, Ward's inclusion of a powerful representation of female sovereignty ruptures *The Reciter*'s generally moralistic construction of gender. One of the book's models for elocution is Queen Elizabeth's speech at Tilbury Camp in 1588, which requires a reader who is simultaneously resistant to and compliant with the dominant gender ideology, for Queen Elizabeth makes a fabulous success out of her failure to be male:

I am come amongst you at this time, not for my recreation or sport, but being resolved in the midst and heat of the battle to live or die amongst you all, and to lay down for my God, and for my kingdom, and for my people, my honour and my blood, even in the dust. I know I have but the body of a weak and feeble woman, but I have the heart of a king, and a king of England too; . . . I MYSELF will take up arms, I MYSELF will be your general, judge, and rewarder of every one of your virtues in the field. (quoted in Ward 1812: 338–39)

Elizabeth's anomalous behavior, like the story about the male sovereign as queen bee, ruptures the text's understanding of natural law. That Elizabeth's royal descendant might also blur the gender boundaries becomes tantalizingly possible when Victoria's journal provides the young queen's description of saluting her troops (with a self-portrait in a man's hat): "The whole went off beautifully; and I felt for the first time like a man, as if I could fight myself at the head of my Troops" (Royal Archives QVJ, September 28, 1837). This passage points up the inconsistency of legally troping woman as slave and child while simultaneously figuring her as parent and sometimes sovereign, whether or not

Queen Elizabeth or Queen Victoria viewed themselves as notable exceptions to gender rules. Thus both of the queens' exclamations implicate the inconsistency of patriarchal law, and, I believe, point out that any woman can, inexplicably, enter the site of power from a position of disempowerment.

Mrs. Thornhill in Elizabeth Helme's *Maternal Instruction: Family Conversations, Moral and Entertaining Subjects* intentionally teaches her children Amelia and George the legality of man's superiority over woman. Explaining her expectations, the widow says that "George . . . will assist me in my accounts, and all that concerns the receipts and expenditure of this estate; for as his father was his own steward, so with my advice shall he." Meanwhile, Amelia "must learn to superintend my domestic concerns, . . . to arrange with strict decorum all my household business" (Helme 1804: 2, 3). But if this distribution of power affirms hierarchical gender relations, Mrs. Thornhill concludes the educational catechism with the "History of Joan Flanders, Countess de Mountford," a true story that does not fit the gender ideology in which Widow Thornhill has so carefully trained her children.

As with the *Commentaries*, female sovereignty disrupts the conduct book's seeming consistency. Joan Flanders is a "remarkable lady" who "united in her own person all the great qualities of both sexes"; she comes to her husband's aid in a civil war over who should occupy the throne. Her husband, John de Mountford, who believes he has prior right to the throne, is imprisoned in Paris and Joan Flanders goes through "uncommon exertions" to free him: "Bold, daring, and intrepid, she fought like a warrior in the field; shrewd, sensible, and sagacious, she spoke like a politician in the council; and endowed with the most amiable manners, and winning address, she was able to move the minds of her subjects by the force of her eloquence, and mould them to her wishes" (Helme 1804: 221). "Instead of depressing her spirits," the knowledge of her husband's imprisonment "appeared only to call forth her courage and fortitude." Hence, "deprived of her natural protector, she shewed the people how able she was to support his interest and honour." Like Queen Elizabeth, the Countess rallies her husband's followers by exclaiming, "For myself, though a woman, I fear no danger . . . I am a wife and a mother, but in this cause I will forget the weakness of my sex, and live or die defending the rights of my country, my husband, and my child." "Put[ting] the spurs to her horse, and, without halting," she gallops to Brest and assembles an army of 500 horsemen, with which she heroically staves off the enemy's attacks until a contingent of allies arrives to end the siege (Helme 1804: 221, 222, 223).

At the conclusion of this narrative Mrs. Thornhill and her children express amazed admiration for the countess, yet they are clearly troubled because she cannot easily be contained within the category of "woman." The seemingly unnatural exchange of power (a woman fights to rescue her beloved husband imprisoned in a tower) cannot help but disturb, for what the children learn is that the so-called generic categories of gender are not eternal and natural but contingent and constructed. Thus, recommencing the process of engendering, Mrs. Thornhill condescendingly pities "Poor Joan of Flanders," while George concludes that "with all her talents and accomplishments, to be necessitated to rush into the rough and turbulent duties of the opposite sex was dreadful. The affection of a wife and mother overcame every other feeling, and enabled her to perform deeds, which in a calmer state she would perhaps have shuddered to hear related" (Helme 1804: 223–24). Amelia, who has been steeped in the ideology of separate spheres, smugly expatiates that she is glad "heaven" will never place her in such a situation. Her mother replies, "I think you are perfectly in the right . . . for I know not who would accept power upon such terms" (Helme 1804: 224). Clearly the troubling issue is that of female empowerment and sovereignty, which the mother attempts to erase neatly with her appeal to moral and legal "right." But the radiant power of the narrative of Joan of Flanders resists the mother's attempts to cover over the possibility of female sovereignty.

In 1838, years after George IV overpowered his estranged wife Caroline in her attempt to accede to the throne as his royal partner, *The Murdered Queen! Or, Caroline of Brunswick, a Diary of the Court of George IV* was published. The fascinated teenage Queen Victoria eagerly discussed this text with Lord Melbourne, who knew Caroline, George IV, and the author, Lady Bury.[2] A diary, a history, a gothic fiction, an essay on sexual politics, and a radical conduct book of sorts, *The Murdered Queen!* features both the terrifying effects of laws that purport to represent all people under the name of "Man" and the courageous resistance of one female writer. Interweaving fact and fiction, the author attacks the Prince Regent's scurrilous conduct towards his wife and prosecutes the king rhetorically if not legally – "the king can do no wrong" – for his part in causing Caroline's death. When George indicted Princess Caroline's sexuality, Lady Bury challenged the man-made law's inconsistency, the inconsistency starkly revealed in the *Commentaries*. Blackstone narrates

the treasonable offense of violating a queen thusly: "if a man do violate
the king's companion, or the king's eldest daughter unmarried, or the
wife of the king's eldest son and heir . . . by violation is understood carnal
knowledge, as well without force, as with it: and this is high treason in
both parties, if both be consenting." The male's need for assurances that
he is the father underlines the biases of patriarchal law: "The plain
intention of this law is to guard the blood royal from any suspicion of
bastardy, whereby the succession to the crown might be rendered
dubious" (Blackstone 1899: II, 1272). The inconsistency, of course, lies in
the fact that Blackstone says absolutely nothing about inspecting a king's
sexual encounters.

One of the most horrifying images in *The Murdered Queen!* occurs in
the representation of one of Caroline's "fearful" dreams. The dream
begins in a blissful, pregendered, lawless state of total gratification:
"How happy, said I to myself, is the childhood of woman, – who derives
pleasure from every thing; and deems that every thing has been created
to please her!" However, the dream becomes a signifier of the terrifying conclusion made possible by the legal condition of coverture.
When she becomes a woman – "A change came over my dream: – I
was grown taller and more stately" – the dream takes on terrifying elements, including the visitation of "a dark figure at the foot of my
couch." This male apparition, with its erect pointing finger, fills her
with "intense and thrilling horror! The head was that of a skeleton, –
from off the back of which fell a monkish cowl. The rest of the figure
was enveloped in a black drapery. I almost ceased to breathe as it stood
mute before me; but at length it made a step forward, and grinned
upon me with mockery, and pointed its bony finger to heaven." At this
point the looming messenger unfurls a scroll upon which the words
"CALUMNY!" and "DEATH!" are inscribed. Then Caroline wakes up
(Bury 1838: 13–15). The raising of Caroline's consciousness raises the
reader's consciousness to the shocking awareness that the would-be
queen's real life – and by induction, any woman's – is more horrific
than any gothic tale. Strongly rejecting the law's depiction of the
male's natural right to dominate women, the narrator of *The Murdered
Queen!* illustrates how the law constructs men as nightmarish monsters
who are authorized, under the guise of royal, masculine imprimatur,
to overpower the female subject. Lady Bury fiercely takes issue with the
notion that the only sovereign self is a male self as she graphically
depicts the ravishment/coverture that occurs under the rubric of the
English man's law.

Reading Victoria's reading logically leads to interpreting Victoria's writing. Though we cannot make direct links between what she read and what she wrote, a number of statements by Victoria about female sovereignty and conduct illustrate the kinds of conflicts she had to resolve on becoming queen, conflicts incorporated in Blackstone's *Commentaries* and the children's books she read. Victoria's mixed emotions about the duty of women to marry and her obvious enjoyment of the role of sovereign appear in her early journals. In 1839 she discussed her aversion to marriage with her prime minister Lord Melbourne, saying, "Why need I marry at all for 3 or 4 years? did he see the necessity? . . . I said I dreaded the thought of marrying" (quoted in Longford 1964a: 106). When Victoria changed her mind and decided to marry Albert immediately rather than wait a few years, Lord Melbourne supported her decision with the comment, "a woman cannot stand alone for long, in whatever situation she is" (quoted in Longford 1964a: 133). Once married, Victoria claimed that she regretted not having married sooner (Grey 1867a: 144).

In the midst of wedded bliss, "Dear Albert's awkward and painful position" – parliament did not give him a title – was cause for royal resentment. The Queen recorded in her journal the following conversation with Melbourne:

talked of . . . its being so strange that *no* provisions had been made for the position of the Queen's Consort, which I wished could be defined, for futurity. The Queen Consort was provided with such rights, and it seemed to me very wrong that the reigning Queen's Husband, should not have the same . . . The position of a Prince Consort, must be painful and humiliating to any man that at times I almost felt it would have been fairer to him for me not to have married him. (Royal Archives QVJ, June 9, 1842)

Likewise, puzzled by the discrepancies in English law regarding gender, Victoria wrote in a memorandum to the prime minister that "It is a strange omission in our Constitution that while the wife of a King has the highest rank and dignity in the realm after her husband assigned to her by law, the husband of a Queen regnant is entirely ignored by the law" (quoted in Hibbert 1984: 152). She detects the "strange anomaly" of this legal omission in a patriarchal culture that views "a Titular King [a]s a complete novelty": "This is the more extraordinary, as a husband has in this country such particular rights and such great power over his wife, and as the Queen is married just as any other woman is, and swears to obey her lord and master, as such, while by law he has no rank or defined position" (quoted in Hibbert 1984: 152).

Such statements indicate that Victoria had learned her conduct lessons well. But in *The Early Years of His Royal Highness the Prince Consort*, a written memorial compiled under the direction of the Queen, the conflicts inherent in the law become issues that Victoria can never quite resolve. If, in Victoria's case, coverture meant that the queen's identity eclipsed that of her spouse, *The Early Years*, as much an apologia for and assertion of Victoria's sovereignty as it is a memorial to Albert, had to wrestle with Queen Victoria's obligation to prove her femininity while yet ruling a male subject. Thus this text features the Queen memorizing and memorializing gender roles that, immediately forgotten, must be relearned again. For example, *The Early Years* praises the Prince Consort's self-sacrificing role as overshadowed partner, symbolized in his response to the Duke of Wellington's offer of a command post in the army: Albert claims that his only desire is "to sink his own individual existence in that of his wife – to aim at no power by himself or for himself – to shun all ostentation – to assume no separate responsibility before the public." Nevertheless, the Prince worries about this obvious coverture of his masculinity when he writes that he is "very happy and contented; but the difficulty in filling my place with the proper dignity is that I am only the husband, not the master in the house" (quoted in Grey 1867a: 256). Victoria expresses equally ambivalent concerns about her gender role. She notes with pleasure in her journal entry of February 3, 1852 that Albert is a natural politician and businessman and that she has grown to "dislike" the duties of sovereignty, for "we women are not made for governing – and if we are good women, we must dislike these masculine occupations." However, immediately thereafter she exclaims, "but there are times which force one to take interest in them *mal gré bon gré*, and I do, of course, intensely" (quoted in Hibbert 1984: 89).

Representing herself as dependent on her consort, on March 1, 1858 Victoria writes in her journal of her "anomalous position" as the "Queen Regnant," for though Albert "God knows, does everything – it is a reversal of the right order of things which distresses me much and which no one, but . . . such an angel as he is – could bear and carry through" (quoted in Hibbert 1984: 103). In another elaborate display of feminine submission, she praises her husband, who

continually and anxiously . . . watch[es] every part of the public business, in order to be able to advise and assist her at any moment in any of the multifarious and difficult questions brought before her – sometimes political, or social, or personal – as the natural head of her family, superintendent of her household, manager of her private affairs; her sole confidential adviser in politics, and only assistant in her communications with the officers of the government. (quoted in Grey 1867a: 255)

Here, again, conflict seems to be the natural state. The Queen's tortuous logic concurrently glorifies the Prince Consort's earnest refusal to usurp her authority while asserting that masculinity is the "natural," original source of sovereign power. The passage incorporates the anomaly that if Albert is the "natural head" of the royal family, then his self-sacrificial masculinity is unnatural or at least suspect. Indeed, submission to the Queen's public identity conflicts with the legally mandated positioning of the feminine as subservient and the masculine as dominant. Furthermore, affirming English law by memorializing Albert's natural masculine superiority, Victoria, the sign of the failure of male issue, simultaneously deposes the law in the implicit assertion that as sovereign she has (un)natural superiority over any Englishman.

That in *The Early Years* Victoria goes to great lengths to rationalize her sovereignty suggests the power of the dominant ideology but also her own powers to resist. In the following wily statement, the persona of Victoria meticulously performs her feminine "sacred obligation" to "'obey' as well as to 'love and honor'" as she resists those who would counsel her "that, as sovereign, she must be the head of the house and the family, as well as of the state, and that her husband was, after all, but one of her subjects":

Fortunately, however, for the country, and still more fortunately for the happiness of the royal couple themselves, things did not long remain in this condition. Thanks to the firmness, but, at the same time, gentleness with which the Prince insisted on filling his proper position as head of the family . . . but thanks, more than all, to the mutual love and perfect confidence which bound the Queen and Prince to each other, it was impossible to keep up any separation or difference of interests or duties between them. (quoted in Grey 1867a: 256)

As this passage indicates subliminally, if the couple was viewed as the prototype of the dominant Victorian gender ideology, their behavior was not normative according to that same ideology. Indeed, the "condition" to which the text obliquely refers is the exceptional one of a woman ruling because of the failure of male issue. Albert ostensibly resolved this "condition" when he insisted, gently or otherwise, on training Victoria to submit to his natural authority. As this passage suggests, in the beginning of the marriage Victoria consciously insisted on ruling without Albert's advice on governmental matters. Thus *The Early Years* implies that the royal couple's married life was a troubled site of gender-bending until it was made to fit the law's model of the natural hierarchical relationship between the sexes.

But the text's protestations that the royal marriage became a conventional one highlights the inconsistencies in the law and the Queen's excessive and often brilliant attempts to accommodate it, at least in her rhetoric. It should not be overlooked that Queen Victoria's declarations of submission to her husband accompany her authorization of the written and monumental memorials to him. These memorials replicate her queenly authority and signify that Albert has been covered in marriage, for while Queen Victoria's memorials to Prince Albert portray him as her idol, such public eulogizing simultaneously displays her monarchical omnipotence. As Margaret Oliphant notes, Victoria's memorials had the unintentional effect of "mak[ing] herself known" rather than her husband (Oliphant 1900: 62). Prince Albert, that is, would not have been the subject of memorialization and thus the autonomous, eternal self he became in textual and sculptural monuments if he were not subject to the Queen's power and pleasure.

I will conclude by looking at the conflicts apparent in two of Victoria's statements about women's rights, the first found in a letter to Gladstone in which the Queen asserts that "God intended" that woman be man's helpmeet:

The Queen is a woman herself – & knows what an anomaly her *own* position is: – but that can be reconciled with reason & propriety tho' it is a terribly difficult & trying one. But to tear away all the barriers wh surround a woman, & to propose that they shld study with *men* – things wh cld not be named before them – certainly not *in a mixed audience* – wld be to introduce a total disregard of what must be considered as belonging to the rules & principles of morality.

The Queen feels so strongly upon this dangerous & unchristian & unnatural cry and movement of "woman's rights," . . . that she is most anxious that Mr. Gladstone & others shld take some steps to check this alarming danger & to make whatever use they can of her name. (quoted in Helsinger *et al.* 1983: 1, 68–69)

Victoria asserts dogmatic loyalty to the doctrine of separate spheres and avows that she has reconciled herself to her anomalous position; in so doing she leaves the "terrible" and "trying" details of that process of reconciliation a mystery, thus mystifying and concealing her power. Likewise, designating her own position as unique, she authorizes herself as identifier if not identity of cultural norms – she is above the law she embodies. Hence, while she asserts that the naturalized category of "woman" is "totally different" from and subordinate to the category of "man," she speaks as powerful sovereign, vigorously and condescendingly teaching the male prime minister his role in the whole debate. By urging her male subordinate Gladstone to use her name – which was the sign of law – to denounce women's rights and urge woman to abide by the Victorian "rules of morality," Victoria at once contests the morality of law and her own sovereignty. A memorial to the doctrine of separate spheres, this statement shows that the Queen is constantly engendering herself, repeatedly memorizing her feminine role because she is engendered to resist it.

Finally, in another deeply conflicted statement, Victoria claims that "I am every day more convinced that *we women, if* we *are* to be *good* women, *feminine* and *amiable* and *domestic*, are *not fitted to reign*; at least it is *contre gré* that they drive themselves to the *work* which it entails." She concludes her observations, though, with the assertion that "this cannot now be helped, and it is the duty of every one to fulfil all that they are called upon to do, in whatever situation they may be!" (quoted in Helsinger *et al.* 1983: 66). Here, Victoria's acceptance of the generic association of masculinity with sovereignty links her to the prevailing norms for women at the same time that it provides a space to defy those standards. For one thing, the Queen refuses to give up the power so "unnatural" for women and implies that her subjects must accept this destabilization of the norms. Thus "duty" works ambiguously to suggest the constraints of institutions at the same time it indicates the means by which to resist the culture's confining boundaries. By arguing that she is the exception to prove the law's consistency, Victoria destabilizes the disciplinary powers of the law and opens a loophole within which Victorians could rationalize their own "duty" to gender norms and consider the possibility of adapting or totally changing those norms.

## APPENDIX
## VICTORIA'S EDUCATION SCHEDULE

Books read by Princess Victoria in the lessons of 1826

### RELIGION

1. *Scriptural Stories,* – by the author of *The Decoy*
2. *A Stranger's Offering, or Easy Lessons of the Lord's Prayer*
3. *Mrs. Trimmer's Description of a Set of Prints of Scripture History, Contained in Easy Lessons*

4. *Scriptural Lessons, Designed to Accompany a Series of Prints from the Old Testament*

### MORAL STORIES

1. *An Easy Introduction to the Knowledge of Nature* – by Mrs. Trimmer
2. *A sequel to No. 1* – by Mrs. Sarah Trimmer
3. *Aunt Mary's Tales*
4. *Maternal Instruction* – by Elizabeth Helme

### HISTORY

1. *True Stories of Modern History* – by a Mother
2. *A Description of a Set of Prints of the English History* – by Mrs. Trimmer

### GEOGRAPHY

1. *Easy Dialogues for Young Children* – by a Lady
2. *Pinnock's Catechism of British Geography*

### GRAMMAR

1. *The Decoy*
2. *The Child's Grammar* – by Mrs. Lovechild

### NATURAL HISTORY

1. *The Rational Dame*
2. *Tales of Birds* – by Mrs. Mathews
3. *A Description of Quadrupeds, Birds, Fishes, Serpents and Insects* – by A. D. M. Luin
4. *Elements of Natural History, in the Animal Kingdom* – by William Mavors

### POETRY

1. *The Infant Minstrel*
2. *Poetry without Fiction* – by a Mother
3. *The Keepsake*
4. *The Literary Box*

### GENERAL KNOWLEDGE

1. *Scenes of British Wealth* – by the Rev'd. I. Taylor

2. *A Picture of the Manners, Customs, Sports and Pastimes of the Inhabitants of England* – by Jehosaphat Aspin
3. *The Natural and Artificial Wonders of the United Kingdom* – by the Revd I. Goldsmith

Books read in the lessons of the year 1827

### RELIGION

1. *Scriptural Lessons, Designed to Accompany a Series of Prints from the Old Testament* – by Mrs. Trimmer – continued
2. *Stories from Scripture* – on an improved plan

### HISTORY

1. *A Concise History of England* – by Mrs. Trimmer
2. *Roman History* – by Mrs. Trimmer

### GEOGRAPHY

1. *Pinnock's Catechism of Geography* – continued
2. *An Introduction to Astronomy, Geography; and the Use of the Globes* – by John Sharman

### NATURAL HISTORY

1. *Elements of Natural History* – by W. Mavor – continued

### GENERAL KNOWLEDGE

1. *A Picture of the Manners, Customs, Sports and Pastimes of the Inhabitants of England* – by Jehosaphat Aspin – continued
2. *Relics of Antiquity*
3. *Picture Gallery Explored*
4. *The Book of Trades*
5. *Polar Scenes* – by Campe
6. *Parry's Three Voyages*

### POETRY

1. *Fables* – by the late Mr. Gay
2. *The Reciter* – by the Revd E. Ward

BOOKS USED FOR DICTATING IN THE GEOGRAPHICAL LESSON

1. *Juvenile Correspondence* – by Lucy Aikin

Books used in the lessons of 1828

### RELIGION

1. *Stories from Scripture* – on an improved plan – continued
2. *The Catechism of the Church of England* – to learn by heart
3. *An Abridgement of the Two Testaments* – by Mrs. Trimmer

### HISTORY

1. *A Concise History of England* – by Mrs. Trimmer – continued

### GEOGRAPHY

1. *An Introduction to Astronomy, Geography; and the use of the Globes* – by John Sharman – continued

### NATURAL HISTORY

1. *Animal Biography* – by the Revd W. Bingley

### GENERAL KNOWLEDGE

1. *The Book of Trades* – continued
2. *Parry's Three Voyages* – continued

### POETRY

1. *The Reciter* – by the Revd E. Ward – continued

### BOOKS USED FOR DICTATING IN THE GEOGRAPHICAL LESSON

1. *Juvenile Correspondence* – by Lucy Aikin – continued

### LATIN BOOKS

1. *The Introduction to the Latin Tongue* – as printed for the use of Eton school
2. *A Radical Vocabulary* – Latin and English – by John Mair

Books read in the lessons of the year 1829

### RELIGION

1. *An Abridgement of the Two Testaments* – by Mrs. Trimmer – continued

### HISTORY

1. *Markham's History of France* – continued

### GEOGRAPHY

1. *Elements of Geography, for the Use of Young Children* – by the author of *Stories of the History of England*

### NATURAL HISTORY

1. *Animal Biography* – by the Revd W. Bingley – continued

### GENERAL KNOWLEDGE

1. *The Book of Trades* – continued

### POETRY

1. *The Poems of Goldsmith*
2. Cowper's *Poems*

### LATIN BOOKS

1. *The Introduction to the Latin Tongue* – as printed for the use of Eton school
2. *A Radical Vocabulary* – Latin and English – by John Mair
3. *A Collection of English Exercises translated from the Writings of Cicero* – by W. Ellis, MA
4. *Delectus sententiarum of historiarum*

Some books listed in "Books Queen Victoria Read from Her Sixth to Thirteenth Year":

*The Cries of London*
*Summer Rambles*
*Rich and Poor*
*Early Lessons*
*Frank*

*Claudine*
*Nursery Morals*
*Harry and William*
*Variety*
*Nursery Morals*
*A Puzzle for a Curious Girl*
*Right and Wrong*
*Illustrations of Political Economy*
*Patriarchal Times*
*The Wandering Jew*
*Southey's Life of Nelson*
*The Rival Crusoe*
*The Life and Adventures of Robinson Crusoe*
*Evenings at Home*
*Harry and Lucy*
*Fabulous Histories*
*The Looking Glass for the Mind*
*Memoirs of the Happy Family*
*Always Happy*
*Sense and Sentiment*

## NOTES

1 Windsor Castle, Royal Archives Z114a; Brigham Young University, Harold B. Lee Library, Special Collections, Victorian Collection.
2 In Royal Archives QVJ, January 11, 1838, Victoria notes, "Spoke of a new and strange book written by Lady Charlotte Bury."

# CHAPTER 10

# The wise child and her "offspring": some changing faces of Queen Victoria

## Susan P. Casteras

The tradition of female royal portraiture is long-standing and venerable in British history and culture. Queen regnants have often been celebrated in art, especially during the reign of the formidable and image-conscious Elizabeth I.[1] Elizabeth exerted considerable control over the ultimately mask-like portraiture of her which proliferated at court and abroad, thereby acknowledging the political power and importance of the royal portrait for its impact beyond artistic value. Like her later counterpart Victoria Regina, Elizabeth I also had a somewhat isolated childhood and had to prove herself as a woman in a decidedly male world. The iconology of Queen Victoria, of course, necessarily reflects another era's perceptions of the sovereign, and during her lifetime there were many significant developments in society, politics, and technology which virtually required the retooling and mass circulation of her image over time. Photography was one revolutionary invention, and with improvements in the mass reproduction of images, it made the Queen's face and person more accessible to her subjects. In fact, Victoria's tacit endorsement of photography by her numerous sittings suggested further identification of herself with this modern way of creating a "likeness." Yet ironically the new mode was far more democratic than portraiture: daguerreotypes and *cartes-de-visite* were affordable by persons of several classes, not just the rich. Even more than the fine arts, the popular and illustrated presses at times made the Queen and her family seemingly unending "victims," for the rising middle-class demanded such information, and visual marketing was aimed largely at satisfying this audience of readers/viewers who voraciously wanted to see and know more of their sovereign. It was arguably the expansion of the printed media that was one of the most crucial factors in disseminating Victoria's image so widely in her own country and abroad. The Queen thus gained a constant presence in the presses and a tangible likeness in the minds and eyes of subjects. The result was that countless homes, however humble, had images of her on their walls, testimony to the affection and loyalty she inspired, the power of popular imagery and mythology, and her tenacity in the public imagination.

The queen's image, in Elizabethan as well as Victorian times, was highly instrumental in reaffirming the primacy of the monarchy as an integral part of British national identity. Queen Victoria understood the power of portraiture and commissioned or sanctioned many state as well as private portraits of herself and family members.[2] By favoring some artists such as the foreign painter Francis Xavier Winterhalter over others, she also exerted some degree of control over her image. Moreover, as an amateur artist herself, in her youth especially Victoria produced images of herself and her personal life and seemed to comprehend in her diaries as well the importance of maintaining appearances both in real life and in art.

Obviously Victoria Regina was not just a woman – she was the monarch, a cultural artifact, and a symbol of political power, patriotism, and public consensus. Her image crystallized not only notions of the sovereign, but also ideas about femininity, nationhood, and the mass marketing of myth. If Elizabeth I was canonized in history as the Virgin Queen wed to her nation, then Queen Victoria paradoxically would serve simultaneously as both symbolic child and mother figure to her own subjects.[3] While the maternal associations that she aroused have been the subject of some analysis, the role of the child in the process of idealization has been neglected.[4] It was precisely the innocence of childhood that became an essential design in the fabric of mythology produced about the Queen, both in early portraits of her before her accession and in ones towards the close of her long reign.[5] An examination of some salient selected images from the realms of both fine and popular art (but excluding caricature or cartoon images) will serve to underscore some of the seminal messages that were generated by the girlish or adolescent queen.

Not surprisingly, early contemporary portraits of Victoria are identical in feeling and content with representations of almost any other wellbred female child. Invariably they show a sweet and chaste girl, often with the semi-mandatory accessory of flowers. This is attested to in numerous instances, for example in an engraving by William Ward (Yale Center for British Art archives) after an 1824 painting by William Fowler, in which the Princess calmly sits, flowers in hand, on a divan. Another unspoiled, but somewhat more lively image is found in Fanny Corbeau's portrayal of Victoria with her curls askew in a somewhat more playful

Plate 10.1 Stephen P. Denning, *Queen Victoria as a Child*, 1823. Oil on canvas.

air. In an 1823 painting of her (plate 10.1, Dulwich College Picture Gallery) by Stephen P. Denning, she is viewed much as any other middle- or upper-class young girl of the period might have been: as a miniature adult woman, surrounded by some floral attributes in a natural setting. Despite the burden of a massive and almost humorously towering hat, the precocious Victoria retains a sense of dignity and character. Her gaze is straightforward and clear, not averted or timid, and her expres-

sion is neither blank nor vapid. A sense of independent spirit or liveliness lurks beneath the layers of elegant attire that obscure her body
almost entirely. The more direct gaze and knowing expression in this
wise child and in many other images of the childish Victoria were often
missing, however, from depictions of her at a later age, when the subject
retreats into a more impassive expression.

Other strands of imagery were overtly aristocratic in staging and
mood, projecting an air of nobility to the youth as a literal lady-in-
waiting (of sorts). For example, in a print published by Colnaghi in 1830
(plate 10.2, Yale Center for British Art archives), some classic Van
Dyckian artistic devices and flair – baroque sweep of drapery, single
column, plumed hat, shafts of light – have been utilized. There is, moreover, emphasis on the figure's face and neck, areas of future bodily
womanliness and sensuality that were often highlighted in aristocratic
portraits of adult women and girls of the upper classes.

By contrast, Richard Westall's 1830 portrait (HM the Queen, Royal
Collection) of the young Victoria casts her more dramatically into the
role of young artist. Like other picturesque girls, she, too, is placed in a
natural setting, but the pose and mood here are bolder than might be
expected. This pictorial princess has allowed her hat to tumble to the
ground and does not stand or sit benignly; instead her arms and legs are
at angles and her hair is loose. She seems to pull back, mid-thought as
well as in the middle of a creative moment or act, in order to contem-
plate nature and presumably draw it in the sketchbook she holds in one
hand. Westall has chosen to reject a stiff or formal pose and instead
creates a sense of a lively, inquiring real child whose persona conveys a
sense of energy, if not high-spiritedness.

There were other works which emphasized these more independent,
less conventionally girlish qualities. For example, in an undated, anonymous wood engraving of Victoria at her lessons (plate 10.3, Yale Center
for British Art archives) she is shown kneeling on the floor studying a
globe. While there are still flowers at her feet, she is more than a pro-
verbial delicate flower of femininity. Instead, she is shown learning geography as well as symbolically mastering the globe or world –
foreshadowing her role as monarch or empress. Her interest in the globe,
however, was one much more typically associated with young boys as the
curious pupils, thus creating a more iconoclastic view of the Princess in
a role that was perhaps more androgynous than gender-specific.

Childhood often seemed short-lived in real life, and the crisis of
female adolescence to some degree was heightened because of the

Plate 10.2 Richard Golding after original painting by William Fowler, *Her Highness the Princess Victoria*, 1830. Engraving.

blurred lines between the appeal of the womanly child and that of the girlish woman, both with shared ideal traits like purity, obedience, and devotion. The pubescent Victoria thus posed a visual challenge, poised as she was on the brink of both childhood and adulthood. An 1834 print of her drawn at Kensington Palace by J. R. Herbert (plate 10.4, Yale Center for British Art archives), captures one such transitional figure.

Plate 10.3 Unknown artist, *Princess Victoria (The Queen) at her Lessons, c.* 1830–32, Wood engraving.

The candor and liveliness of her childhood seem to have utterly vanished and been replaced by the external signs of womanliness. While there was little overt sexuality conveyed in most images of her girlhood, there was greater opportunity to explore her sexual appeal when she was an adolescent, and some of the resulting images make her seem rather like a royal pinup. In place of a child's intense gaze or energetic action is a frozen quality: the Princess looks like she has stepped from the pages

Plate 10.4 John Rogers Herbert, *Princess Victoria*, 1834. Engraving.

of a *Keepsake* book (one of myriad popular tomes filled with mostly light-weight verse and engravings intended for upper- and middle-class lady readers). Her hair is now fashionably and elaborately coiffed, she wears gloves, and her bare shoulders and neck are accentuated. Her body and personality have thus been sexualized to some degree, and although not nubile, she has been objectified into one of the many pretty ladies who dominated the pages of *Keepsake* volumes. For example, her budding breasts are visible, and the curves of her body suggest nascent womanhood. The seemingly omnipresent floral element connoting the delicate blossom of the "weaker" sex is included on a table, but there is also a large book from which Victoria has suspended her reading. With such images there is the sense that Victoria has left childhood behind and taken her prescribed place to continue preparations to assume the duties of her sex.

An even more majestic glimpse into full-blown adulthood is found in George Hayter's 1835 portrait of her (the original in the Royal Collection of Belgium was destroyed by fire, copy at Windsor Castle) at age sixteen. Here the princess is shown as quite womanly, with an intricate coiffure, stylish gown and accessories, and ear-bobs. Despite the lively presence of her beloved spaniel Dash, this princess is perfectly composed in an interior that is framed by baroque trappings and has a view of the castle beyond. Books and a globe, more masculine attributes, to one side at left are counterbalanced at right by a bouquet Victoria fingers and the begging antics of her dog, which she seems to ignore. The days of frolicking with a pet seem to have passed, with less sophisticated pastimes giving way to more adult pursuits and responsibilities.

Other images cast Victoria in a less overtly regal context, as a more identifiably middle-class female of the period. This "masquerade" of bourgeois normalcy is found, for example, in an image from the *Illustrated London News*, which enjoyed a wide readership among middle-class audiences and others. Artists of both sexes indulged in this fantasy of HRH as a middle-class peer, as in this example by a Miss Costell. In an engraving (plate 10.5, Yale Center for British Art archives) of Costell's image, the moment selected is significantly the morning of teenager Victoria's accession in 1837. She is accordingly shown without elegant robes, crown, scepter, jewelry, or other objects that would define her royal status. In visual terms, this tidy, bonneted paragon could be any lady going shopping, not necessarily a member of royalty, much less Victoria on a critical day in her life.

By contrast, there were occasionally more masculinized versions of Victoria, notably an engraving after a work by J. Prentice of *Her Majesty in Military Costume at a Review at Windsor, September 28, 1837* (plate 10.6, Yale Center for British Art archives). While representations of the equestrian queen in riding outfit, mounted side-saddle or reviewing the troops in her Windsor uniform were not uncommon, this close-up of her is rather startling. In lieu of curls, ornament, or ruffles, Prentice's vision of

Plate 10.5 Miss Costell, *The Queen on the Morning of her Accession, June 20, 1837*, 1837.
Wood engraving.

Victoria Regina is quite masculinized in garb and appearance. Her hair
is nearly hidden by the military cap she wears, thereby presenting or dis-
guising her as a surrogate male military officer. Certainly representations
of her ceremonially overseeing the troops would have reminded viewers
of their nation's military fame and glory, but images like this one perhaps
qualify more as "gender bender" iconoclasts to late twentieth-century
eyes.

Plate 10.6 J. Prentice, *Her Majesty in Military Costume at a Review at Windsor, September 28, 1837*, 1837. Engraving.

While images of Victoria as masculinized officer challenged the status quo, the majority of others reaffirmed it. A monarch's authority was supreme, but as a female on the throne, Victoria conveyed a latent element of threat because of the cultural assumptions in prevailing ideology that women were subservient and intellectually inferior. While too many depictions of her in an aggressive or masculinized mode would have sent the "wrong" message to viewers, portrayals of her as a fair flower of girlhood, dignified matron, respectable lady, or dedicated mother would have defused her power and mitigated some of the threat she presumably posed to some viewer/subjects.

One signal moment that was seized upon by various artists focused upon her transition from girl to queen, either in the coronation or in initial meetings with her advisors. In David Wilkie's *Queen Victoria Presiding at Her First Privy Council* (Royal Collection) of 1837, for example, the virginal girl/queen is the center of attention. She is shown wearing white (despite the fact that she was in mourning for her dead uncle) and is the sole female among a large assembly of men. In fact, her light-colored clothing and pose mark her as unique from the dark tones and stiff poses of the men in the group – visually she seems to outshine them. All eyes seem directed toward her as she presides at this event. She is dressed more like a mere girl than a queen in royal robes, yet it is precisely the qualities of innocence and vulnerability which are emphasized visually and ideologically. Wilkie has deliberately chosen to pair an intimate view of her in informal dress with a formal male occasion of power. Unmarried, she requires male guidance, yet she is the monarch, and although outnumbered, she nonetheless exerts a powerful presence among the politically savvy old guard in the privy council.

In a kindred way, Charles Robert Leslie's renowned 1839 painting entitled *Queen Victoria Receiving the Sacrament at Her Coronation* (Royal Collection) reconstructs for his audience a moment of holy truth in which Victoria's equally sacred youth is emphasized. Light streams in from the right as she kneels to receive the sacrament amid countless witnesses. But she is restrained, intense, and pensive, while the onlookers are contrastingly more worldly in appearance. Despite the crown and scepter, she seems relatively simply dressed, modest, dignified, and innocent, all qualities which would have endeared her to her subjects and potentially increased their loyalty to the Crown. Historically, Victoria's accession initially met with mixed feelings because of her youth. Yet it is this quality, above all, that invigorates both this painting and Wilkie's, for Victoria struck many people, as Princess Lieven remarked, as an almost enchanting embodiment of youthfulness and natural grace. "She has an ease, a bearing of superiority and dignity which, combined with her childish face, her small stature and her charming smile, is the most remarkable thing one could imagine" (quoted in Tingsten 1972: 98). In some respects Leslie and Wilkie both invoke Christian iconology, casting Victoria almost as a female equivalent to Jesus among the elders in the temple, as a figure whose inexperience yet wisdom seem to outshine the more dominant (visually as well as otherwise) powers of experience and political acumen.

In another permutation of this theme, George Hayter's celebrated *Coronation of Queen Victoria* of 1838 (Royal Collection), both male and female faces adoringly turn towards the Queen as she sits, enthroned and bearing the symbols of her power, and receives her crown. Divine presence and transmission of authority are suggested by the symbolic shafts of light that pierce the cathedral windows and seem to ordain or empower Victoria as a modern Mary as well as a new ruler. This may be a young queen, but she is shown as strong and ready to accept the duties of service along with whatever else awaits her in her anointed position. As Lytton Strachey remarked, "the spectacle of the little girl queen, innocent, modest, with fair hair and pink cheeks, filled the hearts of the beholders with raptures of affectionate loyalty" (Strachey 1921: 46). Deference to her diminutive size and youth in spite of the enormity of the event and its cavernous setting are implied, and once again the promise of youth itself seems to be a by-product of the visual message.

Hayter's single figure of *Queen Victoria Taking the Oath of Office* (plate 10.7, title of version at the Yale Center for British Art) is a familiar image of the eighteen-year-old dramatically lit from above as she places her hand on the Bible. A teenaged girl who remains "mortal" before she takes the oath and wears the crown nearby, she is depicted as alone yet unafraid – a strong, erect figure who will serve as the newly anointed head of the nation and the Protestant Church of England.

The strength, vigor, and optimism of youthfulness and the Queen's innate poise, competence, and confidence in her role also surfaced in Hayter's 1863 copy (National Portrait Gallery, London) of his 1838 painting of the monarch bathed in light as she sits enthroned on a dais. Although a rose intersects the lion's claws at the base of the throne (as if to soften the male power symbols), the Queen nevertheless possesses considerable dignity and composure and is visually as well as implicitly shown here – as in numerous other depictions of her enthronement – as able to bear the weight of her role and responsibilities.

Plate 10.7 George Hayter, sketch for *Queen Victoria Taking the Coronation Oath*, *c.* 1838. Oil on panel.

As the fiftieth year of her rule approached in 1887, public sentiment and interest in the ageing Victoria had rekindled, and this renewed interest sometimes returned to the imagery of her youth. In the spring of 1889, for example, a museum chronicling the Queen's life opened to the public at Kensington Palace. In addition, there were countless books about her reign, including a well-known volume written by Richard Holmes in 1887. Retrospective romanticizing about her past life became a national obsession, and a commemorative mood settled in, triggering a tidal wave of chauvinistic fervor that swept up the elderly queen and repositioned her as a central icon. There were extravagant ceremonies which fueled popular demand for more and more images of her, and this mood was absorbed into the continually expanding visual mythology of her persona.

This revival of interest in Victoria's private life partly centered on her early, formative years. Accordingly, one major focus of artists in these later years was an imaginative reconstruction of the historical day when the Queen ascended the throne in 1837. The concept is rather voyeuristic, making outsiders instantly "insider" witnesses to what was a quintessentially private and painful event. Nonetheless, what happened behind closed doors fifty years earlier became, perhaps improbably, a stirring subject for art. The morning that Victoria's uncle died, she was summoned to hear the news. As one lady described this poignant moment, the new monarch "in a few minutes . . . came into the room in a loose white night-gown and shawl, her night-cap thrown off, and her hair falling upon her shoulders, her feet in slippers, tears in her eyes, but perfectly collected and dignified" (Wynn 1864: 297).

Evidently Miss Wynn's description inspired the artist Henry Tamworth Wells to tackle this very moment, for he included a long excerpt from her writings when his painting entitled *Victoria Regina: Victoria Receiving the News of her Accession* (plate 10.8, Tate Gallery) was exhibited at the Royal Academy in 1880. The following text accompanied the work, which was subtitled and alternatively known as *"I Will Be Good"*:

On Tuesday at two and a half A.M. the scene closed (death of William IV at Windsor Castle), and in a very short time, the Archbishop of Canterbury and Lord Conyngham the Chamberlain, set out to announce the event to their young sovereign. They reached Kensington Palace about 5; they knocked, they rang, they thumped for a considerable time before they could rouse the procter at the gates; they were again kept waiting in the courtyard, then turned into one of the lower rooms, where they seemed forgotten by everybody. They rang the

*Susan P. Casteras*

Plate 10.8 Henry Tamworth Wells, *Victoria Regina: Victoria Receiving the News of her Accession*, 1880. Oil on canvas.

bell, desired that the attendant of the Princess Victoria might be sent to inform HRH that they requested an audience on business of importance. After another delay and another ringing to inquire the cause, the attendant was summoned, who stated that the Princess was in such a sweet sleep, she could not venture to disturb her. Then they said, "We are come to the *Queen* on business of State, and *even* her sleep must give way to that." It did, and to prove that, she did not keep them waiting, in a few minutes she came into the room in a loose white night-gown, and shawl, her night-cap thrown off, her hair falling upon her shoulders, her feet in slippers, tears in her eyes, but perfectly collected and dignified. (quoted in Graves 1906: VIII, 207–8)

Wells furthermore produced a second, larger and more detailed version of this canvas, which he also exhibited at the Royal Academy seven years later. The Queen ended up buying that version, in part because she wanted to exercise some control over its engraving and also because the artist had lowered the price for Her Majesty.[6]

In both versions, the personification of goodness and self-sacrifice embodied in the subtitle is the young and meritorious Victoria, who, unlike retainers in the text, does not keep the archbishop and chamberlain – or destiny – waiting. Particularly in the 1880 painting, with its three-figure composition and fewer background details, the fullness of Christian symbolism is clearly invoked. Rays of light pour in from the right through a window in the private chambers of the castle, and Victoria stands bathed in this quasi-holy source of illumination. Everything in the room is silent or stilled – the abandoned playthings (in the 1887 version, a ball, books, flowers), an unlit candle, and other still life objects on the table. A portrait of William IV hangs on a wall in the 1887 Royal Collection version, and in both paintings the Queen stands immobile, ignoring the men who have come to announce the news. One is Lord Conyngham, the lord chamberlain, who kneels and kisses her hand, and the other is the Archbishop of Canterbury, who looks at Victoria.[7] The Queen sees neither figure and instead is transfixed and introspective at this crucial juncture of innocence and power, youth and responsibility. She is truly a "wise child," one who must leave behind girlhood and the simpler pleasures of private life to become monarch of an entire nation. As a secular Madonna, her two messengers are not heavenly hosts, but she nonetheless generates an aura of virginity and otherworldliness in the midst of their worldliness. Her figure is erect and incandescent despite the tragic circumstances – she is, if you will, an angel herself as well as a vessel of purity or a modern Madonna, whose visitors approach with a mission of royal annunciation. As in Wilkie's and Leslie's earlier portrayals of the Queen, here, too, she is isolated from mere mortals and human behavior by her divine light, her glowing garments, and her virtuous, if not holy, demeanor. Moreover, her gesture communicated both healing and salvation. Yet because she is female and young (as well as beautiful), she elicits protective instincts along with awe. These men and others will defend and protect her as monarch and symbol of the monarchical system. In return, she will selflessly serve the nation and be the defender of the Protestant faith. Viewed as a heroine as well as a saint, it is nonetheless apparent that Victoria's *thalamus virginis* or secularized chamber of purity has been invaded, providing viewers with an imaginary and melodramatic notion of what was in reality a very personal as well as undoubtedly traumatic moment and experience.

It may seem odd that at the end of her life Victoria was not exactly infantilized, but certainly given a reversal of ageing in some paintings such as Wells's theatrical vignette and paean to her girlhood. Certainly fresh maidenhood was more marketable than withering longevity, but that is only part of the answer. Images such as this one invoke a chain of associations linked with the cult of girlhood – from her untarnished purity in childhood, to her modesty and virtue in adolescence, her Madonna-like qualities in motherhood, and her iconic stature in old age as a symbol or metaphor of an entire empire and era. Lost innocence is recaptured in works with retardataire themes such as Wells's, playing upon viewers' nostalgic desires to preserve the fiction of the past and revive memories of the youthful monarch despite the realities of her advanced age. The Victorian era "grew up" in essence with their monarch, and to be relentlessly reminded in art of her approaching death – or of the termination of that halcyon period of her reign – might be an inadvisable message to send to viewers.

As is apparent even in this brief iconological survey, the use of the monarch's image during her reign shifted and expanded to encompass the different stages of her life. From the outset, formal and informal portraits were created, but there were also genre and history painting elements blended into the portraiture. The Great Exhibition marked a flourishing of her image in unprecedented numbers, but so, too, did her Golden and Diamond Jubilees in 1887 and 1897. The visual culture of her image seemed renewed with the advent of those fiftieth and sixtieth anniversaries on the throne, and artists retroactively began to reinvent the past, sometimes creating genrified historical reconstructions like Wells's painting, with its strong infusions of jingoism, nostalgia, wishful thinking, and fantasy.

Even at the end, when old age limited her public visibility and she settled into nun-like widowhood and somberness, it was images of her that filled the gap by providing countless opportunities for her subjects to "know" her in mass circulation. Royal portraiture forged a certain mystique of the Queen, but to a certain extent, the middle class arguably made/remade her into their own image/s, to identify with, to inspire, and to reinforce national values. In the final accumulation of hundreds, if not thousands, of images made of Victoria during her lifetime, it was the metaphor of the child that remained one of the most compelling, conveying as it did the tensions between innocence and experience, private and public, political and personal, that defined not only the persona of the Queen but also the nation she served.

NOTES

1 On this subject see, for example, Strong 1978b, Gaunt 1980, and Ormond 1973.
2 A forthcoming dissertation on the subject of portraits of the Queen and their political significance is being written by Deirdre Shearman at Harvard University. In this essay, engraved portraits from the Yale Center for British Art archives are found in the Jennings Albums.
3 On the problems that Elizabeth I faced in creating and disseminating images of herself, see, for example, Pomeroy 1989: 35.
4 One insightful interpretation is found in Munich 1987.
5 On Victoria's early years see, for example, Plowden 1981.
6 For additional details on this painting and its creation, see Millar, 1992, text volume: 282–83.
7 See ibid.

# *"I never saw a man so frightened": The young queen and the parliamentary bedchamber*

## Karen Chase and Michael Levenson

I

> It is really a most painful thing to be thus speaking of ladies at all
> in a public debate, or to discuss a question in which they are mixed
> up. But their position and their fortunes have become a matter of
> state. Ladies of the bedchamber are now made public function-
> aries; they are henceforth converted into political engines; they are
> made the very pivot upon which the fate of a ministry turns.
>
> Lord Brougham (Brougham 1841: 418)

This note of mock sorrow and sincere outrage dates from the end of a
fiercely turbulent May in 1839, when the irrepressible and vengeful Lord
Brougham rose in the House of Lords to throw scorn upon his former
allies in the Whig government. Windily recounting the events that we
know as the Bedchamber crisis, Brougham recalled the embarrassing
sequence of misadventures in the early days of the month: the Whig
resignation after the loss of a sustainable majority; the young queen's
turn to the Tories, first to the Duke of Wellington and then to Robert
Peel; the painful clash over Peel's right to replace the members of her
royal household; the Whig defense of Victoria's royal prerogative; the
highly theatrical breakdown of the negotiations between the Queen and
Peel; and the abrupt return of the Whigs to the power they had abandoned just a few days before. In a mood of bitter satire, Brougham
observes that the government has come slinking back into office without
a program or a principle.

The friends of the Government have nothing to say for themselves or their
employers – no merits of their own to plead – no measures to promise for the
future – no defence to make for the past; – all the cry they utter is the name
of "Queen! Queen! Queen!" – all the topic they dwell on is the supposed feelings of their Royal Mistress, the court difference, the Bedchamber quarrel
about promotion; and, to sum up all, in one sentence . . . the event is
announced as matter of ministerial gratulation that Sir R. Peel has in the

attempt to form a government, been defeated by two ladies of the bedchamber! (Brougham 1841: 404)[1]

It was no part of Brougham's account to consider why the episode so violently disturbed the course of political life, why it created so much visible discomfort in elite social circles, or why it generated a sense of failure everywhere, of personal humiliation, of chaos in public opinion. Like so many contemporary observers, Brougham assumed a rigorously public standpoint from which the mere mention of ladies of the bedchamber could only seem a grotesque interference in the responsibility and the decorum of office. But his very tone of visceral disgust points back to the remarkable disruption caused by the young queen's firm refusal to allow any tampering with her ladies. The general nervousness stirred by Victoria's action, the private agitation, the public hysteria, all give a clue to the radically unsettling character of the episode. For Brougham, as for the angry Tories, the debacle was only one more sign of Whig dereliction, but if one escapes the party political wrangle, then it becomes evident that the general moral tipsiness was not only a product of Lord Melbourne's weak ministry, but the effect of a confusion whose roots ran deep into the affective life of an unstable culture.

Who can doubt that the Bedchamber crisis was a spectacle that had been waiting impatiently to erupt? The accession of a young queen, the first reigning queen in more than 100 years, came at a time when the rites of household privacy were achieving unprecedented prominence; the conditions were thus well prepared for a violent conflict between those private ceremonies epitomized by Victoria's sheltered upbringing and the demands of public political theater. The history of kingship has always been a record of tense dealings between the private and public bodies of the sovereign, but in the case of Victoria the tension inevitably sharpened. The problems of her sex and her age, or more exactly the problem of her sex compounded by the problem of her age, meant that Victoria was seen at once to symbolize and to embody a mythology of private experience – its vulnerability, its innocence – even as she was held, and held herself, to the exacting standards of impersonality.

This shuddering instability shows itself in one of Lord Melbourne's letters to the Queen in the early hours of the episode. Announcing that the weak majority on the Jamaica Bill will force the Whigs from power, and still anticipating in these first moments that the Tories will indeed form the next government, the prime minister writes to prepare the Queen for the convulsion.

Lord Melbourne is certain that your Majesty will not deem him too presuming if he expresses his fear that this decision will be both painful and embarrassing to your Majesty, but your Majesty will meet this crisis with that firmness which belongs to your character, and with that rectitude and sincerity which will carry your Majesty through all difficulties. (Victoria 1907: 194–95)

The note sounded here, the careful allusion to the Queen's emotional life and the determined plea for her resolve, suggests the strong mutual awareness that the political change may bring a personal revolution. Through the energetic correspondence that now unfolds hour by hour it becomes plain that the Queen and her first minister had enjoyed an intimacy so comfortable that affairs of state were absorbed into the pleasures of friendship. In a second letter of May 7, Melbourne warns that in her dealings with the Tories Victoria will do well to be "very vigilant" in approving "all measures and all appointments": "It is the more necessary to be watchful and active in this respect, as the extreme confidence which your Majesty has reposed in me may have led to some omission at times of these most necessary preliminaries" (Victoria 1907: 196). Those "omissions," tolerated in the spirit of intimacy, are precisely the omissions of that formal political disposition that the Queen must now abruptly assume, but for all Melbourne's ceremonial prose and his moral delicacy, he cannot forestall the emotional violence created by the prospect. The following morning brought him a turbulent note.

The Queen thinks Lord Melbourne may possibly wish to know how she is this morning; the Queen is somewhat calmer; she was in a wretched state till nine o'clock last night, when she tried to occupy herself and tried to think less gloomily of this dreadful change, and she succeeded in calming herself till she went to bed at twelve, and she slept well; but on waking this morning, all – all that had happened in one short eventful day came most forcibly to her mind, and brought back her grief; the Queen, however, feels better now; but she couldn't touch a morsel of food last night, nor can she this morning. (Victoria 1907: 197)

Melbourne promptly responds: "The situation is very painful, but it is necessary for your Majesty to be prudent and firm" (Victoria 1907: 197). The initial structure of the crisis reveals itself here: the Queen, a center of turbulent affect, must chasten the riot of feeling, while the Prime Minister must tutor her in the athleticism of self-restraint. And in this urgent exercise Melbourne will self-consciously play steady father to wayward daughter. Thus the Queen, in thanking him "for his excellent advice, which is at once the greatest comfort and of the greatest use to her," notes that "she trusts Lord Melbourne will help her and be to her what she told him he was, and begged him still ever to be – a father to one who never wanted support more than she does now" (Victoria 1907: 203).

But even as Victoria asks for a fulfillment of the promises implicit in their relation, Melbourne recedes with a dainty firmness, insisting that the rituals of office be studiously maintained. The negotiations for a new government are now under way, and therefore, intones Melbourne, "it will never do, whilst they are going on, either for appearance or in reality, that Lord Melbourne should dine with your Majesty, as he did before this disturbance" (Victoria 1907: 198). Melbourne's careful use of the third person signifies the will to impersonality, but for the Queen, who had not yet been trained out of the motions of subjectivity, the confusion reaches into the deepest strata of self-representation. Is she an "I" or is she the Queen? Can one possibly be both? In an over-wrought letter of May 8, when it still appears that the Queen will turn to the Tories, she reports to Melbourne on her encounter with the Duke of Wellington, her shifting self-reference exposing the radical uncertainty.

The Queen then said that she felt certain he would understand the great friendship she had for Lord Melbourne, who had been to her quite a parent, and the Duke said *no one felt and knew that better than he did, and that no one could still be of greater use to the Queen than Lord Melbourne.* The Duke spoke of his personal friendship for Lord Melbourne, and that he hoped I knew that he had often done all he could to help your (Lord Melbourne's) Government. The Queen then mentioned her intention to prove her great *fairness* to her new Government in telling them, that they might know there was no unfair dealing, that I meant to see you often as a friend, as I owed *so* much to you. (Victoria 1907: 199)

It was a scene of forced maturation, then, staged there at Buckingham Palace during a few days in May. But although during the first hours of turmoil Victoria fought the very thought of the change, she quickly saw the inevitability of the fall into political impersonality – a fall into, as it were, the British constitution – and so actively took on the role that was in any case forced upon her. On the morning of the 8th she is distraught, but by the evening of the 9th she has fashioned a political face. After a tense meeting with Peel she informs Melbourne that "I was calm but very decided, and I think you would have been pleased to see my composure and great firmness; the Queen of England will not submit to such trickery" (Victoria 1907: 205).

II

Although the immediate effect of the shock was to force the Queen to assume the public airs of her royal role, the equally important result – still more important for being disavowed – was the entanglement of public men within the web of private life. The crisis *reactivated* the engine of private experience in those who habitually conducted government under the secure cloak of impersonality. Nowhere is this clearer than in the fortunes of the word "confidence" during these anxious days.

The Melbourne ministry had resigned on May 7 because its margin of only five on the Jamaican question indicated a decisive failure to sustain parliamentary confidence. As Melbourne put it to the Lords, the vote showed "such a want of confidence on the part of a great proportion of that House of Parliament, as to render it impossible that we should continue to administer the affairs of her Majesty's Government in a manner that can be useful or beneficial to the country" (*Hansard* 1839: 974). To construe the issue of parliamentary "confidence" in terms of a voting margin within the Commons is clearly (and uncontroversially) to follow well-established political conventions that ignore the emotional state of the dissenting members. "Confidence" here is a matter of public votes on public questions.

Against this conventional background of a technical, political "confidence," the reaction of the Queen appeared all the more disruptive. In the first hours after the resignation, Lady de Grey had sent to Peel her astute anticipation of the form the disruptions would take. "The Queen," she writes bluntly, "has always expressed herself much impressed with Lord Melbourne's open manner, and his truth. The latter quality you possess, the former not." Then, having praised Peel's character, she indicates her fear "that even with such qualities you may not succeed in gaining the Queen's confidence, as I think your bearing too reserved and too cautious" (Peel 1899: 389). Indeed, when the Queen meets the Tory leader, she responds as Lady de Grey had imagined, informing Melbourne that she finds Peel "such a cold, odd man she can't make out what he means. He said he couldn't expect me to have the confidence in him I had in you (and which he never can have) as he has not deserved it. My impression is he is not *happy* and sanguine . . . The Queen don't like his manner after – oh! how different, how dreadfully different, to that frank, open, natural and most kind, warm manner of Lord Melbourne" (Victoria 1907: 200). The Queen, in effect, restores confidence to its full semantic density and its older political meanings,

according to which the confidence of the sovereign is not merely a
matter of political congruity, but implies deep affirmations of a personal
will. Confidence, then, takes on extralegal meanings, both older ones
that we know as ancient regal prerogatives, and newer ones that belong
to an age of private life; in both senses, it belongs to a family of emotions and attitudes including trust, fondness, devotion, care.

The powerful collision of these distinct meanings occurs when
Robert Peel decides that his own political weakness requires a special
show of queenly favor. Indeed later, after the game has been lost (or
perhaps won through the losing), he will defend in the Commons his
dogged insistence on the Bedchamber question, asking whether he
could "overlook this important fact, that in the House of Commons I
should not commence my career commanding a majority? . . . Being
invited to take upon myself the responsibility of conducting public
affairs, and taking it without the confidence of the House of
Commons, could I ask for less, than that I should have, at least, the
unqualified confidence of the Crown" (*Hansard* 1839: 988). Exactly
because he was weak in Parliament, he felt the need to be strong with
the Queen. Bulwer Lytton, speaking in high Whig dudgeon, disdained
this principle, pointedly asking whether a Ministry "*not having a majority in the House of Commons should make that very reason the pretext for demand-
ing a peculiar show of countenance from the Crown?*" (Bulwer Lytton 1839:
135) Could Peel's political weakness possibly justify the personal, the
intimate, demand? The further question of course, is why the "peculiar show" of favor should have become so tightly bound to the fate of
the royal household. Why should the ladies of the bedchamber have
come to matter like this?

It cannot have been, of course, because the Queen's domestic
arrangements were remotely representative. Rather, it may well have
been precisely their exceptional character and the exceptional demands
place upon them that made the affairs of the Queen's bedchamber a
privileged scene in an unfolding narrative of domesticity. Just to the
extent that common private needs existed here, too, in the most public
of private lives, they took on an amplification that gave dramatic
urgency to the crisis. When Peel demanded that the Queen exhibit her
confidence by yielding him the power to appoint the membership of the
royal household, and when she blankly refused to accept him on those
terms, the two laid the ground not only for a new constitutional struggle
over the relations between Crown and Parliament, but also for a struggle over the definition of the domestic realm.

How did it happen? How did they all arrive here in the swamp of public confusion? It had started so well two years earlier, the meeting of the Queen and her minister in the first hours of her accession: he with his solicitous ceremony, she with her eager desire to learn the posture of her power. On June 20, 1837, after her first long day as queen of England, she recorded the charged encounter in her journal.

At 9 came Lord Melbourne, whom I saw in my room, and of *course quite alone* as I shall *always* do all my Ministers. He kissed my hand, and I then acquainted him that it had long been my intention to retain him and the rest of the present Ministry at the head of affairs, and that it could not be in better hands than his. He again then kissed my hand. He then read to me the Declaration which I was to read to the Council, which he wrote himself and which is a very fine one. I then talked with him some little time longer, after which he left me. He was in full dress. I like him very much and feel confidence in him. He is a very straightforward, honest, clever, and good man. (Victoria 1907: 98)

Here, at the start, can be seen the exciting confusion of personal and public connections, neatly captured in the slippage between a figure of speech and the formal touch of two bodies: the ministry "could not be in better hands than his. He then again kissed my hand." Within her general wariness of the fawning officials around her, she decisively chose Melbourne as the one to trust: "the more I see him, the more confidence I have in him" (Victoria 1907: 103), and he quickly transformed his life to nurture this new tie.

Together constantly, even in violation of rules of precedent, they felt more than easy affection; they clearly met deep needs for one another. On Melbourne's part, the friendship with the Queen utterly changed his official standing; after the sharp awkwardness of his relation with King William, Melbourne now bathed richly in the warmth of his tie to Victoria. A year before he had been exposed to the humiliation of the sensational adultery charge brought by George Norton; now, all was easy harmony. And then, beyond the happy political reversal, he clearly enjoyed the affective luxury of this intimacy – as Greville put it, "I have no doubt he is passionately fond of her as he might be of his daughter if he had one, and the more because he is a man with a capacity for loving without having anything in the world to love" (Greville 1885: 113). Months later, Greville comments more fully on the remarkable change that has allowed Melbourne to overcome the force of habit so completely as to endure the life he leads. Month after month he remains at the Castle, submitting to this daily routine: of all men he appeared to be the last to be broken in to the trammels of a Court, and never was such a revolution seen in anybody's occupations and habits. Instead of indolently sprawling in all the attitudes of luxurious ease, he is always sitting bolt upright; his free and easy language interlarded with "damns" is carefully guarded and regulated with the strictest propriety, and he has exchanged the good talk of Holland House for the trivial, labored, and wearisome inanities of the Royal circle. (Greville 1885: 129–30)

The Queen, needless to say, saw her court and her minister with other eyes, but then on her side of the relation, there were still more subtle adjustments to make. Melbourne had only to change his manner; she had to determine the conditions of her sovereignty. In that project, she chose him as the trusted minister who would give clarity through the political haze. But she also frankly understood the paternal relation that bemused those around her. Transcribing the intensities of the coronation ceremony, she recalled that "My excellent Lord Melbourne, who stood very close to me throughout the whole ceremony, was *completely* overcome at this moment, and very much affected; he gave *such* a kind, and I may say *fatherly* look" (Victoria 1907: 155). The Queen and Melbourne together built a delicate structure of affect, within which he was both deferential minister and doting father, while she was his sovereign and his daughter.

To say that the daughterly role was only a reassuring metaphor while the sovereignty was urgently real is to miss the necessarily fictive aspect of those first years of queenship. So little was given to Victoria, so much had to be invented. With no precedent of a queen regnant in over 100 years and with a succession of recent kings who had offered so many incompatible styles of sovereignty, Victoria's political role was no more firmly scripted than the role of friendship. Throughout the early relation with Melbourne, it was never quite clear whether she was a queen impersonating a daughter, or a daughter impersonating a queen.

What is at once most uncanny and most impressive is Victoria's resourcefulness in using each side of this ambiguity to control the instability of the other. Obligingly, and with desires of his own to satisfy, Melbourne offered himself as a prop in the Queen's delicate drama. As queen, she could allow herself to indulge useful forms of intimacy, secure in the thought that sovereignty set crisp limits to the claims of his paternal emotion. And as daughterly young woman to ageing fatherly man, she could keep her distance from the royal harness, experimenting with tones and styles of queenship. In effect, she played at being a daughter as she played at being a queen, with Melbourne shifting easily between the father above and the minister below. Early on, she saw that Melbourne would be "of the greatest use to me both politically and privately" (Victoria 1907: 103), and as it happened, the best use of all was to move so quickly between those realms that the very distinction lost its clarity.

And then, of course, though it was Melbourne supremely, it was not Melbourne alone who disturbed the division of realms; it was the set of his political friends and allies who joined the Court; and most fatefully, it was the ladies of the bedchamber. Was it Whig cunning or only Whig exuberance? Whatever the motive or the cause, the result was that the royal household was populated with the relations of Melbourne's cabinet ministers, their wives, their sisters, and their daughters.[2]

For the Tories this was a political construction of the bedchamber that only extended the conditions of Victoria's early upbringing. Lord Ashley captures party frustration when he writes to Peel that "from her earliest years she has been taught to regard us as her personal enemies. I am told the language at Kensington was such as to inspire her with fear and hatred. And certainly Melbourne's hedge of male and female Whigs was not adapted to remove this prejudice by letting in Tory light" (Peel 1899: 405).[3] In a prescient piece of invective published in the *Quarterly Review* in 1837, J. W. Croker – still a leading Tory tactician and polemicist – had brightly italicized the objections to the Whig arrangement.

It is neither constitutional in principle, nor convenient or becoming in practice, that the Sovereign should be *enclosed* within the *circumvallation* of any particular *set*, however respectable – that in the hours of business or amusement, in public or in private, she should see only the repetition of the same family faces, and hear no sound but the different modulations of the same family voices; and *that the private comfort of the Queen's interior life should be, as it inevitably must, additionally exposed to the fluctuations of political change, or what is still worse – that political changes should be either produced or* PREVENTED *by private favour or personal attachments.* (Croker 1839: 233)

Croker brazenly evokes the specter of political indoctrination, what would come to be called "brainwashing," achieved through the relentless manipulations of private life – the looming nightmarish control exercised by those "same family faces."[4] The essay puts into play a theory of influence that will circulate wildly through the Bedchamber debates and according to which the domestic sphere is a closed realm of affective energies that can create tastes, dispositions, and ultimately political beliefs.

And yet, nothing is clearer than that this theory does not apply universally; not everyone, not every monarch, is vulnerable to the pressures of intimacy. The theory, which comes bearing principles of high generality, in fact exists to explain the glaringly special case of Victoria, whose sex and youth expose her to the powers lurking within the household. On both sides of the dispute, indeed, resided an acute consciousness of the anomaly embodied in this queen. It was not simply that for more than 100 years the country had known only male monarchs; it was also that the female monarch was twenty years old. As Croker laid out the case, "A princess of the age of eighteen years and one month, who had been educated in a perhaps proper, but certainly very remarkable seclusion from general society, and whose experience of what is called the world was even less – if less be possible – than might have been expected from her tender years, is suddenly called to the government of a great empire" (Croker 1839: 235). And then beyond these provoking conditions of sex and age, lay the changing character of domestic life, at once more sharply defined and more passionately valued than in the time of the most recent and most ambiguous precedent, Queen Anne. After a meeting with Peel, Lord Ashley recalls him saying that "I remember that I am to provide the attendants and companions of this young woman, on whose moral and religious character depends the welfare of millions of human beings. What shall I do? I wish to have around her those who will be, to the country and to myself, a guarantee that the tone and temper of their character and conversation will tend to her moral improvement" (Peel 1899: 393). An image of the drawing room as the privileged site of *bildung*, perhaps the only site, creates the much-expressed worry not only that the Queen will have partisan opinions but also that her character will harden permanently into Whiggish shape.

For their part, the Whigs, no less than the Tories, invested the domestic circle with extravagant significance; only in their case, the high value of the private household lay not in its power to create public character, but precisely in its distance from the workings of power, its status as refuge from the field of politics. From this standpoint, the application of Peel's principle would bring a domestic catastrophe. It would mean, in Bulwer Lytton's words, that "the Sovereign was to be debarred from the privileges enjoyed by her meanest subject – condemned to feel that every association, every intimacy, every friendship, was held upon the tenure of ministerial jealousy and fear – chopped and changed with each fluctuation of party – living not in a home but an inn" (Bulwer Lytton 1839: 135). This, indeed, is how the Queen understands the challenge. In a journal entry of

May 9, she records the difficult conversation with Peel earlier that day, in which she had defended her right to keep the mistress of the robes and the ladies of the bedchamber: "I said . . . that I never talked politics with them" (Victoria 1907: 208). She recalls taunting the Duke of Wellington with the question, "Was Sir Robert so weak that *even* the Ladies must be of his opinion?" (Victoria 1907: 209). To Melbourne she writes, "The Queen would not have *stood so firmly* on the Grooms and Equerries, but her *Ladies* are *entirely* her own affair, and *not* the Ministers" (Victoria 1907: 206); and when on the following day, the 10th, the danger seems averted, she writes again to say that "she must rejoice at having got out of the hands of people who would have sacrificed every personal feeling and instinct of the Queen's to their bad party purposes" (Victoria 1907: 211).

It is right, but only partly right, to see the two parties as holding incompatible views on the relation of domestic and political life. But behind the round rhetoric of high principle stands a dirty tactical conflict. The Whigs, having seized the ground of the Queen's private comfort, trap Peel into the role of political bully, coarsely insensitive to the ideals of home life. Once control of the household has become the sign and token of power, Peel has little choice but to persist in his demand for that special show of confidence, what he calls the "public proof of your majesty's entire support and confidence" (Peel 1899: 397). To the degree that the Queen placed the bedchamber outside the reach of politics, as a *refuge* from politics, to that very degree it became an arena of political desire. Only by winning his point in that sacred space – by winning "permission to make some changes in that part of your Majesty's household which your Majesty resolved on maintaining entirely without change" (Peel 1899: 397) – would Peel feel that he had achieved the "confidence" to govern.

The Whig polemic moved on ground just as treacherous. The lofty claims on behalf of sacred domesticity and personal affection grew murky, even paradoxical, when the private emotions were those of the monarch. Quickly and inevitably, the Whig argument shifts from a defense of domestic privacy to an improbable defense of the rights and privileges of the sovereign. ("Strange doctrine in Whig mouths," wrote Greville in his diary [Greville 1885: 183]). On the 9th an aroused and perhaps renewedly ambitious Melbourne writes to the Queen that "if Sir Robert Peel presses for the dismissal of those of your Household who are not in Parliament, you may observe that in so doing he is pressing your Majesty more hardly than any Minister ever pressed a Sovereign before." And further: "They press upon your Majesty, whose personal feelings ought from your circumstances to be more consulted, a measure which no Minister before ever pressed upon a Sovereign" (Victoria 1907: 204). At this point it becomes clearer why the episode aroused such immediate popular passion: as Melbourne's remarks show, the sovereign – indeed sovereignty – has become cast as the emblem of personality oppressed by party politics; the Queen had suddenly become the spectacular limiting case of the rights of private will within a coarsely public world. In these uncanny circumstances of the crisis, to defend those rights was to defend the high privileges of monarchical will. In his speech before the House of Lords, justifying his return to office, Melbourne concludes with a grand rhetorical gesture that sustains the flourishing confusions of sovereignty and domesticity.

I now, my Lords, frankly declare, that I resume office unequivocally and solely for this reason – that I will not abandon my Sovereign in a situation of difficulty and distress, and especially when a demand is made upon her Majesty, with which I think she ought not to comply – a demand, in my opinion, inconsistent with her personal honour, and which, if acquiesced in, would make her reign liable to all the changes and variations of political parties, and render her domestic life one constant scene of unhappiness and discomfort. (*Hansard* 1839: 1015)

That the royal household should be the household of a reigning Queen, that she should be a young queen, that she should begin her reign at a time of both great political instability and increased devotion to domestic security – all this created a richly welcoming context for the uncanny transgressions between politics and domesticity. No one knew what to say; awkwardness was everywhere. Continually, the principals in the closet drama improvise verbal routines that have the look of ceremonial formality; but in fact the guiding conventions by which these figures would understand themselves – the dependence of a girl or the strength of a monarch; the quiet of home or the deep voice of political authority; the merely technical meaning of "confidence" or its urgent psychic claim – all collide and disarm one another. The absurdity of the episode, well appreciated by those caught within it, should not mislead.[5] Much can be discharged and displayed within the convulsions of embarrassment.

IV

Lord Brougham's consternation, though rhetorically exaggerated, had ample justification: "Never before did I know, never did I hear, of a Whig

Government establishing itself upon a bedchamber question, – resting its whole claim to the support of the country upon its care for the personal feelings of the monarch" (Brougham 1841: 416). He did not add, though he might well have, that the sight of Tories as jealous defenders of parliamentary right against the claims of the monarch carried its own strong peculiar savor. Croker, who saw the absurd tangle, complained to Lord Hertford that the Queen, in turning against the Tories, has rejected "her natural allies"[6] (Croker 1885: 344).

Certainly, the comedy of such party cross-dressing continues to tickle anyone with a taste for political ironies. But what throws a new tangle into the confusion is the recognition that the monarchy was itself undergoing a profound historical evolution, which could not have been fully grasped by the participants in the comic drama. One way to describe the change is to see it as the *feminizing* of the monarchy, a development begun well before Victoria's reign but given heightened force by the conspicuous fact of her sex.[7] The loss of monarchical prestige under the fourth of the Georges; the flailing, largely futile, attempts of William IV to impose his political will upon Parliament; and the popular mythology of those heartier days "when George III was king"; all contributed to a notable weakening of a still-potent image of the sovereign as the concentrated sight of masculine authority. Then, too, stands the fact that more even than in the case of royal sovereignty, Parliament had always been the quintessential male preserve, a condition giving added point to the Queen's satiric comment that she would retain her mistress of the robes because Peel had "said *only* those who are *in Parliament* shall be removed. I should like to know if they mean to give the *Ladies* seats in Parliament?" (Victoria 1907: 206). The Court, on the other hand, whether or not led by a reigning queen, had retained a space for its ladies. Always less uniformly male, by the end of the age of Victoria the Court began to seem irrevocably female.

No one could have known that when William IV dismissed the Melbourne ministry, this was a last, and indeed a desperate, attempt to employ the sovereign right of dismissal in order to assert royal influence on government policy.[8] In the event, William was unable to keep the Tory ministers he desired, and so his defiant gesture only dramatized the limits of monarchical authority (Newbould 1990: 160). Within the long historical logic of parliamentary rise and monarchical decline, the tempest in the bedchamber appears less random and foolish; it suggests the painful locking into place of the "womanly" character of all modern sovereignty. Melbourne's very choice of metaphor in describing Peel's assertion – Peel "is pressing your Majesty more hardly than any Minister ever pressed a Sovereign before" – teases out the sexual figure in the relationship between a parliament, conscious of the potency of its broadened legitimacy, and a monarch placed in a condition of female vulnerability. No doubt part of the provocation of a queen sitting on the throne at this historical moment in time is that it *confirms* this feminizing of sovereignty – as if the truth about changing power relations between Parliament and the monarch were finally revealed in the accession of Victoria: relative to Parliament, the monarch is placed in just that defensive and vulnerable position which women held in relation to men.

## v

In his parliamentary explanation after the return to office, Melbourne recalled that during his visit to the Queen after tendering his resignation, he never even mentioned the ladies of the household, because he never imagined that their tenure would be at issue. Instead he undertook only to inform Victoria of her historical responsibilities. In another howling, sneering essay in the *Quarterly Review* – whose main lines seem to have been commissioned by Peel himself[9] – J. W. Croker wonders how this "*historical lecturer*" could have construed his responsibilities when "*that* which it most concerned her to know – *that* of which there had been no example for *one hundred and thirty* years, was a *change of ministers in a female reign*, and what it might be proper and constitutional to do in *such an almost unprecedented emergency*" (Croker 1839: 245). Melbourne ignored "the special circumstances and peculiarities of the case of a *female sovereign*" when this was "the only novelty in the case that required any advice" (Croker 1839: 246). That the last close precedent was in the reign of Anne – "a period in every way remarkable, but in none more so than in the important, the overwhelming influence which *female ministers* under the title of *court ladies*, had obtained over the destinies of England and of Europe" (Croker 1839: 245), when "the momentous struggle between Godolphin and Marlborough on one side, and Oxford and Bolingbroke on the other, was conducted in the recesses of the Queen's apartments between the Mistress of the Robes and the Woman of the Bedchamber" (Croker 1839: 255) – is what Melbourne had spectacularly failed to inform the Queen. He had ignored Mrs. Masham ("she was only a bedchamber-woman, but she soon became the pivot of the political world"), and had kept a ludicrous silence on the subject of the Duchess of Marlborough: "Not a word of her! though she is the strongest example, perhaps in the history of the world, certainly in the history of this empire, of the abuse of female favoritism, and the most flagrant instance of the incalculable influence of household familiarity on the destinies of mankind" (Croker 1839: 253). And so on, crescendo beyond crescendo.

A much nearer precedent, which Croker had special reason to remember but also tactical reasons to forget,[10] loomed close behind the present frenzy. For all of its own complex determinations within a densely cultural environment, the Queen Caroline affair of 1820/21 stood as a harshly lit image of political/domestic conflict. Laqueur has persuasively identified Caroline's cause as "perhaps the first of those nineteenth-century political causes – opposition to the bastardy clauses of the New Poor law was another – in which women acted as defenders of familial values and communal morality" (Laqueur 1982: 442). Davidoff and Hall have extended this insight in order to argue that the episode marked a first precipitate of an emerging discourse of marriage and domesticity: "Public opinion had decreed that the royal family must indeed be a family; kings and queens must be fathers and mothers in their own home if they were to be fathers and mothers to the people" (Davidoff and Hall 1987: 155).[11] Set against the figure of a sexually degraded male sovereign, Caroline came to stand as the improbable site of domestic virtue.

But it is one thing to identify a queen consort as the representative of an injured respectability, whose reputation has been mutilated by a king's rude morals; it is quite another to make the young queen regnant into a compound of wounded domesticity and unchallenged sovereignty. If that compound became more stable later in the reign, then this was surely due both to the reassuring mythology of Victoria's marriage to Albert and to her recession into the more comfortable space of symbolism. But in 1839 the Queen still figured as a concretely embodied woman who had not yet disappeared behind the harness of ceremony.

A pro-Tory pamphlet entitled *The Household, or What Shall We do with the Ladies?* bitterly criticized that phrase in the Queen's letter of refusal describing Peel's request as not only "contrary to usage" but also "repugnant to her feelings." *Feelings,* insists the anonymously aggrieved pamphleteer, must always be sacrificed "upon the altar of duty" (Croker 1839: 260). And yet everywhere in the affair there loomed the disruptive presence of feeling, of irreducible sensation and emotion surging beneath the rites of politics. Undoubtedly, much of what made the affair so absorbing to the public mind was that the political stresses became a convenient frame around a crisis of feeling that took on the aspect of domestic catastrophe. Exceptional though her position inevitably remained, the Queen gave a heavily stylized performance of several distinct domestic gestures that were recognizable and in many ways representative. Victoria, who asks Melbourne to give her a father's support, will mock the Tory "attempt to see whether she could be led and managed like a child" (Victoria 1907: 206). But it is worth emphasizing that the position of the child was only one disruptive affective site. A scandalized Greville tells his diary that "the Queen was in communication with Sir Robert Peel on one side, and Lord Melbourne on the other, at the same time" (Greville 1885: 182), and though Greville means only to refer to the political impropriety, his words inevitably evoke a picture of the Queen in the role of unattached young woman choosing between two suitors. When she has broken with the "cold, odd" Peel – failed father, failed suitor – she gaily invites the graceful Melbourne to dine. As one of history's most famous cuckolds, the ageing husband of Caroline Lamb could now enjoy his own (erotically tinged) theft.

Beyond these more available symbolic resonances, the constant chanting together of those words "age" and "sex" can reasonably be taken as a substitution for the unutterable word "virgin." Speculative though the idea must be, one might still fairly surmise that at a deeper level of the collective psyche the disturbance of the Bedchamber crisis gained great energy from the unspoken conflation of "sovereignty" and "virginity." The awful hush before the Queen, the excessive scruple, the zealous preservation of distance, all this so palpable in the behavior of the male principals, might be seen as an overdetermined product of both her constitutional authority and the authority of her intact innocence. Although the parliamentary speech and the diverse written texts naturally avoid the taboo of the Queen's sexual status, the persistent preoccupation with her "unworldliness" suggests an appreciation, at whatever level of consciousness, that the Queen was not yet initiate in the ways of normative adult sexuality.

Indeed, what is perhaps most disruptive of all in the event, and what gives special edge to the sexual implication, is the Queen's aggressive assertion of a world beyond the realm and reach of men. Those "Ladies," with whom she never discusses politics, mark out a female household space, which according to usual understandings existed as refuge and support for the responsible male domestic authority. But in the young queen's royal household she herself embodied that authority, thus creating the uncanny condition of a family without men. When she recounts the tale of her refusal, she speaks as the proud head of house-hold, fiercely reluctant to imperil a single member of the circle: "the Queen maintains *all* her ladies . . . her *Ladies* are *entirely* her own affair, and *not* the Ministers." To the images of queen as daughter to paternal ministers and as blushing adolescent caught between two eligible admir-ers, one must add the still more startling figure of the Queen as chief among a tribe of women.

The conversations among those women disappeared in the surround-ing air. Among the many documents in this heavily textualized affair, we have no register of what the mistress of the robes said to the first lady of the bedchamber; their laughter is unrecorded. But we have every reason to suppose that during this perplexing week, when their intimacy was the subject of raucous public debate, these privileged women used their tongues in self-defense. Whatever was said and whatever its tone, it would have helped give Victoria the temerity to speak back to the looming men. "Sir Robert Peel has behaved very ill," she reports to Melbourne in the second of her three letters to him on the 9th, "and has insisted on my giving up my Ladies, to which I replied that I never would consent, and I never saw a man so frightened" (Victoria 1907: 204).

Few at the time could have known of the Queen's flashing anger and her pleasure in Peel's fear. But though the details have had to wait for history, the structure of the agon was all too conspicuous at the time. This strong-willed, hedged-in adolescent of a queen had defeated the usurping Tory male, and though party affiliation was likely to dictate individual reactions, those of all parties bestowed rapt attention upon those hints of turmoil behind the screen. Among all the rapidly circu-lating images of crisis, the one most sharply etched was that of the roused woman refusing to surrender the rights of her bedchamber. Just six months later the engagement of the Queen to Albert would begin her assimilation into the role of wifely exemplar. But for the space of that period of crisis and its shuddering aftermath, Victoria lived out an asser-tion of royal privilege that was at the same time a glaring exposure of stresses within an emerging domestic ideal. From the summit of her high anomaly, she transformed the household into a brightly lit theater where the spasms of private life were exposed to hungry public view.

### NOTES

1   For several years Brougham had been an eloquent tangle in the hair of the Whigs. He and Melbourne had clashed sharply in 1837, and over the next few years, even when the conflict was not so direct or open, Brougham's

insinuations were a chronic irritant. See, for instance, Lord Holland's remarks in his diary entry for May 1839, in *The Holland House Diaries* (Lord Holland 1977: 402).

2  A seething J. W. Croker summarizes the tableau:

> The *wife* of the *Lord President of the Council* was *First Lady of the Bedchamber*; one *sister* of the *Secretary for Ireland* is *Mistress of the Robes*, and another, *Lady of the Bedchamber* – as was also the *wife* of the *Lord Lieutenant of Ireland*: the *sister* of the *Secretary* at War is *Bedchamber Woman*; the *sister-in-law* of the *Home Secretary* and the *daughter* of the *Chancellor of the Exchequer* are *Maids of Honour* – not to mention the *wife*, *sister*, and *daughter* of Lords Durham, Spencer, and Grey, who though not now in the Cabinet, are even more prominent in the Whig party than any of the Ministers. (Croker 1839: 236)

3  On the other hand, Lord Liverpool, in his own letter to Peel, resists the prevailing overstatement. Drawing on his personal connection to the Queen (through his daughter), Liverpool writes that "it is but fair and just for me to say that no objection was made by Lord Melbourne in several instances to appointments, or offers of appointments, to persons of adverse politics to himself." Liverpool goes on to note that "Lady Manvers was offered a ladyship of the bedchamber, Lady Harriet Clive was made Bedchamber Woman, and Miss Pitt and Miss Cox were made Maids of Honour." Still, whatever the scale of Whig intentions, no one tried to deny that the domestic circle of the Queen had been given a sharply political character (Peel 1899: 402).

4  All through Croker's gnashing anger runs the thought that the Queen will disappear so far into the recesses of privacy that she will be a toy in the hands of her advisors. It is a terror of a space removed from the public arena, a space not regulated by Parliament or the press. So Croker warns that the Whigs have promulgated "a doctrine by which the nearest interests of the Sovereign – the hourly attendance on her person – the daily participation of her society – and all the influences, both personal and political, of an intimate familiarity, might be irrevocably committed to the meanest, or the most mischievous, or the most mercenary hands, freed from any visible control, and exempt from all legal or even moral responsibility" (Croker 1839: 261).

5  As Brougham put it in his characteristically bright colors, "It seems the fate of these household discussions to be attended with constant misapprehension, and to involve all concerned with them in ridicule and discredit" (Brougham 1841: 418).

6  Letter to Lord Hertford, May 29, 1839 (Croker 1885: 344).

7  Margaret Homans has shown how Victoria inherited a "paradigm of queenship" from Queen Caroline, a "queenly identification with vulnerable femininity" (Homans 1994: 246). And between Caroline and Victoria, we suggest, there stands the additional vulnerable femininity of weakening male monarchs.

8  Ian Newbould provides a detailed discussion of the events leading up to and down from this last royal dismissal of a ministry (Newbould 1990: 152–59).

9  In a memorandum to Croker, Peel outlines in detail the structure of argument that will govern Croker's *Quarterly Review* essay: "What, in a constitutional point of view, had the country to do with the youth of the sovereign,
   or the sex of the sovereign? No more than with the nature, or the beauty"
   (Croker 1885: 341). As it assumed published form, Croker's essay, with its
   extravagant bitterness and brazen accusation – it names Melbourne guilty
   of "enormous lying" – suggests the smooth conversion of measured parliamentary rhetoric into passionate polemical discharge. The press, as it were,
   could say what the politicians meant.
       It is worth noticing that this view of 1839 stands in significant conflict with
   the position that Peel offered to Croker in July 5, 1837, when he wrote that
   "The theory of the Constitution is, that the King has no will, except in the
   choice of his Ministers – that he acts by their advice, that they are responsible, &c. But this, like a thousand other theories, is at variance with the fact.
   The personal character of the Sovereign, in this and all other Governments,
   has an immense practical effect" (Croker 1885: 314).
10 Croker had written a vastly popular pamphlet on the royal marriage, *A Letter
   from the King* (Croker 1820).
11 Davidoff and Hall argue further that "The reaction to the whole episode
   marks one of the first *public* moments at which one view of marriage and of
   sexuality was decisively rejected in favour of another . . . The domestic had
   been imprinted on the monarchical" (Davidoff and Hall 1987: 152).

# CHAPTER 12

# The "Widdy's" empire: Queen Victoria as widow in Kipling's soldier stories and in the Barrack-Room Ballads

*Dagni Bredesen*

> 'Ave you 'eard o' the Widow at Windsor
>   with the hairy gold crown on 'Er 'ead?
> She 'as ships on the foam, – she 'as millions at 'ome
>   An' she pays us poor beggars in red . . .
>     ('Ow poor beggars in red!)

As the unofficial poet laureate of the empire, Rudyard Kipling is not the first writer one looks to for a critique of the subject he lauded. Nor does he spring to mind immediately as a source for fictional treatments of widows in general, or the widowed Empress in particular; one might more readily turn to Dickens or Trollope for the one and to the many biographers and historians of the House of Windsor for the other. Yet, for the low-ranking military men in Kipling's stories of the Anglo-Indian army and in the later collection of poems, *The Barrack-Room Ballads*, widowhood becomes a constitutive element of Queen Victoria's identity. References to "the Widow," "the Widder" or "the Widdy" frequently reflect the warm affection of "Misses Victorier's Sons" for their sovereign. Self-designated as both the Widow's sons and her property, Kipling's soldiers protect the Queen's goods and her borders, and enforce her will. Yet equally as often, these references to Victoria's widowhood signal the private soldier's ambivalence towards his devalued position in the task of empire building; towards the very empire the soldiers are called upon to extend and maintain; and finally, towards the Queen on whose behalf and in whose name they labor.

For the men in her armed forces, Victoria *Regina et Imperatrix* personifies the abstract powers that have sent them to the ends of the earth, to guard India: her prize possession, the jewel in her crown. The idea of service to the queen endows the drudgery of the soldier's life with a sense of significance. But this chivalrous fiction obscures the political and business interests that motivate their presence in India. Further, the relationship between soldier and monarch does not allow for any interaction;

her titles alone serve to mark rather than bridge the vast social gulf
between the Queen on her throne and her lowly foot soldiers.
Widowhood, however, is a condition that cuts across wealth, rank, and
class, striking women in every social strata, uniting women in a common
bond of loss. Representing Victoria as "the Widow," despite article and
capital letters, blurs the distinctions between sovereign and subject in
ways that make the Queen appear more approachable, even accessible
to affection and solicitude, but necessarily also to critique. By personal-
izing the imperial project and then constructing an identity for Victoria
on the basis of her widowhood, Kipling's soldiers also have someone
they can hold directly accountable for the hardships they face.

While scholarship has begun to reevaluate earlier assumptions concerning Rudyard Kipling's jingoism, the connection between his critique
of empire and his representations of Victoria as widow has been perceived as incidental.[1] Yet in emphasizing Victoria's widowhood, Kipling
taps into the traditionally vexed status of the widow that encourages a
range of strong, often ambivalent responses. The diffuse societal unease
generated by widowhood combines with tensions created by the
anomaly of a female monarch to add an affective and ambivalent charge
to criticism of imperial policies and practices. Conversely, mention of
Victoria in terms of her widowhood rather than in terms of her royal
titles serves to contain the radical potential of Kipling's critique because
it construes the relations between monarch and soldiers as familial
rather than political.

By the late 1880s, when Rudyard Kipling was writing tales of Anglo-
Indian life, Prince Albert had been dead for nearly thirty years. In the
decades that followed the Prince Consort's death, Queen Victoria's pro-
tracted mourning – the lengthy self-imposed seclusion, the invariably
black apparel, the persistence in morbid household rituals and the more
public demonstrations of sorrow in the innumerable statues and monuments commemorating Albert – continuously impressed upon the
Queen's subjects her status as widow. But Victoria's strict, even excessive
observance of mourning and prolonged absence from public life pro-
voked criticism from royalist and antiroyalist alike. Dorothy Thompson
notes the problems brought on by the Queen's extended mourning:

> Those of her subjects who sympathized with her withdrawal from public life
> considered that she should do so properly and hand over her public role to a
> man. Those who wished her to remain on the throne, or who respected her deci-
> sion not to abdicate, not unnaturally expected her to fulfill all the demands of
> her position after a decent interval of mourning. For the Queen to continue in

a public role distinct from that of wife or mother was again to except her from the rules of behaviour by which her subjects were increasingly governed. (Thompson 1990: 58)

On the surface, Queen Victoria's identification with the role of widow appears to have conflicted with her public duties as monarch. Yet, on a more complex level, widowhood appears to have bolstered the Queen's resistance to relinquishing the throne and to have offered her one way of resolving various tensions inherent in her position of female monarch, a position even she admitted to be anomalous.

Without minimizing Victoria's sense of loss for the man she had regarded as "father, protector, guide, advisor in all and everything, mother, as well as husband" (Journal, June 9, 1858, quoted in Tingsten 1972: 76), widowhood gave the Queen a new rationale for her continued participation in government in an era in which the dominant gender ideology discouraged political power and public display of women. Writing shortly after Albert's death to the uncle who had been to her both confidant and counselor prior to her marriage, Victoria insists:

I am also anxious to repeat *one* thing, and *that one* is *my firm* resolve, my *irrevocable decision*, viz. that *his* wishes – *his* plans – about everything, *his* views about *every* thing are to be *my law*! And *no human power* will make me swerve from *what he* decided and wished . . . I am *also determined* that *no one* person, may *he* be ever so good, ever so devoted among my servants – is to lead or guide or dictate *to me*. I know *how he* would disapprove of it. And I live *on* with him, for him. (quoted in Tingsten 1972: 83)[2]

Evidently, the influence over the Queen that Uncle Leopold, King of Belgium, and other male advisors had enjoyed in the past would be sanctioned no longer; Victoria's stated aim was now to attend solely to the wishes of her dead husband. As Albert's relict, Victoria conformed to a gender ideal of self-effacing womanhood that, at the same time, empowered her to act, since she alone could claim full knowledge of Albert's intentions.[3] In this position, Victoria was supported by historical and legal precedent dating back to Roman times, which permitted unusual economic and social independence for a woman if she were widowed.[4] Embracing the responsibilities of widowhood solved one problem: that of finding a socially consonant role permitting the exercise of female authority. Nevertheless, a widow in the Victorian period – whether queen or commoner – had to negotiate numerous social, legal, and cultural contradictions.

At a time when women were considered "relative creatures" – that is, that a woman's worth is determined by her relationship to father, husband, son – "widow" signifies the loss of what has been for that woman a primary relationship and, during much of the nineteenth century, the primary legal means of constituting her identity. Yet her very survival belies the notion of female dependency. In an era when respectable single women were uniformly expected to be chaste and sexually naïve, widows were respectable, single, yet sexually experienced. Similarly, despite the ideal of the subjection of a woman to a man – on the grounds of hierarchical familial relations that grant husbands authority over wives, fathers authority over daughters – many widows were the heads of their own households. Further, although the notion of the fully privatized domestic sphere was widely approved, when forced by circumstances to support themselves, widows frequently turned the home into a source of income; thus, by inheriting their husband's property or by establishing a small business at home, widows might be economic entities in their own right.[5] The challenge to ideas of respectable femininity posed by the widow reinforces the association of widowhood with notions of ambiguity already in place because of her relation to the deceased.

In the Victorian period as in times past, the "good" widow was a *memento mori*, a living reminder of the deceased and of human mortality: her very clothing marks her relation to death. On the one hand, the widow could be perceived as an emblem of timelessness in her association with the grave and eternity. On the other, she often appeared stuck in time; one has only to think of Queen Victoria's refusal to change the style of her dress after Albert's death in 1861. Ostensibly preoccupied with the realm of the spirit, the widow was pressed by circumstances to concern herself with the things of this world: funeral arrangements, mourning garb, physical survival if poor, inheritance issues if rich, and affairs of state if queen. The problem with this involvement in public and economic affairs lies in the implicit contradiction of widowhood, which is, to quote Tony Weller, "widders are 'ceptions to evry rule." Though wary, society tolerates the widow's special status because she serves as a link in the familial chain between father and son. Ideally, then, her position is both exceptional and temporary: she holds a place in the family business or conserves family property on behalf of the son who will one day reach maturity.[6]

Quite apart from the widow's exceptional legal and social status, there are contradictory cultural associations that augment the ambiguity of widowhood. At once sinister in her proximity to death and pathetic in expressions of grief, the widow elicits responses that range from fear and revulsion to sympathy and a sense of filial or societal obligation. The power of widowhood to evoke strong responses may be one reason that a multitude of contradictory, often comic, cultural resonances have accrued to the figure of the widow. In folklore and literature since Petronius, the widow has been depicted variously as comic, tragic, gullible, scheming, parasitic, independent, defenseless, dangerous, sexually rapacious, eternally devoted. Rudyard Kipling draws on the already ambiguous status of widowhood in his construction of the widowed Empress as seen through the eyes of the common foot soldier characters in the military tales and ballads. When the soldiers use the appellation "The Widow," or its colloquial variations "Widdy" and "Widder," to denote the Queen, the chivalric impulse and national pride inherent in the idea of defending queen and country is spliced with a cynicism that exposes an underlying class- and gender-related antagonism toward the female monarch.

Upon his return to London after seven years in India, Rudyard Kipling launched his career as a successful writer with an eye to the market, and, as Ann Parry notes, with the intent to "educate and undeceive the 'sunward-gazing nation' about its Empire" (Parry 1992: 32).[7] For him, this entailed telling the story from the inglorious point of view of the common foot soldier. With their emphasis on "the rigors of military life, the isolation of the foreigner in a strange land, and the harshness of the Indian climate" (Bauer 1994: 30), the military stories in *Soldiers Three* and elsewhere focus on the exploits and attitudes of three representatives of the common Anglo-Indian foot soldier: Terence Mulvaney (an Irishman), Stanley Ortheris (a Cockney), and John Learoyd (a Yorkshireman) – each characterized by his own distinctive, if at times incomprehensible, dialect. The adventures of these "three musketeers," as Kipling introduced them to the reading public, primarily consist of elaborate hoaxes and schoolboy pranks played on superiors, rebellious regiments, truculent recruits, Eurasian neighbors, and, sometimes, even on each other. Though couched in comedy, these military stories and ballads register many of the soldiers' complaints concerning the conditions under which they extend and defend imperial holdings. The ballads not only address issues abroad, but bring the critique close to home in their protest over the soldier's lot after leaving active service. According to Kipling's soldier/spokesman, having survived the rigors of army life, the soldier returned to England only to face insult, mistreatment, and neglect at the hands of London civilians.

But even the most explicit expressions of dissatisfaction uttered by the returning soldiers are meant to encourage reform rather than incite riot. For example, in the ballad "Tommy," Kipling's archetypal Tommy Atkins promises to "wait for extry rations if you treat us rational" (Kipling 1989: 397, line 34); this promise calls the attention of an unknowing or unfeeling audience to a social problem – the neglect of the returned soldier – yet assuages anxiety over the returned soldier's potential for unrest. A similar strategy for expressing discontent or criticism while at the same time deflecting its radical force comes into effect when soldiers refer to Victoria in terms of her marital status rather than by her titles.

At first glance, references to Victoria as queen in comparison to Victoria as widow in Kipling's military tales and ballads might not indicate a substantive difference. A comparable notion of the honor due to the Queen is evinced in reference to "the Widow." Military dress is called "the Widow's Uniform" as well as the Queen's. An elision of class hierarchies can occur when a soldier pledges allegiance to the Queen as well as when he claims an affiliation with the widow.[8] The difference lies in that, for Kipling, when potential for actual disorder among the ranks manifests itself, a widow can bear association with the disorder of war and the troops' unruly nature better than a monarch.

Repeatedly in *Soldiers Three* and in other military tales, Victoria is denoted as widow when referred to in the context of a disreputable behavior or event. Having turned civilian upon marriage, Mulvaney one day leaves to meet members of his old regiment: he wears, despite his wife's reproaches, "his best coat . . . to do honour to the Widdy. I cud ha' done no less" (Kipling 1909: III, 352). The loyalty to the Queen indicated by this courtly gesture, and perhaps the gentlemanly pretensions, are punctured by the diminutive "Widdy," and the valiant deed he does in the Widdy's name is correspondingly reduced: Mulvaney quells, not a hoard of rioting natives, but a mob of drunken soldiers. The appellation "Widdy" not only points to Mulvaney's common roots, but also enables the mention of such a ruckus in proximity to the Queen, while the cuteness of the term assuages anxiety among readers concerning the real problem of unruly troops both at home and abroad. A comparable example occurs in another story about Private Mulvaney. In "With the Main Guard," Mulvaney recalls that his "first rig'mint was Oirish – Faynians an' rebils to the heart av their marrow was they, an' so they fought for the Widdy betther than most, bein' contrary – Oirish" (Kipling 1909: II, 154). The "go figure" contrariness attributed to this band of soldiers elides the real contradiction of an Irish–Catholic regiment in the British army. The inevitable hostility is expended without threat in the use of the diminutive "Widdy," which for these particular soldiers could scarcely be purely affectionate. But simultaneously, the fighting Irish might find it conceptually less grating to wage war on behalf of a widow, whereas Victoria's title serves as an irritating reminder of Ireland's colonized status.

But the proximity to violence implied when the term "Widow" or "Widdy" is used also implicates the Widow herself in the excesses of war as described in Kipling's *Barrack-Room Ballads*. Abroad, the soldiers who beat and kick "niggers" while pillaging their homes – atrocities described in the infamous ballad "Loot" – wish "good luck to those that wears the Widow's clo'es" (Kipling 1989: 409, line 47). At home, Kipling's Tommy needs his metropolitan audience to "prove it to our face / The Widow's uniform is not the soldier-man's disgrace" (Kipling 1989: 397, lines 35–36). While Tommy's demand is a plea primarily for better treatment, read in conjunction with "Loot" this *Barrack-Room Ballad* presumes at least the perception of a taint upon those who "wear the Widow's clo'es." Indeed, the Widow seems an appropriate presiding figure over the mayhem of war since, in the process of extending Britain's empire, Victoria's soldiers continually add more women to the ranks of the widowed.

Kipling endorses neither the violence nor the attitudes he depicts in poems like "Loot"; nevertheless, he makes clear in other ballads and short stories that the actions of these soldiers have been conditioned by their nominal pay, exposure to danger and disease, the arbitrariness or incompetence of commanders, and the mind-numbing boredom of camp life. Significantly, in three of the most explicit examples of critique, Kipling establishes a metonymic relationship between the widowed Queen and her far-flung empire. In the ballads "The Widow at Windsor" and "The Widow's Party" and the short story "The Madness of Private Ortheris," the complicated relation of widowhood to gender ideals, property, and death provides a set of organizing terms for the complaint voiced by Kipling's foot soldiers.

In the *Barrack-Room Ballad* "The Widow at Windsor" (Kipling 1989: 411–12), issues of money, property, and inheritance generate intense ambivalence towards the Queen, who is represented as both shopkeeper and mother, as well as towards the soldier's own vexed status as both beggar and son. As the epigraph excerpted from the ballad indicates, the poor pay soldiers earned while in active service and the paltry pensions they later received was cause for great concern.[9] Nor did the disparity in the respective fortunes of sovereign and soldier pass unnoticed: the

Widow wears a "hairy gold crown" and "'as millions at 'ome / an' she pays us poor beggars in red." The word "pays" implies an arrangement between the worker and an employer whose books do not balance, and as one of Kipling's later propaganda pieces, "The Absent-minded Beggar," makes clear, "beggar" was not just a demeaning expression. Often, the military pensions of returned soldiers were completely inadequate and had to be supplemented by panhandling. Despite its foregrounding in the first verse, payment for services rendered is not the primary issue between the Imperial Mother and her sons; in each of the three verses, however, the affective tie displaces the economic contract when the soldiers identify themselves as either "Missis Victorier's sons" (Kipling 1989: 411, lines 14–15) or as "sons of the Widow" (Kipling 1989: 411–12, lines 21, 41).

Designating "Misses Victorier" as the Widow facilitates the slippage from soldier to sonship; one can only ever be a "soldier of the Queen," but one can be a "son of the Widow." As her son, the soldier is imbued with a measure of the Queen's own authority: "Hands off o' the sons o' the Widow, / Hands off o' the goods in 'er shop, / For the Kings must come down an' the Emperors frown / When the Widow at Windsor says 'Stop'!" (Kipling 1989: 411, lines 20–23). But any reflected glory immediately is undercut by the two phrases that seem to conflate sons with goods. As becomes evident throughout the ballad, these claims to sonship can only be ironic because this widow is not holding a place for these sons in her shop. The pleasant fiction of familial relations breaks down as soon as one remembers that Victoria is not the typical widow; she does not hold a place formerly occupied by her dead husband until her son comes of age. The ambiguous status of the Prince Consort meant that his was not a position that could be passed on to a son. The place Queen Victoria held was hers until death. Though Victoria's prolonged mourning for Albert may have forestalled this recognition, her eldest son "Bertie" could attest to the fact that the Widow's power was far from temporary. As evinced in the parenthetical aside "(Poor beggars! we're sent to say 'Stop!')" (Kipling 1989: 411, line 24), the only place the Widow grants her soldiers is a place at the edge of her empire as enforcers of her will and her sentries by sea and land.

For Kipling's soldier-narrator, perhaps the most disturbing fact about the Widow of Windsor is that, though a woman, she is the Lockean Propertied Subject on a grand scale. The ballad obsessively ponders the extent of her holdings. Not only is "'er nick on the cavalry 'orses . . .'er mark on the medical stores" (Kipling 1989: 411, lines 6–7), she also owns

"'alf of creation" (Kipling 1898: 411, line 16). In this ballad, the association between the widow and a notion of excess conjures up a nightmarish vision of empire in which the "Lodge o' the Widow" runs from "The
Pole to the Tropics" (Kipling 1989: 412, lines 25–26). In the second verse,
the Widow's shop metamorphoses into a masonic lodge. In describing
the Widow's empire thus, the narrator conflates *petit bourgeois* economics
and a mysterious network that cannot be escaped. As the imagery
changes, so the tone changes. By the third verse, no metaphor is adequate and the last line is one of despair. Though a source of national
pride, the extent of the British Empire is characterized as oppressive in
its very expansiveness. Even if one could:

> Take 'old o' the wings o' the mornin';
> An' flop round the earth till you're dead;
> . . . you won't get away from the tune that they play
> To the bloomin' old rag over 'ead.
>
> (Kipling 1989: 412, lines 35–38)

The Widow's domain is uncontainable and unwieldy; nevertheless, it is
the soldiers' responsibility to secure, with their lives if need be, the
Widow's pervasive control: "We brought 'er the same with the sword an'
the flame, an'. . . salted it down with our bones" (Kipling 1989: 411, lines
17–18). In the last couplet, the final parenthetical aside "(Poor beggars!
– they'll never see home!)" (Kipling 1989: 412, line 44) turns a godspeed
home into a warning of certain death.

Whereas the ballad "The Widow at Windsor" might be said to pro-
blematize some of the more abstract ideals of empire – military valor
exerted to extend Britain's territories and protect her interests – "The
Widow's Party" (Kipling 1989: 419–20) lodges more concrete complaints
about the hardships endured by "Johnnie" during his tour of duty, in
order to dislodge frivolous metropolitan notions concerning the soldier's
life. Far from attending either picnic or party, conscription for Johnnie
means unpalatable rations, uncomfortable living conditions, and constant danger to life and limb. In one particularly gruesome passage,
Johnnie deliberately plays off a question about eating utensils in order
to discuss military action:

> And some was sliced and some was halved,
> And some was crimped and some was carved,
> And some was gutted and some was starved,
> When the Widow give the party.
>
> (Kipling 1989: 419, lines 22–25)

The lines never make clear to whom the "some" refers. Could it be the fowls referred to in the previous stanza, or Johnnie's messmates, or the "niggers" mentioned in the fifth stanza? In a similarly enigmatic fashion, Johnnie sums up one of the chief rationales for his presence in this hinterland: "We broke a King and we built a road – / A court-house stands where the Reg'ment goed" (Kipling 1989: 420, lines 26–27). The line that follows, "And the river's clean where the raw blood flowed"(Kipling 1989: 420, line 28), exposes the civilizing mission's brutal underside and replaces this now empty explanation with an equally absurd one, that such things happen "When the Widow give a party" (Kipling 1989: 420, line 29). Of course, the party trope does more than cast aspersions on Victoria's abilities as hostess. Imagining the empire as a shop or as a party trivializes the magnitude of British holdings, and turns the Queen into a widow who presides over her little mercantile venture or her picnic in the park. This fantasy, while diverting, fails when the soldier admits that the invitation to the Widow's party is one he cannot refuse. And clearly, this is one party he would like to miss.

Unlike the explicit critique conveyed in the widow ballads, dissatisfaction with the hardships of military life is "manfully" suppressed, and only occasional remarks concerning the poor pay or unfair treatment spike the narrative in the stories collected in *Soldiers Three*. Yet in "The Madness of Private Ortheris" (Kipling 1909: II, 25) the Cockney private expresses a far more intense ambivalence towards the widowed Empress than that seen in the preceding examples. Stanley Ortheris rants:

An I lef' all that for to serve the Widder beyond the seas, where there ain't no women and there ain't no liquor worth 'avin' and there ain't nothin' to see, nor do, nor say, nor feel, nor think. Lord love you, Stanley Orth'ris, but you're a bigger bloomin' fool than the rest o' the reg'ment and Mulvaney wired together! There's the Widder sittin' at 'Ome with a gold crownd on 'er 'ead; and 'ere am Hi, Stanley Orth'ris, the Widder's property, a rottin' Fool! . . . What's the use of grousing there and speaking against the Widow? (Kipling 1909: II, 25–26)

Ortheris's complaint points to an irresolvable crux the soldier faces: he wants to be loyal to the Queen and what she stands for, but he hates what he is doing. His strategy for retaining the Queen as an icon while criticizing her is twofold: first, he refers to Victoria as "Widder," and second, he turns the critique against himself. Ortheris's rant against the deprivations of military life takes as its starting point his initial intent to serve "the Widder" beyond the seas. The use of "widder" conveys more than a mere sense of Cockney speech patterns, recalling as it does the reiterated warning in Dickens's *Pickwick Papers* to "be wery careful o' widders all your life" (Dickens 1837: 353). The comical "widder," with its Dickensian associations already has the effect of destabilizing Ortheris's indictment even as it provides a focal point for his disaffection. Combined with the discrediting title of the story, the use of "widder" in reference to the Queen diffuses the power, if not the poignancy, of Ortheris's critique.

For Ortheris, the "widder" is justifiably sinister. His devotion to the widowed Empress has led him not to adventure beyond the seas, but into what even an uneducated private recognizes as an existential absurdity. Yet because overt condemnation of class system, military institution, or sovereign is unthinkable, Ortheris turns his critique upon himself: he is the "bloomin' fool" (Kipling 1909: II, 25–26). He labels himself a "rottin' fool" for cooperating with what he recognizes are the inequities of class relations that enable "the Widder" to sit "at 'ome" while he is reduced to mere chattel.[10]

Professing a desire to help the raving private return to his senses, the journalist-narrator construes Ortheris's tirade against his status as the "Widder's property" as a personal attack on the widow. Such an interpretation calls attention to the gender issues at stake when a woman who, as widow and as ruler, overturns the conventional subordinate feminine status that reassures males of even the lowest class. Ortheris, however, immediately rejects this assessment and insists "S'elp me Gawd, I never said a word agin 'er, an' I wouldn't – not if I was to desert this minute." Ortheris's apparent recantation gives his friends all the proof they need of the mental instability heralded in the title of the story. The sources of his distress are overlooked in the joint effort to restore him to sanity.

Happily for his comrades and the readers, Ortheris's derangement proves temporary, and he is cured by a few hours of judicious isolation in the bush. But even the Kiplingesque newspaperman who narrates the story does not settle for the easy resolution effected by the kind of jocular ending or edifying moral that conclude the other stories. Nor does he attempt either to mend or conceal the cracks in the dreams of empire exposed by Ortheris's breakdown. Instead, he models the appropriate response: "I left, and on my way home thought a good deal over Ortheris in particular, and my friend Private Thomas Atkins whom I love, in general. But I could not come to any conclusion of any kind whatever" (Kipling 1909: II, 31). Coming to a conclusion would mean either denying the validity of Ortheris's argument or admitting that empire has been built on the backs of the English soldier. Kipling's refusal of closure in this story encourages the reader to continue pondering the plight of the British Tommy while it absolves Kipling of actually attacking government policy.

As contemporary criticism continues to formulate the political consequences of nineteenth-century colonial texts, the ambivalence reflected in the soldier stories and *The Barrack-Room Ballads* towards Queen Victoria calls attention to the meaning of widow as a suggestive category of analysis that complicates Victorian and colonialist studies. Kipling's representation of Victoria as widow makes apparent the centrality of her role in the production of a nineteenth-century nationalistic logic of imperialism even as this category allows narrators of the ballads to interrogate the positions they occupy in relation to the Queen as her servants, sons, or chattel. The two widow ballads and the story just recounted reflect the ambivalence of soldiers who, as loyal English subjects, take pride in their nation's strength and in serving their monarch. Yet, as men, these same soldiers find their position as property humiliating. This mortification is exacerbated rather than soothed when they identify themselves as "*Sons* of the Widow," because they know they will never enjoy directly the material prosperity their labor produces. The critique made by these soldiers of the conditions under which they labor, the nightmare proportions of empire, and the treatment they receive once their active service is over forces a re-examination of assumptions concerning Kipling's status as jingoist supporter of British imperialism. Part of that reexamination involves recognizing how the troping of Queen Victoria as widow inscribes familial relations into the rhetoric of empire.

NOTES

I would like to thank David Baulch, Robert Corbett, Tamara Kaplan, and Nancy Kool for their insightful reading of this chapter. I am indebted also to Kathleen Blake, Marsanne Brammer, Gary Handwerk, and Margaret Homans for their critical contributions to earlier stages of this work.

1 Peter Keating is one of the few critics who does more than mention in passing the two ballads "The Widow at Windsor" and "The Widow's Party." Yet, after a brief discussion of the differences between the two poems, Keating turns to the questions these ballads raised about "whether the young author from India was a flag-waving imperialist or a dangerous radical" (Keating 1994: 74); he does not examine the representation of Victoria as widow.

2 Letter to King Leopold of Belgium (December 24, 1861).

3 Victoria's status as widow also justified the prolonged withdrawal from the state ceremonies and public appearances that she diffidently sought to avoid:

> That the public should wish to see her she fully understands, and has no wish to prevent – quite the contrary; but why this wish should be of so unreasonable and unfeeling a nature, as to *long* to *witness* the spectacle of a poor, broken-hearted widow, nervous and shrinking in *deep mourning*, ALONE, in STATE as a SHOW, where she used to be supported by her husband . . . is a thing *she cannot* understand. (quoted in Tingsten 1972: 115)

4 Having only passed in 1882, The Married Woman's Property Act, which allowed wives in Great Britain to own property independent of their husbands, was a fairly recent development.

5 To name but a few sources that have contributed to what appears to be a burgeoning field of "widow studies": o'Faolain and Martines 1973; Lopata 1979: introduction; Klein 1992; Mirrer 1992; Walker 1993; Bremmer and van den Bosch 1995.

6 The supra-exceptional case of the Queen's relation to the Prince of Wales illustrates on a grand scale the problems when the widow's power is not temporary. Victoria's longevity and her refusal to relinquish any responsibility to her eldest son prevented "Bertie" from effectually coming to power until well into middle age, thus confining the playboy prince to a kind of stasis.

7 For evidence that Kipling's concern for the general disregard of the army was justified, see Brian Bond's "The Late-Victorian Army," in which Bond calls attention to the unpopularity of the army in the country at large and its neglect by the government in peacetime (Bond 1961: 616).

8 Reference to the Queen has the ostensible effect of leveling the class playing field. Everyone in the army is a servant to the Queen, at least in the minds of soldiers like Ortheris, who asserts in the story, "His Private Honour," "I'm a private servin' of the Queen, an' as good a man as 'e is . . . for all 'is commission an' 'is airs an' 'is money" (Kipling 1989: 257). The effect of leveling class differences intensifies when the British Tommy claims a familial relationship to Victoria as he does in a number of the *Barrack-Room Ballads*.

9 The concern over poor pay becomes a dominant theme in the military tales and *Barrack-Room Ballads*. Although the most overt expressions of dissatisfaction are linked to the Widow, this commentary often includes oblique glances at the Queen. In the story "The Man Who Was," Kipling's soldiers toast the Queen "upon whose pay they were falsely supposed to settle their mess bills" (Kipling 1909: II, 400). The ballad "A Shillin' a Day" ends every stanza of complaint with an emphatic if ironic "GAWD SAVE THE QUEEN" (Kipling 1989: 427), while in "Private Ortheris's Song" (a piece that did not make it into the *Barrack-Room Ballads*) the narrator begins his lament over life in the army with the line "The Queen gave me a shillin' / To fight for her over the seas" (Kipling 1989: 425), wryly indicating that the wages earned did not quite compensate the soldier for the hardships he has endured.

10 Kipling uses the same rhetorical move in the ballad attributed to the same Cockney soldier, "Private Ortheris's Song." In the song like the story, a recitation of victimage is turned back upon the speaker when he admits "My very worst friend from beginning to end / By the blood of a mouse was myself!" (Kipling 1989: 426).

PART IV

*Afterlife*

# CHAPTER 13

# Queen Victoria in the Funnyhouse: Adrienne Kennedy and the rituals of colonial possession

## Janet Winston

In her memoirs *People Who Led to My Plays*, the African American play-wright Adrienne Kennedy describes her life's work, through a frag-mented array of verbal and visual snapshots, in terms of images that influenced her psyche. Notable among these is a statue of Queen Victoria, which embodied for Kennedy her ambivalent connection to England through her maternal white grandfather and those "people who had colonized [her] West African ancestors" (Kennedy 1990: 105). Recalling her voyage to London in 1960 before traveling to a newly inde-pendent West Africa, Kennedy explains: "Queen Victoria [would] come to [haunt my mind]. The statue we saw of Victoria in front of Buckingham Palace was the single most dramatic, startling statue I'd seen. Here was a woman who had dominated an age" (Kennedy 1987b: 118). In what follows, I examine this monumental image of Queen Victoria and its significance in one of Kennedy's dramatic works.

Uttered in response to Victoria's statue and within the context of *People*, Kennedy's remarks above speak as much to Victoria's influence iconographically as to her power politically. While the Queen reigned over "an Empire which by 1890 comprised more than a quarter of all the territory on the surface of the world" (Abrams 1979: 927, 936), the Queen's image exerted its influence both domestically and globally. Indeed, although Victoria spent much of her reign within the small radius of London, Windsor, Balmoral, and the Isle of Wight, and for many years in near seclusion, her eidetic presence was ubiquitous throughout the British Empire (Longford 1964a: 311–14; Ormond 1973: 478). As biographer Stanley Weintraub notes, by the time of Victoria's Diamond Jubilee in 1897, "few homes in Britain or among expatriates in the Empire were without some representation of the youthful or aged Queen – on calendars, oleographs, cabinet photos, jubilee mugs, com-memorative plates – and on every postage stamp of the millions printed and posted since 1840 . . . For most of her subjects, the Queen had

already metamorphosed . . . into myth" (Weintraub 1987: 579–80). And
of the Victorian "[s]culpture [that] quite literally followed the globe" in
the form of exports to the colonies of British monuments commemorating imperial figures, the Queen was a common subject (Read 1982:
368). Her graven image presided in cities around the world – in
Rangoon, Colombo, Calcutta, Bombay, Lucknow, Lahore, Karachi,
Kingston, Durban, Port Elizabeth, Montreal, Belfast, and Dublin, to
name just a few.[1]

Such "monumental sculpture," Edward Said reminds us, in contrib-
uting to "the physical transformation of the imperial realm," was part
of the imposition of "an ideological vision [of empire] implemented and
sustained not only by direct domination and physical force but much
more effectively over a long time by *persuasive means,* the quotidian processes of hegemony" (Said 1993: 109). Relying on notions of racial and
cultural supremacy – the so-called white man's burden to "spread
Western civilization" and "give good government to other races" presumed inferior (Eldridge 1978: 2, 1) – Britain's "ideological vision"
required an icon of an infallible yet benevolent empire (Spurr 1993: 32).
Thus, as Lytton Strachey explains, "[t]he Queen was hailed . . . as the
mother of her people and as the embodied symbol of their imperial
greatness" (Strachey 1921: 383): the "Great White Mother" (Fredeman
1987: 8).

Victoria's inscription on the globe did not always exert the ideological
control intended of it, however – in Dublin, for example, her statue was
dubbed "the Hippopotamus" (Read 1982: 371) – nor does her maternal
image function monolithically. As Adrienne Munich demonstrates,
Victoria's actual and iconic status as a maternal monarch in Victorian
England's ethos of separate spheres is a cultural paradox, which manifests itself in late nineteenth-century literature and art as an "excess of
representation" (of Victoria and of excessive female rulers) and a representation of Victoria as excess (Munich 1987: 265–70, 278). As icon of
empire and "excess of representation," Victoria comes to represent in
twentieth-century literature both colonialism's excesses and the powers
and limits of colonial representation.[2] For although postindependence
governments and former colonial subjects have been in the process of
removing statues of Queen Victoria and other monuments of empire,
by either dismantling them or physically displacing or abandoning them
in overgrown parks or uninhabited reliquaries[3] (see plate 13.1), postcolonial writers have been appropriating such images for their literature.
They do so, not to memorialize or mythologize imperialism further, but

Plate 13.1 Statue of Queen Victoria overthrown in Georgetown, Guyana after independence in 1966.

to engage in a form of what Said calls "decolonizing cultural resistance" – writing that disrupts the West's conception of culture and history by "enter[ing] into the discourse of Europe and the West, to mix with it, transform it, to make it acknowledge marginalized or suppressed or forgotten histories" (Said 1993: 216). Constituting a type of postcolonial revisionist practice, this literature employs ekphrasis – the verbal representation of a work of visual art (Meltzer 1987: 21; Krieger 1992: 6) – to recontextualize and refigure imperial monuments for the purpose of representing notions of empire, such as the mythos of a benevolent imperialism.

Mary Lou Emery historicizes the use of ekphrasis from *The Iliad* to "My Last Duchess" within the context of colonial expansion, demonstrating how the trope has been deployed as both a tool of and a weapon against the European imperialist project (Emery 1994). In doing so, she expands on the argument made in recent studies that ekphrasis foregrounds the power of representation to pass itself off as nature (Meltzer 1987: 215–17; Krieger 1992: 258–59) and the implication in W. J. T.

Mitchell's work that ekphrasis "is a trope for representation itself *and* for what lies beyond representation" (Emery 1994). According to Emery, "[t]hese traditions [of ekphrasis] formalize the power of the colonizing patriarchal gaze embedding it in a trope that then links the gazer with divine authority and lends access to the real and natural as it structures founding myths of nations and empire" (Emery 1994). As Emery's work on ekphrasis and Caribbean literature makes clear, postcolonial writers rework ekphrasis in order to counter imperialist representations as well as to reveal the use of the trope and, by extension, the power of representation in the project of colonization (Emery 1994; 1997).

If within this postcolonial context we consider Françoise Meltzer's notion of ekphrasis as "the attempt of writing to overcome the power of the image in a mimetically oriented culture of images" (Meltzer 1987: 102), then the representational excess that Munich identifies – Victoria "as contradiction, nonsense, massiveness" (Munich 1987: 278) – as well as the proliferation of Victoria's image as an imperial icon may be, in part, what these twentieth-century ekphrastic texts seek to bring under their discursive control. The image of an expansive yet contradictory queen is either contained by a textual frame or immobilized as statuary and further subordinated by an all-pervasive verbal field.

Furthermore, if, through metonymic extension, Queen Victoria represents the Victorian Empire, and if, as Emery claims, ekphrasis represents representation, then ekphrastic images of the Queen can be said to represent colonial discourse itself. As with Victoria's image of maternal monarchy, this discourse is "constructed around an ambivalence" (Bhabha 1984: 126). According to Homi Bhabha, "the colonial presence is always ambivalent, split between its appearance as original and authoritative and its articulation as repetition and difference . . . The 'part' (which must be the colonialist foreign body) must be representative of the 'whole' (conquered country), but the right of representation is based on its radical difference" (Bhabha 1985a: 150, 153). As a result, colonial discourse – the system of signs constructed to explain and authorize this presence – is contradictory also, fraught with "discursive doubleness" (Bhabha 1985b: 74). Bhabha describes this contradictory mode of colonial discourse as "mimicry": "the desire for a reformed, recognizable Other, as *a subject of a difference that is almost the same, but not quite*" (Bhabha 1984: 126). By exploiting its own inherent ambivalence, mimicry not only institutes colonial power but also threatens it. Resistance, therefore, "is not necessarily an oppositional act of political intention, nor is it the simple negation or exclusion of the 'content' of an other culture" (Bhabha 1985a: 153). Rather, "[it] is the effect of [this] ambivalence" – a *"menace"* – that "disrupts [colonial discourse's] authority" through "the sign of the inappropriate" (Bhabha 1985a: 153; 1984: 126–27, 129).

Statues of Queen Victoria reveal this ambivalence. On the one hand, imperial texts themselves, such monuments are intended to signify and through such signification to enforce British authority and dominion abroad. They represent Britain in the image of the "Great White Queen" (Morris 1978: 369) as omnipotent and omnipresent – a dominating "difference" from the colonized peoples of the territories in which many of these statues stand. Forged in metal and stone by Victorian sculptors according to European aesthetic conventions, they *stand in* for "the violent dislocation, the *Entstellung* [displacement] of the act of colonization" itself, which imposes English political, economic, and cultural conventions at the same time that it displaces indigenous social structures and peoples (Bhabha 1985a: 156).

On the other hand, the sculpted images of the Queen as imperial mother also attempt to interpellate colonial peoples as *her children* – rightful inheritors and obedient subjects of the British Empire. Such maternal images are implicated, then, in representing Britain as a consolidating force of sameness. Describing such paradoxes of colonial discourse, David Spurr explains that "the desire to emphasize racial and cultural difference as a means for establishing superiority takes place alongside the desire to efface difference and to gather the colonized into the fold of an all-embracing civilization" (Spurr 1993: 32). Thus, statues of Queen Victoria represent the ambivalence of the colonial presence at the same time as they attempt to produce discursively colonial subjects who are "almost the same, but not quite."[4]

Consider, for example, Sir Thomas Brock and Sir Aston Webb's *Victoria Memorial* outside Buckingham Palace[5] – the monument that so captivated Kennedy. Atop the central group of statues stands a winged figure of "Victory." Beneath her, as the human embodiment of this mythic symbol of triumph (Ricks 1987: 136–37), sits Victoria, looking stalwart and impassive (see plate 13.2). In one hand, the Empress-Queen holds a royal scepter; in the other, an orb suggestive of the globe of the imperial world. Opposite Victoria, and in stark contrast to these emblems of victory in battle and stern rule, is a sculpture of a mother with her infant and two small children. Smaller sculptures representing the colonies adorn "gateposts surrounding the main Memorial" (Read 1982: 379). In "West Africa," for example, a cherub figure resembling one of the children in

Plate 13.2 Statue of Queen Victoria by Sir Thomas Brock from the *Victoria Memorial*,
1910–24, London.

"Motherhood" holds back a leopard and an eagle – representative, presumably, of the supposedly savage forces of this land. This monument
memorializes, then, the imperial queen *and* the imperialist ideology of her
reign: Victoria is figured by association as both unvanquishable force and
"Great White Mother," who civilizes and protects her so-called children
– those subjects of territories colonized by her gaze.

Significant to my discussion here, this monumental statue informs not
only Kennedy's imagination but also that of her heroine Negro-Sarah
of *Funnyhouse of a Negro*, Kennedy's first published play. As Kennedy
describes in her memoirs, "In my play I would soon have the heroine,
Sarah, talk to a replica of this statue. *Finally* the dialogue with a statue
would be explicit and concrete. And the *statue* would reply; the *statue*
would inform my character of her *inner* thoughts. The *statue* would reveal
my character's secrets to herself" (Kennedy 1987b: 118). In *Funnyhouse*, as
in *People Who Led to My Plays*, Kennedy foregrounds the powerful influence of images on the psyche – that aesthetic representations such as
photographs and statues are, in Kennedy's words, "forces that caused me
to act" (Kennedy 1987b: 116; 1989: 145, 148). In this one-act play – begun
during Kennedy's visit to Ghana in 1961 (Wilkerson 1992: 71–72), published in 1962, and first produced in 1964 – Queen Victoria quite literally and figuratively takes center stage: a replica of her statue serves as
the play's dominant stage prop and an animated version of the statue
inhabits the protagonist's psyche.

Kennedy's evident fascination with royalty[6] reveals itself in an even
earlier work, the short story "Because of the King of France" (1961), her
first published piece. In it a young man tries to escape racial persecution
in the United States by fleeing to the Virgin Islands. He writes himself
into a narrative of royal patronage in which he becomes the favored
pianist of Louis XIV. His escape fantasies – narrated in epistolary form
to his class-conscious cousin (the story's narrator) – are thwarted,
however, when he witnesses in the palace's "Hall of Mirrors" his seven-
teenth-century Corsican double being publicly humiliated by the king.
The story suggests the enduring nature of racism – spanning centuries,
cultures, and narrative plots only to subsume its victims in repetitions of
humiliation and violence. Significantly, as Lois Overbeck notes,
"Because of the King of France" foreshadows several of the themes and
textual strategies that Kennedy later develops in *Funnyhouse of a Negro*
(Overbeck 1992: 23): the pressures to assimilate into white middle-class
culture, the internalization and repetition of racist stereotypes, the metaphor of the hall of mirrors, and the menacing lure of European royalty.

The fact that the story was published in *Black Orpheus*, the premier literary journal of Anglophone Africa, is equally important to my discussion here. In the company of literature by African, West Indian, and other African American authors – Camara Laye, Wole Soyinka, Ama Ata Aidoo, Aimé Césaire, Richard Wright, and Langston Hughes, to name just a few (Benson 1986: 26–28) – Kennedy's work was firmly established within the context of African diasporic writing, as Paul Bryant-Jackson explains (Bryant-Jackson 1992: 55). Several critics, such as Bryant-Jackson, Paul Harrison, and James Hatch, acknowledge Kennedy's commitment to African cultural and aesthetic traditions.[7] Their perspectives offer a necessary supplement to readings that place Kennedy "at the periphery of [the more polemical] Black Theatre Movement" of the 1960s and 1970s and, consequently, characterize her work as exploring instead universal themes of oppression and human alienation (Williams 1985: 133–34), individual psychosis, and a singularly American sensibility (Blau 1984: 521, 531–32).

Although the notion of a Pan-African approach to literature is not new (Ngugi 1986: 97–98), Carole Boyce Davies reconceptualizes diasporic writing within the specific context of international black women's literature. She uses the term "uprising textualities" to designate works that offer an anti-imperialist critique and represent resistance to multiple kinds and dimensions of oppression (Davies 1994: 86–89, 96, 108). With this conceptual framework – black women's resistance literature of the African diaspora – and the insights of postcolonial discourse theory, I approach *Funnyhouse of a Negro*. In interviews and autobiographical writings, Kennedy underscores the sense of connection she feels to African writers and the profound influence her West African trip had on her writing in general and on *Funnyhouse* in particular:[8]

I would say almost every image in *Funnyhouse* took form while I was in West Africa where I became aware of masks. I lived in Ghana at a most fortunate time. Ghana had just won its freedom. It was wonderful to see that liberation . . . I couldn't cling to what I'd been writing – it changed me so . . . I think the main thing was that I discovered a strength in being a black person and a connection to West Africa. (Kennedy 1987a: 248–49, quoted in Overbeck 1992: 23).

Set in a New York City brownstone in the mid-twentieth century, *Funnyhouse of a Negro* features a young African American woman – the protagonist, Negro-Sarah – being possessed by several mythohistorical figures, who are aspects of herself – Queen Victoria, the Duchess of Hapsburg, Jesus, and Patrice Lumumba – as well as a vision of her

father coming back from Africa to find her. At the end of the play, Sarah
hangs herself in her rented room in front of a statue of Queen Victoria.
Afterwards, two white characters – her Jewish boyfriend Raymond and
her landlady Mrs. Conrad – discover her corpse, laugh, and tell stories
about her life. Sarah's many selves most often are played onstage by
different actors, a circumstance necessitated by Kennedy's use of language in the play, which includes repetitious lines often spoken in unison
or in intricate patterns of call and response.

Both the trope of postcolonial ekphrasis and the discourse of colonial
mimicry work together in this play to suggest a metatextual reading: that
*Funnyhouse* is about representation. In particular, the play concerns the
consolidation and imposition of static identities as a means of social
control as well as theatricality,[9] how performance can be a process for
dispossessing such identities and moving beyond circumscript roles.

The *funnyhouse* of the play's title is itself a trope of representation. A
funhouse with ubiquitous mirrors of distortion offering grotesque
images from warped lenses and evincing terror, Kennedy's funnyhouse
serves as a metaphor for whites' constructions of black identity. And as
with funhouse mirrors that face each other, Negro-Sarah's many selves
interminably reflect grotesque images of blackness (Diamond 1992: 136)
in their relentless ridiculing of Sarah's father for his skin color and his
desire to return to Africa to "heal the race" (Kennedy 1988: 14): "My
father is a nigger who drives me to misery"; "He comes through the
jungle to find me"; "He is the blackest one of them all"; "He haunted
my conception, diseased my birth"; "He was a wild black beast who
raped my mother"; "He is the wilderness" (Kennedy 1988: 11, 3, 8, 17,
10, 21). Throughout the play, blackness, and in particular the black man,
is associated with the jungle, bestiality, and rape in keeping with cen-
turies-old white stereotypes about Africans and their descendants as
belonging to a primitive "backward race" (Said 1979: 206; Stepan 1990:
42).

Such stereotypes are rooted, of course, in the rhetoric of European
imperialism, which in *Funnyhouse* is emblematized by the statue of Queen
Victoria. Kennedy appropriates this statue as imperialist icon and recon-
textualizes it within her own narrative of decolonization. Specifically,
she takes the statue of Victoria out of the memorials and colonial "pleasure parks" erected for its display (Morris 1968: 330, 354–55) and *displaces*
it in a pleasure park of her own making – the grotesque funnyhouse – in
order to critique and ultimately fracture its colonizing imperial gaze. Set
constructions for productions of *Funnyhouse*, such as the 1968 Petit

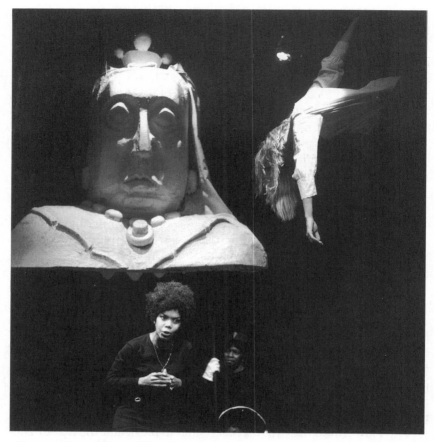

Plate 13.3 Bust of Queen Victoria from the Paris production of *Funnyhouse of a Negro* (*Drôle de baraque*) at the Petit Odéon, 1968, directed by Jean-Marie Serreau.

Odéon production in Paris and the 1995 Signature Theatre Company production in New York, feature statues ranging from the macabre to the sublime (see plates 13.3 and 13.4). In the 1968 production, Queen Victoria's statue takes the form of a monstrous, disembodied head; in the recent production, the statue represents the entire body of a younger, thinner, and less menacing Victoria, who has been decapitated.[10] The emphasis in both statues on Victoria's head – either by its massiveness or by its violent exclusion[11] – underscores the Queen's position as head of the empire and, as such, the power of her *commanding gaze*.

Whatever the statue's form on stage, Kennedy's text makes clear that

Plate 13.4 Sculpture of Queen Victoria from Signature Theatre Company's production of *Funnyhouse of a Negro*, New York, 1995, directed by Caroline Jackson Smith. Set design by E. David Cosier. Sculpted by Tom Moore.

it has nightmarish implications for her protagonist's psyche. As Negro-Sarah describes in her first monologue:

[My room] is also Victoria's chamber. Queen Victoria Regina's. Partly because it is consumed by a gigantic plaster statue of Queen Victoria who is my idol and partly for other reasons . . . It is a sitting figure, a replica of one in London, and a thing of astonishing whiteness . . . Raymond says it is a thing of terror, possessing the quality of nightmares, suggesting large and probable deaths. And of course he is right. (Kennedy 1988: 5)

As the embodiment of the "Great White Queen" and the emblem of empire, this statue serves as a monument to an Anglo-European supremacy erected upon the foundation of racism. Modeled after the figure of Queen Victoria at Buckingham Palace, the statue also represents European aestheticism in opposition to a supposed African primitivism.

Kennedy highlights this contrast by incorporating the black mask into the play's repertoire of images. The black mask symbolizes both African aesthetics and white stereotyping. Although originally constructed and used for ceremonial purposes, African masks (and other cultural artifacts) were plundered by European explorers, who ripped them out of their ritual contexts and took them to Europe. European scholars and artists either dismissed their artistic value or fetishized them for supposedly embodying a so-called primitive aesthetic.[12] Such misreadings served to confirm racist assumptions about African cultures as primitive and thus helped consolidate European notions of cultural superiority used to justify colonialism.

The black mask is also suggestive of "blackface," which whites and later blacks donned in minstrel shows – those crude imitations of black folk life performed for the amusement of whites[13] – and thus signifies the belittling roles that the dominant culture forces African Americans to assume (Fabre 1983: 120, 123, 218). In one of the play's many versions of reality, Negro-Sarah "bludgeoned [her] father's head with an ebony mask" (Kennedy 1988: 6, 13). According to *Webster's*, "bludgeon" means both "to strike with a heavy club" and to "coerce." Thus, Negro-Sarah's attack on her father can be read as a symbolic murder: her rejection of his pride in his African heritage and her coercion of him to wear the whites' masks of Black identity, to become the "wild black beast," "the rapist," "the wilderness" of her besieged imagination (Kennedy 1988: 5, 10). By transforming a sacred object of African ritual into an instrument of coercion and destruction, Negro-Sarah rejects her black identity and aligns herself with the European:

My friends will be white. I need them as an embankment to keep me from reflecting too much upon the fact that I am a Negro. For, like all educated Negroes – out of life and death essential – I find it necessary to maintain a stark fortress against recognition of myself. My white friends, like myself, will be shrewd, intellectual and anxious for death. Anyone's death. I will mistrust them, as I do myself. But if I had not wavered in my opinion of myself, then my hair would never have fallen out. And if my hair hadn't fallen out, I wouldn't have bludgeoned my father's head with an ebony mask. (Kennedy 1988: 6)

Identifying with her light-skinned mother, who believes "she had trapped herself in blackness" by marrying a dark-skinned man committed to "heal[ing] the pain of the race" (Kennedy 1988: 15, 19), Sarah is one of "the assimilated women" in black women's writing, who, according to Mary Helen Washington, are "victims . . . of a kind of psychic violence that alienates them from their roots and cuts them off from real contact with their own people and also from a part of themselves" (Washington 1982: 213). Kennedy depicts this psychic violence as the internalized hatred of blackness and the consequent striving to efface one's blackness to gain white approval. Desiring assimilation into Euro-American culture, Sarah "long[s] to become even a more pallid Negro . . . pallid like Negroes on the covers of American Negro magazines; soulless, educated and irreligious" and "to live in rooms with European antiques and my [statue of] Queen Victoria" (Kennedy 1988: 5–6).

This statue of Victoria forms the centerpiece of Negro-Sarah's growing collection of European artifacts: her "imitations of Edith Sitwell,"[14] "walls of books," and "photographs of castles and monarchs of England" and "Roman ruins" (Kennedy 1988: 5–6). Correspondingly, the persona of the "Great White Mother" dominates Sarah's burgeoning assimilationist consciousness (Sollors 1991: 512–13). In contrast to the play's father figures – Sarah's father and Patrice Lumumba – who, as Werner Sollors explains, "[represent] the quest for African origins" (Sollors 1991: 510), the statue of the white imperial matriarch signifies the ethos of assimilationism in the United States as it encodes colonialist domination abroad (Curb 1980: 181–82). As Sarah says in her first monologue: "Victoria always wants me to tell her of whiteness. She wants me to tell her of a royal world where everything and everyone is white and there are no unfortunate black ones. For as we of royal blood know, black is evil and has been from the beginning. Even before my mother's hair started to fall out. Before she was raped by a wild black beast. Black was evil" (Kennedy 1988: 5).

Several critics read Sarah's identification with her light-skinned

mother and her desire for assimilation within the context of the convention of the "mulatto" character in (particularly African) American literature, who is "[t]orn between the inseparable yet irreconcilable black
and white worlds."[15] This biracial character embodies both the history
of the violence of racism during slavery (the forced concubinage and
rape of the enslaved African woman by the white slave master) and the
continuing strife of black–white relations in the United States (Berzon
1978: 53). Yet, rather than signifying merely a dichotomy between white
and black worlds, England and African America, or Europe and Africa,
Kennedy's use of the mulatto figure in *Funnyhouse* suggests a triangula-
tion of identity: a metaphoric transcription on the body of Negro-
Sarah's imagination of the terrible *triple passage* – the movement of slave
ships from England to West Africa and then to the Americas. For Negro-
Sarah is not merely a "divided soul" (Berzon 1978: 62); she is multiply
fractured, and her fractured being incorporates figures from multiple
locations along the "triangular" slave trade's devastating route:[16] Queen
Victoria, the Duchess of Hapsburg (and Empress of Mexico), and Jesus
– as figures of imperial acquisition, colonial rule, and Christian missionary intrusion – represent Europe; Patrice Lumumba – as Zaire's first
African prime minister and a symbol for Kennedy "of a freed Africa"
(Kennedy 1987b: 119) – represents West Africa;[17] and Negro-Sarah – as
an African American victim of the violence of racism in the United
States, a legacy of that triple passage – represents America.

However, despite Sarah's psyche being inscribed with the violence of
both contemporary racism and the historical slave trade, this multiplicity of locations and identifications gestures toward a potentially libera-
tory subject position,[18] one which embodies what Carole Boyce Davies
and Mae Henderson refer to respectively as "migratory subjectivity"
and "speaking in tongues" (Davies 1994: 36; Henderson 1990: 122).
Theorizing black women's writing and identity in the African diaspora
as crossing boundaries and existing in multiple locations and times,
Davies argues that "Black female subjectivity . . . can be conceived not
primarily in terms of domination, subordination or 'subalternization,'
but in terms of slipperiness, elsewhereness," which leads to a "path of
movement outside the terms of dominant discourses" (Davies 1994: 36,
37).

In a related move, Henderson argues that "[w]hat is at once
characteristic and suggestive about black women's writing is its inter-
locutory, or dialogic, character, reflecting not only a relationship with the
'other(s),' but an internal dialogue with the plural aspects of self that

constitute the matrix of black female subjectivity" – "'the other in ourselves'" (Henderson 1990: 118, 119). Using the religious practice of "speaking in tongues" as a "trope for both glossolalia ['intimate, private, inspired utterances'] and heteroglossia ['polyphony, multivocality, and plurality of voices']" (Henderson 1990: 123, 124), Henderson delineates how "black women writers weave into their work competing and complementary discourses – discourses that seek both to adjudicate competing claims and witness common concerns" (Henderson 1990: 124). As Henderson explains, "[t]he notion of speaking in tongues . . . leads us away from an examination of how the Other has written/read black women and toward an examination of how black women have written the other(s)' writing/reading black women" (Henderson 1990: 125). Thus, in theorizing black women's writing, both Davies and Henderson conceive of the multiple social, geographical, and discursive locations of black female subjectivity represented within it as making possible a dislocation from and critique of dominant discourses.

*Funnyhouse* launches just such a critique by foregrounding mobility and multivocality in its representation of Negro-Sarah. Eschewing assertions of authentic black identity, such as those found in realist African–American dramas of the 1950s (Harrison 1989: xvi–xviii), Kennedy's play dislocates itself from the dominant discourses it contains by drawing on African and African-influenced cultural practices to shape its form.[19] Specifically, *Funnyhouse* relies on the art of mimicry characteristic of the social and religious rituals of African masquerade and spirit possession.

During colonial occupation in Africa, African masquerades, such as the masked comedies of the Anang and the Afikpo peoples of southeastern Nigeria, frequently parodied Europeans, including colonial officials and the king of England (George VI), as Fritz Kramer documents (Kramer 1993: 167–70; Messenger 1971: 217). Accompanied by masked dancers and singers in the case of the okumkpa plays of the Afikpo, and by dancers, "acrobats, conjurers, tight-rope walkers . . . stilt dancers, [and] marionettes" in the ekong plays of the Anang, players wore specially created or acquired masks and costumes as they acted out scenes caricaturing the white man and those villagers who affectedly imitated him (Kramer 1993: 167–70). Although the political importance of these masked dramas has been contested, according to Kramer they "did sometimes take on a leading role in the polemics against the foreign culture" (Kramer 1993: 164–70) and were regarded by some Africans as "our force against the foreigner."[20]

Similarly, African–Caribbean Carnival masquerades served as a means of mocking colonial authority and frequently led to large-scale anticolonial uprisings.[21] Providing a few days of release for enslaved West Indians from the oppressive system of labor and the rigid social hierarchy enforced by the white plantocracy, these festivals were punctuated with parodies of European people and culture: black West Indians donned masks or powdered their faces and hair with white flour, dressed in elaborate costumes, and performed imitations of European dances and British plays.[22] Such performances often included satirical songs denouncing the slave masters, and processions featuring caricatures of well-known European figures, such as the Archbishop of Canterbury, Admiral Nelson, "Brittania," King William IV, and Queen Victoria (Abrahams and Szwed 1983: 242–43, 250, 270).

Parodies such as these performed by indigenous and enslaved peoples in resistance to colonial domination inform *Funnyhouse of a Negro*. For the *funnyhouse* of the play's title is not merely a metaphor for the protagonist's psychic fragmentation. Nor is it solely a reference to an "'amusement park attraction whose gates are flanked by two enormous grimacing figures – a metaphor for America' . . . where one can feel the 'white world . . . ridiculing the Negro,'" as several critics, quoting Kennedy herself, explain (Fabre 1983: 119; Sollors 1991: 514). Clearly, the funnyhouse is an allusion to the Caribbean festival of Carnival. The "whiteface" called for in the scene directions for the actors playing Queen Victoria and the Duchess of Hapsburg (Kennedy 1988: 3; Fabre 1983: 119–20) is suggestive of the masks of Europeans constructed and worn during Caribbean Carnival and African masked comedies: "*It is an alabaster face, the skin drawn tightly over the high cheekbones, great dark eyes that seem gouged out of the head, a high forehead, a full mouth and a head of frizzy hair. If the characters do not wear a mask then the face must be highly powdered and possess a hard expressionless quality and a stillness as in the face of death*" (Kennedy 1988: 3). The Queen's and Duchess's white faces resemble death masks, suggestive of the "large and probable deaths" associated with the Queen's statue in Sarah's room (Kennedy 1988: 5). Such white masks suggest the wearers' distance from the white roles they represent,[23] and in reversing the convention of blackface used to ridicule African Americans, they serve in Kennedy's play as a potent reminder of the transgressive power of carnivalesque "turn about" (Emery 1990: 76–77; Bakhtin 1968: 11). If, according to Mikhail Bakhtin, medieval and early modern European "carnival celebrated temporary liberation from the prevailing truth and from the established order" and signified "the feast of becoming, change, and renewal" (Bakhtin 1968: 10), then in *Funnyhouse* the Carnival trope celebrates forms of dramatic practice implicated in a more far-reaching process of liberation and social transformation.[24]

These practices of African masquerade and African Caribbean Carnival celebrated in *Funnyhouse* illustrate Bhabha's concept of colonial mimicry. Indeed, they enact the "process by which the look of surveillance returns as the displacing gaze of the disciplined, where the observer becomes the observed and 'partial' representation rearticulates the whole notion of *identity* and alienates it from essence" (Bhabha 1984: 129). Queen Victoria's surveillant look as embodied in her ubiquitous statue becomes in *Funnyhouse* what is looked at – the object of anticolonial mockery and narrative displacement. Neither Sarah nor any of her selves offers the reader or viewer an essential black or white identity. All are masks aimed at "producing a partial vision of the colonizer's presence" (Bhabha 1984: 129). Occasionally these masks are dropped to reveal, not "Black consciousness," but the lie of white mythologies. As Sarah says in her second monologue, "I clung loyally to the lie of relationships, again and again seeking to establish a connection between my characters. Jesus is Victoria's son . . . A loving relationship exists between myself and Queen Victoria, a love between myself and Jesus, but they are lies" (Kennedy 1988: 7).

Rather than interpreting such lines and indeed the play as a whole as a Surrealist exploration of the unconscious, as critics – following Kennedy's lead (Kennedy 1977: 47) – often do, we must acknowledge the invocation of another African cultural practice, the ritual of spirit possession.[25] In place of an essential black consciousness, Kennedy offers an African–inspired dramatic form complete with incantational language, foreign beings taking possession of the protagonist's body and spirit, a sculpted figure used as an idol, and a ritual sacrifice at the performance's conclusion.[26]

Closer to incantation than to ordinary speech, Kennedy's repetitious language in *Funnyhouse* contributes to the play's overall ritualistic quality.[27] The repetition of such lines as "My father is a nigger who drives me to misery" and "he was a wild black beast who raped my mother" (Kennedy 1988: 10–11) ultimately serves to undermine the very narrative these words propose. Uttered in "whiteface," these lines exemplify Bhabha's concept of discursive mimicry, which "repeats rather than re-presents" (Bhabha 1984: 128). As Trinh T. Minh-Ha explains, "rehashing stereotypes to criticize stereotyping can . . . constitute a powerful practice . . . When repetition reflects on itself as repetition, it constitutes this doubling back movement through which language . . . looks at itself exerting power and, therefore, creates for itself possibilities to repeatedly thwart its own power" (Trinh 1991: 190). Through repetition, the racist language in *Funnyhouse* is exposed as a technology of domination. Revealing only "authorized versions of otherness" (Bhabha 1984: 129), such words point to "what lies between them" (Trinh 1991: 191): Negro-Sarah's "migratory subjectivity," to use Davies's phrase – an identity that cannot be fixed or named.[28]

Kennedy's use of language overall in *Funnyhouse* suggests the practice of "speaking in tongues" – Henderson's term, drawn from the linguistic traditions of the Pentecostal Holiness church, for black women's discourse that is both "dialogic" ("testimonial") and "dialectical" ("competitive") (Henderson 1990: 121). As Henderson explains,

[S]peaking unknown tongues (tongues known only to God) is in fact a sign of election, or holiness . . . But there is a second connotation to the notion of speaking in tongues – one that suggests not glossolalia, but heteroglossia, the ability to speak in diverse languages. While glossolalia refers to the ability to "utter the mysteries of the spirit," heteroglossia describes the ability to speak in the multiple languages of public discourse. (Henderson 1990: 122–23)

As are the elect through whom God speaks, the protagonist of Kennedy's play is possessed with the spirits of others who speak through her: not God, but Victoria, the Duchess, Jesus, and Lumumba. And this "heteroglossia" of Negro-Sarah's multiple selves is also a kind of "glossolalia" or "inspired [utterance]" suggestive of religious ritual (Henderson 1990: 124).

Yet, instead of uttering "ecstatic, rapturous, inspired speech, based on a relation of intimacy and identification between the individual and God" (Henderson 1990: 123), Negro-Sarah's selves recite the rhetoric of European colonial domination. Consider, for example, the following lines in *Funnyhouse* spoken by Jesus:

JESUS. Through my apocalypses and my raging sermons I have tried to escape him, through God Almighty I have tried to escape being black . . . I am going to Africa and kill this black man named Patrice Lumumba. Why? Because all my life I believed my Holy Father to be God, but now I know that my father is a black man. I have no fear for whatever I do, I will do in the name of God, I will do in the name of Albert Saxe Coburg, in the name of Victoria, Queen Victoria Regina, the monarch of England, I will. (Kennedy 1988: 19–20)

Here the invocation of God, Albert, and the Queen to sanction the assassination of the African leader, and the satirical twist on the debate over Jesus' racial identity (Lincoln 1973: 63–65) mock the ritualized rhetoric of empire. Jesus' sermon exemplifies not another example of repetition to undo stereotyping, but a specific instance of mimicry in which "the sign of the inappropriate" arises from "the ambivalent world of the 'not quite/not white'" (Bhabha 1984: 126, 132).[29]

Such gestures of mimicry, in which representative "spirits of colonization" (Stoller 1989: xxii) come to life imitating colonial customs, characterize the spirit possession rituals enacted in parts of colonial Africa. In response to Europe's occupation of Africa, several of these possession cults evolved for the express purpose of opposing white rule and later were responsible for "[s]ome of the greatest insurrections in the early colonial period" (Kramer 1993: 128). One group, the Hauka cult, practiced by the Songhay people in French colonial Niger and later by the Songhay and the Zerma in the former British colonial Gold Coast, set up their own social and political system in "bold defiance of French rule" (Kramer 1993: 134; Stoller 1992: 147, 155; 1989: 152). They further opposed European rule by mocking colonial officials through elaborate rituals: "Imagine a Songhay medium who aped a colonial administrator. His body was contorted. His eyes bulged. Saliva frothed at his mouth. To add insult to injury, he spoke a mixture of Pidgin French and Songhay. All in all, a terrifying burlesque" (Stoller 1989: 153–54). In his controversial film *Les maîtres fous*, Jean Rouch documents one occasion of a Hauka ritual in Ghana in which cult members, possessed by the spirits of Europeans, exaggeratedly imitated British colonial customs of speech and gesture. The ritual included chanting a debased version of an official address, marching and saluting extravagantly, performing an animal sacrifice, and making an offering to a mock imperial statue of a British governor-general (Stoller 1989: 148, 150).

Clearly, Kennedy borrows from such possession theatrics in *Funnyhouse*, including the ritualized mimicry of colonial figures, to create her own ritual of resistance to colonialism. In place of the makeshift statue of a British governor-general – the centerpiece of the Hauka possession ritual – *Funnyhouse* incorporates a replica of an official statue of Britain's imperial queen. Read within the context of spirit possession ritual, the play's reference to this statue as Sarah's "idol" (Kennedy 1988: 5) suggests not merely her mock admiration for the Queen but also the use of the Queen's statue for ritualistic purposes. Specifically, the statue of Queen Victoria in *Funnyhouse* becomes, through Kennedy's artistic powers, one of the "objects of worship [used in African spirit rituals and in the black church] – idols, icons, fetishes, symbols – that own a potency for animism" (Harrison 1974: 12). Victoria's statue has the power to come to life; the character of Victoria – one of Sarah's many selves – speaks as the embodied spirit of that static statue.

And in the tradition of possession rituals, whose gestures of mimicry result in the release of the foreign spirit, *Funnyhouse* animates the statue of Queen Victoria in order to release through ritual its power over those subjects in the Queen's *possession*. Thus, the figure of Queen Victoria functions in the play as both the spirit of colonialism possessing Negro-Sarah and the fetish necessary to perform that spirit's ritual dispossession. Significantly, in his discussion of colonial discourse, Bhabha compares mimicry to a fetish (here, with a psychoanalytic inflection), noting that "the fetish mimes the forms of authority at the point at which it deauthorizes them" (Bhabha 1984: 131–32). The result of colonial mimicry is that colonial texts "loose their representational authority. Black skin splits under the racist gaze, displaced into signs of bestiality, genitalia, grotesquerie, which reveal the phobic myth of the undifferentiated whole white body" (Bhabha 1984: 132–33, quoted in Kintz 1992: 151).

As a text of colonialism, the statue of the imperial queen – whether whole, decapitated, or disembodied – represents the mythic "whole white body" to which Bhabha refers. The consolidation of Empire authorized by this statue and *re*-represented in the written play, therefore, is temporarily disrupted in *Funnyhouse* by mimicry – both textually, on the written page, and ritually, through the performance process itself.[30] And if ekphrasis demonstrates the unfulfilled desire of the language arts to subsume the visual arts, as Françoise Meltzer and Murray Krieger assert, then the tension represented in the play *in performance* between the static visual monument and ritual's mobile verbal field *enacts* the trope of ekphrasis. In doing so, *Funnyhouse* permits an ironic play on Meltzer's description of the trope as "the image colonized by writing" (Meltzer 1987: 67): here the image *of colonialism* is "colonized by writing" (and spoken language).

At the play's conclusion, Negro-Sarah hangs herself in her room next to her statue of Queen Victoria. Read within the symbolic economy of spirit possession, Sarah's suicide represents the sacrifice that completes the ritual. Yet, although she is symbolically released from the terrifying spirits that possessed her, her lifeless body – hanging next to the statue of "the Great White Queen" – continues to be written over by the scripts of whites: "The poor bitch has hung herself," the landlady declares, laughing, and Raymond responds, "She was a funny little liar" (Kennedy 1988: 22–23).

I began this chapter with Kennedy's verbal snapshot of London, in which she describes the statue of Queen Victoria that she saw on her first visit to England. After *Funnyhouse* was produced, Kennedy would return to London to live for three years. In her autobiographical piece "A Theatre Journal," she concludes with the following sketch from her second London stay: "The crazed old woman living in the house on Rothwell Street screamed, standing in the yard, some days, 'Go back to India where you belong.' Despite the enchantment, there was a subplot to England that I couldn't perceive" (Kennedy 1990: 124). Regardless of her claim to the contrary, Kennedy clearly perceives the irony of her neighbor's invective, being acutely aware of the violent displacement brought about by England's imperialist project and of the racism it upholds and engenders. In *Funnyhouse*, Kennedy explores her newly found connection to Africa using masks and ritual; at the same time, she exploits her "enchantment" with England – probing her fascination with Victoria's statue to expose this "subplot" and the role of visual images within it.

NOTES

1 Read 1982: 368–71; Ormond 1973: 489, 490, 491, 492, 493; Morris 1978: 369; 1968: 105n1, 254–55, 339, 416; Christopher 1988: 1, 140; Judd 1970: 183; Spielmann 1901: 18, 65, 135, 142, 143, 161.
2 I want to thank Mary Lou Emery for her help with this point.
3 Christopher 1988: 143; Morris 1978: 63; Read 1982: 371.
4 I want to thank Mary Lou Emery for her help with this point.
5 The following description is based on photographs and text in Benedict Read's *Victorian Sculpture* (Read 1982: 379).
6 Kennedy 1992: 4; 1977: 45–46; 1987b: 118–20.
7 Harrison 1974: 9–10; Hatch 1987: 26–27; Bryant-Jackson 1992: 49–51; Freedman 1992: 214.
8 Kennedy 1990: 109; and 1987b: 116, 121; Bryant-Jackson 1992: 55; Wilkerson 1992: 71.
9 Genevieve Fabre makes this point regarding Kennedy's work as a whole (Fabre 1983: 123).
10 I want to thank Laura Harris for suggesting this to me.
11 In conversations with the Signature Theatre Company's sculptor, Tom Moore, and the set designer, E. David Cosier, I learned that originally a separate head was constructed for Victoria and was attached to her body for the dress rehearsal; however, the production company and Kennedy agreed that the headless statue worked best.

12  Steele 1987: 31–32; Henry Louis Gates, Jr. quoted in Traylor 1987: 48–49; Graham-White 1974: 24, 38; Blier 1993: 144, 149–50, 156, 158; Kramer 1993: 192–93.

13  Traylor 1987: 49–52; Fabre 1983: 5–6; Harrison 1989: xli.

14  Significantly, Edith Sitwell wrote a flattering biography of Queen Victoria, *Victoria of England* (1936). Kennedy read Elizabeth Longford's biography of Victoria (Kennedy 1990: 119).

15  Fabre 1983: 119, 122; Sollors 1991: 512–13, 515, 516; Hay 1973: 7; Forte 1992: 159–64.

16  Griffiths 1993: 46. In related gestures, Paul Bryant-Jackson argues "that Kennedy's travelers are existentially suspended in the historic middle passage" (Bryant-Jackson 1992: 56) while Rosemary Curb contends that "the bodies of black women in Kennedy's plays become sites for the reenactment of the European imperialist colonization of Africa," including Sarah, whose "consciousness [is] set on three continents at war" (Curb 1992: 143, 151).

17  In a related fashion, Werner Sollors suggests that "[t]he antithesis between Victoria and Lumumba may . . . be seen as that between empire and anti-colonialism" (Sollors 1991: 509); Margaret Wilkerson reads these four characters as representing the "historical confrontation between white Europeans and black Africans" (Wilkerson 1992: 73).

18  Paul Bryant-Jackson argues in a similar vein that Kennedy's characters demonstrate a "restlessness" indicative of a "matrilineal diasporic" identity of resistance, although he also reads Sarah's multiple and conflicting identities as an indication of madness (Bryant-Jackson 1992: 54–56).

19  Numerous critics have explored the influences of African religious and cultural practices, in particular dramatic forms, on African American drama, emphasizing the ritualistic quality of many plays, including those of Kennedy: Harrison 1974: 3–29; 1989: xi–lxiii; Fabre 1983: 4, 205, 218, 225–30; Hatch 1987: 13–29; Traylor 1987: 47–49; Brown-Guillory 1988: 1, 80–81; Steele 1987: 30–32; Benston 1992: 62–63, 70–77; Williams 1985: 7; Bryant-Jackson 1992: 55–56.

20  Quoted in George Balandier, *Ambiguous Africa: Cultures in Collision* ([New York: Pantheon, 1966], 110), quoted in Graham-White 1974: 59.

21  Robert Dirks, "Slaves' Holiday," *Natural History* 84.10 (1975): 82–84, 87–88, 90, quoted in Abrahams and Szwed 1983: 226.

22  Abrahams and Szwed 1983: 226, 229–30, 231, 233, 235, 236, 239–40, 249, 256, 260, 269; Fabre 1983: 232.

23  Graham-White 1974: 24; Kramer 1993: 132, 165; Fabre 1983: 218.

24  Although Linda Kintz acknowledges a connection between *Funnyhouse* and Bakhtinian and Caribbean Carnival, she sees in the play only the dominant white culture being "released from constraints" (Kintz 1992: 150–51).

25  As Amiri Baraka asserts, "the Afro-American has always been trying to evolve . . . an art that comes out of the basically dionysian, basic African spirit possession" (Amiri Baraka, interview, *The Drum* [1987], 16–17 quoted in Harrison 1989: xvi).

26 Elinor Fuchs and Robert Scanlan acknowledge the ritualistic quality of Kennedy's work, including *Funnyhouse*, although they read it within the context of ritual theater of the European and New York avant-garde (Fuchs 1992: 76; Scanlan 1992: 96, 106). In contrast, Paul Bryant-Jackson, Billie Allen, and Linda Kintz recognize a connection between Kennedy's work and African ritual (Freedman 1992: 214; Allen 1992: 223; Kintz 1992: 154, 160).

27 Sollors 1991: 512–13; Fuchs 1992: 79; Curb 1980: 180, 194.

28 Linda Kintz arrives at a similar conclusion using Henry Louis Gates, Jr.'s theory of "signifying" (Kintz 1992: 160).

29 Kintz sees such mimicry in *Funnyhouse* as merely unsuccessful "overimitation" rather than subversive parody although she recognizes its potential as a "[strategy] of resistance" (ibid.: 152–53, 161).

30 This tension between the statue of Victoria and the ritual of mimicry is connected to what Kimberly Benston describes as "the contrast in *Funnyhouse of a Negro* between the Jungle and the Room (emblems of reified stasis – statuary, walls, repetition – versus signs of wildness – hair, screams, movement) as synecdochic enactment of a larger defining tension between classicism (such as colonialism, the unified bourgeois subject, modernism) and its disruption or interruption by the Uncanny (such as revolutionary resistance, the subject-in-progress, the Imaginary)" (Benston 1992: 114).

# Bibliography

Abbot, Jacob 1849, *History of Queen Elizabeth*, New York.

1850, *The Life of Elizabeth, Queen of England*, London.

Abbot, Willis J. 1913, *Notable Women in History: the Lives of Women who in all Ages, all Lands and in all Womanly Occupations have Won Fame and put their Imprint on the World's History*, Philadelphia: John C. Winston.

Abrahams, Roger and John Szwed (eds.) 1983, *After Africa: Extracts from British Travel Accounts and Journals of the Seventeenth, Eighteenth, and Nineteenth Centuries Concerning the Slaves, their Manners, and Customs in the British West Indies*, New Haven: Yale University Press.

Abrams, M. H. 1979, "The Victorian Age," in *The Northern Anthology of English Literature*, 4th edn, vol. II, New York: Norton.

Adams, Henry 1961, *The Education of Henry Adams*, Boston: Houghton Mifflin. First edn 1918.

Adams, William Henry Davenport 1884, *Celebrated Englishwomen of the Victorian Era*, 2 vols., London: F. V. White.

Aikin, L. 1811, Juvenile correspondence, London.

Allen, Billie 1992, "An Interview with Billie Allen," with Paul Bryant-Jackson and Lois More Overbeck, Bryant-Jackson and Overbeck (eds.) 1992.

Allen, Helena G. 1982, *The Betrayal of Liliuokalani, Last Queen of Hawaii, 1838–1917*, Glendale, Calif.: Clark.

Altick, Richard 1987, "Signs of the Times, 1837–1887," *Victorian Poetry* 25.3–4.

Always Happy!!! 1814, London.

Anglo-Saxon Race 1848, "An Inquiry into the Causes of its Unrivalled Progress, with Some Considerations Indicative of its Future Destiny," *American Whig Review* January.

Archer, Thomas 1888, *Our Sovereign Lady Queen Victoria: her Life and Jubilee*, 4 vols., London: Blackie.

Armstrong, Nancy 1987, *Desire and Domestic Fiction*, New York: Oxford University Press.

Arrowsmith, William 1982, "Ruskin's Fireflies," in *The Ruskin Polygon: Essays on the Imagination of John Ruskin*, ed. John Dixon Hunt and Faith M. Holland, Manchester University Press.

Auerbach, Nina 1982, *Woman and the Demon: the Life of a Victorian Myth*, Cambridge, Mass.: Harvard University Press.

Austin, Linda 1987, "Ruskin and the Ideal Woman," *South Central Review* 4.

Bagehot, Walter 1966, *The English Constitution, 1867*, Ithaca: Cornell University Press. First edn 1867. Reprinted 1995.

Bakhtin, Mikhail 1968, "Introduction," *Rabelais and His World*, trans. Helene Iswolsky, Cambridge, Mass.: MIT Press. First edn 1965.

Ball, Charles 1981. *The History of the Indian Mutiny*, 2 vols., New Delhi: Master Publishers reprint. First edn 1858–59, London: London Printing and Publishing Company.

Ballard, George 1775, *Memoirs of Several Ladies of Great Britain: who have been Celebrated for their Writings or Skill in the Learned Languages, Arts and Sciences*, London: T. Evans.

Barker, Mary E. 1850, "Mary, Queen of Scots," *Ladies' Repository* April.

Barrett Browning, Elizabeth 1973, *The Complete Works of Elizabeth Barrett Browning*, 6 vols., ed. Charlotte Porter and Helen A. Clarke, New York: AMS Press reprint. First edn 1900.

Bartlett, Franklin Weston, D. D. 1901, *The Good Queen: a discourse in Memory of her Most Gracious Majesty Queen Victoria*, Rockport, Mass.: Sidney A. Savage.

Bauer, Helen Pike 1994, *Rudyard Kipling: a Study of the Short Fiction*, New York: Twayne.

Baym, Nina 1995, *American Women Writers and the Work of History, 1790–1860*, New Brunswick: Rutgers University Press.

Beckwith, Martha Warren (ed. and trans.) 1972, *The Kumulipo: a Hawaiian Creation Chant*, Honolulu: University of Hawaii Press.

Benson, Peter 1986, *Black Orpheus, Transition, and Modern Cultural Awakening in Africa*, Berkeley: University of California Press.

Benstock, Shari 1986, *Women of the Left Bank: Paris, 1900–1940*, Austin: University of Texas Press.

Benston, Kimberly 1992, "Locating Adrienne Kennedy: Prefacing the Subject," in Bryant-Jackson and Overbeck (eds.) 1992.

Berzon, Judith 1978, *Neither White nor Black: the Mulatto Character in American Fiction*, New York: New York University Press.

"The Betrothal of Victoria," 1867, *The Ladies' Repository* November.

Bhabha, Homi 1984, "Of Mimicry and Man: the Ambivalence of Colonial Discourse," *October* 28.

  1985a, "Signs Taken For Wonders," *Critical Inquiry* 12.

  1985b, "Sly Civility," *October* 34.

Birch, Dinah 1988a, *Ruskin's Myths*, Oxford: Clarendon.

  1988b, "Ruskin's 'Womanly Mind," *Essays in Criticism* 38.

  1989, "*The Ethics of the Dust*: Ruskin's Authorities," *Prose Studies* 12.

Blackman, William Fremont 1899, *The Making of Hawaii: a Study in Social Evolution*, London: Macmillan.

Blackstone, W. 1899, *Commentaries on the Laws of England*, ed. James Dewitt Andrews, 4th edn, 2 vols. Chicago.

Blau, Herbert 1984, "The American Dream in American Gothic: the Plays of Sam Shepard and Adrienne Kennedy," *Modern Drama* 27.

Bleackley, Horace 1909, *Ladies Fair and Frail: Sketches of the Demi-Monde During the Eighteenth Century*, London: John Lane.

Blier, Suzanne Preston 1993, "Truth and Seeing: Magic, Custom, and Fetish in Art History," in *Africa and the Disciplines*, ed. Robert Bates, V. Y. Mudimbe, and Jean O'Barr, Chicago: University of Chicago Press.

Bloom, Harold 1969, "Introduction," in *The Literary Criticism of John Ruskin*, Harold Bloom. Gloucester, Mass.: Peter Smith.

Bolton, Sarah Knowles 1892, *Famous Types of Womanhood*, New York: Thomas Y. Crowell.

"Books read by Her Hghness the Princess Victoria in the lessons of 1826, 1827, 1828 and 1829," Victorian Collection, Special Collections, Brigham Young University, Harold B. Lee Library.

Bond, Brian 1961, "The Late Victorian Army," *History Today*, 11.9.

Bordo, Susan 1993, *Unbearable Weight: Feminism, Western Culture, and the Body*, Berkeley: University of California Press.

Bradley, J. L., (ed.), 1984, *Ruskin: the Critical Heritage*, London and Boston: Routledge & Kegan Paul.

Brantlinger, Patrick, 1988, *Rule of Darkness: British Literature and Imperialism, 1830–1914*, Ithaca, N.Y.: Cornell University Press.

Brantôme, Abbe de (Pierre de Bordeille) 1902, *The Book of the Ladies*, trans. Katharine Prescott Wormeley, Boston: Hardy, Pratt.

Braudy, Leo 1986, *The Frenzy of Renown: Fame and its History*, Oxford: Oxford University Press.

Bremmer, Jan and Lourens van den Bosch 1995, *Between Poverty and the Pyre: Moments in the History of Widowhood*, London and New York: Routledge.

British-American Association 1887, "Faneuil Hall: Who are its Conservators? The Story of the Victoria Jubiliee Banquet Re-Told for the Benefit of the American Public,"[Boston]: no publisher.

Brooke, Rupert 1941, "The Soldier," in *The Poetical Works of Rupert Brooke*, ed. Geoffrey Keynes, London: Faber & Faber.

Brougham, Henry 1841, *Speeches of Henry Lord Brougham*, Philadelphia: Lea & Blanchard.

Brown, Howard N. 1901, "A Lesson from the Life of Queen Victoria: a Sermon Delivered in King's Chapel, January Twenty-Seven, MDCCCCI," Boston.

Brown-Guillory, Elizabeth 1988, *Their Place on the Stage: Black Women Playwrights in America*, New York: Praeger.

Bryant-Jackson, Paul 1992, "Kennedy's Travelers in the American and African Continuum," in (eds.) Bryant-Jackson and Overbeck 1992.

Bryant-Jackson, Paul and Lois More Overbeck (eds.) 1992, *Intersecting Boundaries: the Theatre of Adrienne Kennedy*, Minneapolis: University of Minnesota Press.

Bulwer Lytton, Edward 1839, *Edinburgh Review* 70.

Bury, C. 1838, *The Murdered Queen! Or, Caroline of Brunswick, A Diary of the Court of George IV*, London.

Bush, Catherine 1988, *Elizabeth I*, New York, revised edn. London.

Byron, George Gordon, Lord 1980–93, *Lord Byron: the Complete Poetical Works*, 7 vols., ed. Jerome J. McGann, Oxford: Oxford University Press.

Calder, Jenny 1976, *Women and Marriage in Victorian Fiction*, London: Thames & Hudson.

Campbell, Hugh 1825, *The Case of Mary Queen of Scots and of Elizabeth Queen of England . . .*, London.

Carey, Alice 1848, "Death of Cleopatra," *Ladies' Repository* March.

Carey, Rosa Nouchette 1899, *Twelve Notable Good Women of the XIXth Century*, London: Hutchinson.

Cate, George Allan 1988, *John Ruskin: a Reference Guide*, Boston: G. K. Hall.

Chakrabarty, Dipesh 1992, "Postcoloniality and the Artifice of History: Who Speaks for 'Indian' Pasts?," *Representations* Winter.

Chamber of Commerce of the State of New York 1901, "Tribute to the Memory of Her Majesty Queen Victoria," New York: no publisher (February 7).

Chamberlain, Joseph E. 1877, "A Dream of Anglo-Saxondom," *The Galaxy* December.

Charlot, Monica 1991, *Victoria, The Young Queen*, Oxford: Basil Blackwell.

Christ, Carol 1977, "Victorian Masculinity and the Angel in the House," *A Widening Sphere: Changing Roles of Victorian Woman*, ed. Martha Vicinus, Bloomington and London: Indiana University Press.

Christopher, A. J. 1988, *The British Empire at its Zenith*, London: Croom Helm.

Clarke, Mary Cowden 1858, *World-Noted Women*, New York: Appleton.

*Claudine: Or, humility the Basis of all Virtues* 1835, London.

Comer, James P. 1990, "Great Lives, Great Examples," *Parents Magazine*, January.

Comstock, Harriet T. 1914, *The Girlhood of Elizabeth: a Romance of English History*, London.

Coningsey 1861, *A Chapter of the Bengal Mutiny, as Seen in Central India, by one who was There in 1857–58*, London: Blackwood.

Conner, Patrick 1979, *Savage Ruskin*, Detroit: Wayne State University Press.

Conway, Moncure D. 1887, "The Queen of England," *The North American Review* August.

Cox, Philip 1933, *The Rani of Jhansi*, London: Allen & Unwin.

Croker, J. W. 1820, *A Letter from the King to his People*, London: W. Turner.

1839, "The Household and the Ministry," *Quarterly Review* 64.

1885, *The Croker Papers*, vol. II, ed. Louis J. Jennings, London: John Murray.

Cumming, J. G. 1842, "Apostrophe to Mary, Queen of Scots," *The Ladies' Companion* May.

Curb, Rosemary 1980, "Fragmented Selves in Adrienne Kennedy's *Funnyhouse of a Negro* and *The Owl Answers*," *Theatre Journal* 32.

1992, "(Hetero)Sexual Terrors in Adrienne Kennedy's Early Plays," in Bryant-Jackson and Overbeck (eds.) 1992.

David, Deirdre 1987, *Intellectual Women and Victorian Patriarchy*, London: Macmillan.

1995, *Rule Britannia: Women, Empire, and Victorian Writing*, Ithaca N.Y.: Cornell University Press.

Davidoff, Leonore and Hall, Catherine 1987, *Family Fortunes: Men and Women of the English Middle Class, 1780–1850*, London: Hutchinson.

Davies, Carole Boyce 1994, *Black Women, Writing and Identity: Migrations of the Subject*, London: Routledge.

Davis, Richard Harding 1903, "The Queen's Jubilee," in *A Year from a Reporter's Note-Book*, New York and London: Harper & Brothers.

Dellamora, Richard 1990, *Masculine Desire: the Sexual Politics of Victorian Aestheticism*, Chapel Hill: University of North Carolina Press.

Diamond, Elin 1992, "Mimesis in Syncopated Time: Reading Adrienne Kennedy," in Bryant-Jackson and Overbeck (eds.) 1992.

Dickens, Charles 1972, *The Posthumous Papers of The Pickwick Club*, ed. Robert Patten, London: Penguin. First edn 1837.

Disraeli, Benjamin 1895, *Sybil*, London. First edn 1845.

Doane, Mary Ann 1987, *The Desire to Desire: the Woman's Film of the 1940s*, Bloomington: Indiana University Press.

Dougherty, Charles 1963, "Of Ruskin's Gardens," in *Myth and Symbol: Critical Approaches and Applications*, ed. Bernice Slote, Lincoln: University of Nebraska Press.

Douglas, Ann 1977, *The Feminization of American Culture*, New York: Alfred A. Knopf.

Doyle, Laura 1994, *Bordering on the Body: the Racial Matrix of Modern Fiction and Culture*, New York: Oxford University Press.

Duff, David 1972, *Victoria and Albert*, New York: Taplinger.

Edgeworth, M. 1827, *Harry and Lucy*, 4 vols., London.

1836, *Frank*, New York.

Editor's Easy Chair 1868, *Harper's New Monthly Magazine* April.

Edwards, Harry 1994, "The Athlete as Role Model: America's Sports Past?," *Sport* November.

Eldridge, C. C. 1978, *Victorian Imperialism*, Atlantic Highlands: Humanities Press.

Eliot, George, "The Modern Hep! Hep! Hep!," in *The Essays of Theophrastus Such*, New York: William Allison, n.d. First edn 1879.

Emerson, Sheila 1994, *John Ruskin: the Genesis of Invention*, Cambridge: Cambridge University Press.

Emery, Mary Lou 1990, *Jean Rhys at "World's End": Novels of Colonial and Sexual Exile*, Austin: University of Texas Press.

1994, "Refiguring the Postcolonial Imagination: Tropes of Visuality in Writing by Rhys, Kincaid, and Cliff," essay in progress, University of Iowa.

1997, "'Space Sounds' in Wilson Harris's Recent Fiction," in *The Review of Contemporary Fiction* (special issue on Wilson Harris, ed. Joyce Sparer Adler).

Erskine, Walter 1861, *A Chapter of the Bengal Mutiny, as Seen in Central India by One who was There in 1857–8*, London: Blackwood.

Ezell, Margaret J. M. 1993, *Writing Women's Literary History*, Baltimore: Johns Hopkins University Press.

Faberman, Hilarie 1983, "Augustus Leopold Egg, RA (1816–1863)", Ph.D. dissertation, Yale University.

Fabre, Genevieve 1983, *Drumbeats, Masks, and Metaphor: Contemporary Afro-American Theatre*, trans. Melvin Dixon, Cambridge, Mass.: Harvard University Press. First edn 1982.

Fellows, Jay 1975, *The Falling Distance: the Autobiographical Impulse in John Ruskin*, Baltimore: Johns Hopkins University Press.

 1981, *Ruskin's Maze: Mastery and Madness in his Art*, Princeton: Princeton University Press.

Fitch, Raymond 1982, *The Poison Sky: Myth and Apocalypse in Ruskin*, Athens: Ohio University Press.

Flint, Kate 1993, *The Woman Reader, 1837–1914*, Oxford: Clarendon Press.

Forster, E. M. 1936, "Notes on the English Character," in *Abinger Harvest*, New York: Harcourt Brace Jovanovich.

Forte, Jeanie 1992, "Kennedy's Body Politic: the Mulatta, Menses, and the Medusa," in Bryant-Jackson and Overbeck (eds.) 1992.

Fradenburg, Louise Olga 1992, "Introduction: Rethinking Queenship," in *Women and Sovereignty*, ed. Louise Olga Fradenburg, *Cosmos: the Yearbook of the Traditional Cosmological Society*, Edinburgh University Press, 7.

Fraser, George MacDonald 1989, *Flashman in the Great Game*, New York: Plume. First edn 1975, London: Blackwood.

Fredeman, William E. 1987a, "A Charivari for Queen Butterfly: *Punch* on Queen Victoria," *Victorian Poetry* 25.

 1987b, "Introduction: England Our Home, Victoria Our Queen," *Victorian Poetry* 25.

Fredeman, William E. (ed.) 1987, "Jubilee Odes," *Victorian Poetry* 25.

Freedman, Gerald 1992, "An Interview with Gerald Freedman," with Paul Bryant-Jackson, in Bryant-Jackson and Overbeck (eds.) 1992.

Freiwald, Bina 1988, "Of Selfsame Desire: Patmore's *The Angel in the House*," *Texas Studies in Language and Literature* 30.

Froude, James Anthony 1888, *The English in the West Indies; or The Bow of Ulysses*, New York: C. Scribner's Sons.

Fuchs, Elinor 1992, "Adrienne Kennedy and the First Avant-Garde," in Bryant-Jackson and Overbeck (eds.) 1992.

Galloway, Samuel 1845, "Female Character and Education," in *The Literary Emporium; a Compendium of Religious, Literary, and Philosophical Knowledge*, vol. I–II, New York: J. K. Wellman.

Gaunt, William 1980, *Court Painting in England*, London: Constable.

Gernsheim, Helmut and Alison 1959, *Victoria R.: A Biography with Four Hundred Illustrations based on her Personal Photograph Albums*, New York: G. A. Putnam's Sons.

Gilbert, Sandra M. and Susan Gubar 1979, *The Madwoman in the Attic: the Woman Writer and the Nineteenth-century Literary Imagination*, New Haven: Yale University Press.

Graham-White, Anthony 1974, *The Drama of Black Africa*, New York: Samuel French.

Graves, Algernon 1906, *Complete Dictionary of the Contributors to the Royal Academy*, 8 vols. London: Henry Graves & George Bell.

*Great Women Paper Dolls* 1994, Santa Barbara, Calif.: Bellerophon Books.

Green, J. R. 1875, *A Short History of the English People*, New York.

Greville, Charles C. F. 1885, *The Greville Memoirs*, second part, vol. 1, ed. Henry Reeve, New York: D. Appleton.

Grey, C. 1867a, *The Early Years of His Royal Highness the Prince Consort*, New York.

1867b, Review of *The Early Years of His Royal Highness the Prince Consort, Compiled Under the Direction of Her Majesty the Queen, Harper's New Monthly Magazine* October.

Griffiths, Ieuan L. 1993, *The Atlas of African Affairs*, London: Routledge. First edn 1984.

Hale, D. G. 1971, *The Body Politic: a Political Metaphor in Renaissance English Literature*, The Hague: Mouton.

Hale, Sarah J. 1870, *Woman's Record; or, Sketches of all Distinguished Women from the Creation to AD 1868. Arranged in Four Eras with Selections from Authoresses of Each Era*, 3rd revised edn, New York: Harper.

Haley, Bruce 1978, *The Healthy Body and Victorian Culture*, Cambridge, Mass.: Harvard University Press.

*Hansard's Parliamentary Debates* 1839, Third Series, London: Thomas Curson Hansard.

Hardie, Frank 1935, *The Political Influence of Queen Victoria, 1861–1901*, London: Humphrey Milford.

Hardy, Thomas 1925, "Drummer Hodge," in *Collected Poems of Thomas Hardy*, New York: Macmillan.

*Harlequin and Good Queen Bess, or, Merrie England in the Olden Time. A Grand Historical! Metaphorical!! Allegorical!!! and Diabolical!!!! PANTOMIME, Performed for the First Time, on Wednesday, 26th December, 1849 at the Theatre Royal, Drury Lane. Written by the Author of "Bluff King Hal,"* 1849, London.

Harrison, Frederic 1977, *The Dark Angel: Aspects of Victorian Sexuality*, New York: Universe.

Harrison, Paul 1974, "Introduction," in *Kuntu Drama: Plays of the African Continuum*, ed. Paul Harrison, New York: Grove.

1989, "Mother/Word: Black Theatre in the African Continuum: Word/Song as Method," in *Totem Voices: Plays from the Black World Repertory*, ed. Paul Harrison, New York: Grove.

Hatch, James 1987, "Some African Influences on the Afro–American Theatre," in Hill (ed.) 1987.

Haven, Revd Gilbert 1863, "Pictures of Travel: the Sacred Places of England," *The Ladies' Repository* March.

Hay, Samuel 1973, "African–American Drama: 1950–1970," *Negro History Bulletin* 36.

Hayman, John 1978, "Ruskin's *The Queen of the Air* and the Appeal of Mythology," *Philological Quarterly* 57.

1989, "John Ruskin's *Hortus Inclusus*: the Manuscript Sources and Publication History," *Huntington Library Quarterly* 52.

Hays, Mary 1821, *Memoirs of Queens: Illustrious and Celebrated*, London: Allman.

Helme, E. 1804, *Maternal Instruction: Family Conversations, Moral and Entertaining Subjects*, New York.

Helsinger, Elizabeth 1982, *Ruskin and the Art of the Beholder*, Cambridge, Mass.: Harvard University Press.

Helsinger, E., Sheets, R. L., and Veeder, W. 1983, "Queen Victoria and 'The Shadow Side,'" in *The Woman Question: Society and Literature in Britain and America 1837–1883*, 3 vols., Chicago: University of Chicago Press.

Henderson, Mae Gwendolyn 1990, "Speaking in Tongues: Dialogics, Dialectics, and the Black Woman Writer's Literary Tradition," in *Reading Black, Reading Feminist: a Critical Anthology*, ed. Henry Louis Gates, Jr., New York: Meridian. First edn 1989.

"Her Majesty the Queen" 1897, *Review of Reviews* January 15.

Hewison, Robert 1976, *John Ruskin: the Argument of the Eye*, Princeton: Princeton University Press.

Hill, Errol (ed.) 1987, *The Theatre of Black Americans: a Collection of Critical Essays*, New York: Applause Theatre.

Hilton, Tim 1985, *John Ruskin: the Early Years 1818–1859*, New Haven: Yale University Press.

Himmelfarb, Gertrude 1987, *Marriage and Morals Among the Victorians and Other Essays*, New York: Random House.

Hodges, Katherine 1887, *Fifty Years a Queen*, New York: Belford, Clarke.

Holland, Lord 1977, *The Holland House Diaries 1831–1840*, ed. Abraham D. Kriegel, London: Routledge & Kegan Paul.

Homans, Margaret 1993, "'To the Queen's Private Apartments': Royal Family Portraiture and the Construction of Victoria's Sovereign Obedience," *Victorian Studies* 37.

    1994, "The Powers of Powerlessness: the Courtships of Elizabeth Barrett and Queen Victoria," in *Feminist Measures: Soundings in Poetry and Theory*, ed. Lynn Keller and Cristanne Miller, Ann Arbor: University of Michigan Press.

    1995, "Queen Victoria and Victorian Queens," unpublished lecture, Louisiana State University, February 24, 1995.

    1997, *Queen Victoria: Power, Representation, and the Woman Monarch*, forthcoming.

Horsman, Reginald 1981, *Race and Manifest Destiny: the Origins of American Racial Anglo-Saxonism*, Cambridge, Mass. and London: Harvard University Press.

Houghton, Walter 1957, *The Victorian Frame of Mind, 1830–1870*, New Haven and London: Yale University Press.

Howitt, Mary (ed.) 1868, *Biographical Sketches of the Queens of England, from the Norman Conquest to the Reign of Victoria; or Royal Book of Beauty*, London: Virtue.

Huff, Cynthia 1988, "Private Domains: Queen Victoria and Women's Diaries," *Auto/Biography Studies* 4.

Hughes, Thomas 1971, *Tom Brown's Schooldays*, Harmondsworth: Penguin. First edn 1857.

Hunt, John Dixon 1982, *The Wider Sea: a Life of John Ruskin*, New York: Viking.

[Ireland, William Henry] 1805, *Effusions of Love from Chatelar to Mary Queen of Scotland . . .*, London.

Jackson, Helen Hunt 1888, *Verses*, Boston: Roberts Brothers.

James, Robert Rhodes 1984, *Prince Albert: a Biography*, New York: Knopf.

Jameson, Anna 1832, *Memoirs of Celebrated Female Sovereigns*, 2 vols., New York: J. and J. Harper.

1834, *Memoirs of Celebrated Female Sovereigns*, 2nd edn, London.

Judd, Denis 1970, *The Victorian Empire*, New York: Praeger.

Kasson, Joy 1990, *Marble Queens and Captives*, New Haven: Yale University Press.

Keating, Peter 1994, "Soldier, Soldier," in *Kipling the Poet*, London: Secker & Warburg.

Kennedy, Adrienne 1961–2, "Because of the King of France," *Black Orpheus* 10.

1977, "A Growth of Images," *Drama Review* 21.4.

1987a, Interview, in *Interviews with Contemporary Women Playwrights*, ed. Kathleen Betsko and Rachel Koenig, New York: Beach Tree.

1987b, *People who Led to my Plays*, New York: Knopf.

1988, *Funnyhouse of a Negro. In One Act*, Minneapolis: University of Minnesota Press. First edn 1962.

1989, "An Interview with Adrienne Kennedy," with Elin Diamond, *Studies in American Drama, 1945–Present* 4.

1990, "A Theatre Journal," in *Deadly Triplets*, Minneapolis: University of Minnesota Press.

1992, "Adrienne Kennedy: an Interview," with Paul K. Bryant-Jackson and Lois More Overbeck, in Bryant-Jackson and Overbeck (eds.) 1992.

Kent, Noel J. 1983, *Hawaii: Islands Under the Influence*, New York: Monthly Review.

Kestner, Joseph A. 1989, *Mythology and Misogyny: the Social Discourse of Nineteenth-Century Classical Subject Painting*, Madison: University of Wisconsin Press.

Kiernan, V. G. 1989, *Poets, Politics and the People*, London: Verso.

Killham, J. 1958, *Tennyson and the Princess: Reflections of an Age*, London: Athlone.

Kingsley, Charles 1871, *At Last: Christmas in the West Indies*, London: Macmillan.

1873, "Sir Walter Raleigh and His Time," in *Plays and Puritans and Other Historical Essays*, London.

Kintz, Linda 1992, "Theatrical Subjects: the Plays of Adrienne Kennedy," in *The Subject's Tragedy: Political Poetics, Feminist Theory, and Drama*, Ann Arbor: University of Michigan Press.

Kipling, Rudyard 1909, *The Writings in Prose and Verse of Rudyard Kipling: Soldiers Three and Military Tales*, vol. II, III, New York: Charles Scribner's Sons.

1910, "Gloriana", *Rewards and Fairies*, London.

1940, *Rudyard Kipling's Verse. Definitive Edition*, New York.

1989, *The Complete Verse: Definitive Edition*, New York: Doubleday.

Kirchhoff, Frederick 1976, "A Note on Ruskin's Mythography," *Victorian Newsletter* 50.

1977, "A Science Against Sciences: Ruskin's Floral Mythology," in *Nature and the Victorian Imagination*, eds. U. C. Knoepflmacher and G. B. Tennyson, Berkeley: University of California Press.

Kissane, J. 1962, "Victorian Mythology," *Victorian Studies* 6.

Klein, Joan Larsen 1992, *Daughters, Wives and Widows: Writings by Men about Women and Marriage in England, 1500–1640*, Chicago: University of Illinois Press.

Kramer, Fritz 1993, *The Red Fez: Art and Spirit Possession in Africa*, trans. Malcolm Green, London: Verso. First edn 1987.

Krieger, Murray 1992, *Ekphrasis: the Illusion of the Natural Sign*, Baltimore: Johns Hopkins University Press.

Kuykendall, Ralph and A. Grove Day 1961, *Hawaii: a History*, Englewood Cliffs, N.J.: Prentice-Hall.

Landor, Walter Savage 1846, "Queen Elizabeth, Cecil, Duke of Anjou, and De la Motte Fenelon," in *Imaginary Conversations* (1824–9), *The Works of Walter Savage Landor*, 2 vols., London.

Landow, George P. 1971, *The Aesthetic and Critical Theories of John Ruskin*, Princeton: Princeton University Press.

Lang, John 1861, *Wanderings in India and Other Sketches of Life in Hindostan*, London: Routledge.

Langland, Elizabeth 1995, *Nobody's Angels: Middle-Class Women and Domestic Ideology in Victorian Culture*, Ithaca, N.Y.: Cornell University Press.

Laqueur, Thomas 1982, "The Queen Caroline Affair: Politics as Art in the Reign of George IV," *Journal of Modern History* 54.

Lebra-Chapman, Joyce 1986, *The Rani of Jhansi: a Study in Female Heroism*, Honolulu: University of Hawaii Press.

Liliuokalani 1991, *Hawaii's Story by Hawaii's Queen*, Rutland, V.T.: Charles E. Tuttle. First edn 1898.

Lincoln, C. Eric 1973, *The Black Muslims in America*, Boston: Beacon.

Longford, Elizabeth 1964a, *Queen Victoria: Born to Succeed*, New York: Harper & Row.

  1964b, *Victoria R.I.*, London: Weidenfeld & Nicolson.

  1981, *Eminent Victorian Women*, New York: Knopf.

Lopata, Helena Znaniecka 1979, "Widowhood, Other Places, Other Times and in America," in *Women as Widows: Support Systems*, New York: Elsevier.

Lucas, John 1987–88, "Love of England: the Victorians and Patriotism," *Browning Society Notes* 17.

Lutyens, Mary 1967, *Millais and the Ruskins*, London: John Murray.

Macaulay, Thomas Babington 1952, "The Minute on Indian Education," in *Macaulay Prose and Poetry*, Cambridge, Mass.: Harvard University Press.

McLeod, Glenda 1991, *Virtue and Venom: Catalogs of Women from Antiquity to the Renaissance*, Ann Arbor: University of Michigan Press.

Marshall, Beatrice 1916, *Queen Elizabeth*, London.

Martin, Theodore 1875–80, *The Life of His Royal Highness the Prince Consort*, 5 vols., New York: Appleton.

  1908, *Queen Victoria as I Knew Her*, Edinburgh: Blackwell.

May, Joseph 1901, "Victoria and her Era: an Address Delivered on Sunday, February 3, 1901, at a Service Commemorative of Queen Victoria at the First Unitarian Church of Philadelphia," [Philadelphia?].

Meltzer, Françoise 1987, *Salome and the Dance of Writing: Portraits of Mimesis in Literature*, Chicago: University of Chicago Press.

Merrill, Arthur Lawrence 1901, *Life and Times of Queen Victoria* [Philadelphia?].

Messenger, John 1971, "Ibibio Drama," *Africa* 41.

Millar, Oliver 1992, *The Victorian Pictures in the Collection of Her Majesty the Queen*, Cambridge: Cambridge University Press.

Millett, Kate 1970, "The Debate over Women: Ruskin Versus Mill," *Victorian Studies* 14.

Mirrer, Louise (ed.) 1992, *Upon My Husband's Death: Widows in the Literature and Histories of Medieval Europe*, Ann Arbor: University of Michigan Press.

Mirzoeff, Edward (producer and director) 1994, *Elizabeth R*. BBC film production.

Morgan, Peter 1988, "Ruskin's Queen of the Air," in *Poetics of the Elements in the Human Condition, II*, ed. Anna-Teresa Tymieniecka, Dordrecht, Netherlands: Kluwer.

Morris, James 1968, *Pax Britannica*, New York: Harcourt Brace Jovanovich.

1978, *Farewell the Trumpets*, New York: Harcourt Brace Jovanovich.

Müller, F. M. 1861, *Lectures on the Science of Language*, First Series, London.

1864, *Lectures on the Science of Language*, Second Series, London.

Munich, Adrienne Auslander 1984, "Capture the Heart of a Queen: Gilbert and Sullivan's Rites of Conquest", *Centennial Review*, 28.

1987, "Queen Victoria, Empire, and Excess," *Tulsa Studies in Women's Literature* 6.

1989, *Andromeda's Chains: Gender and Interpretation in Victorian Literature and Art*, New York: Columbia University Press.

1996, *Queen Victoria's Secrets*, New York: Columbia University Press.

Musick, John R. 1898, *Hawaii: Our New Possessions*, New York: Funk.

Nadel, Ira B. 1987, "Portraits of the Queen," *Victorian Poetry* 25.

Newbould, Ian 1990, *Whiggery and Reform: 1830–41*, Basingstoke: Macmillan.

Newell, D. 1848a, "First Impressions of England and the English," in Newell (ed.) 1848.

1848b, "Lady Jane Grey," in Newell (ed.) 1848.

1848c, "London – Westminster Abbey," in Newell (ed.) 1848.

Newell, D. (ed.) 1848, *The Family Circle and Parlor Annual*, New York.

Ngugi wa Thiong'o 1986, *Decolonizing the Mind: the Politics of Language in African Literature*, Nairobi: Heinemann. First edn 1985.

Nord, Deborah Epstein 1988, "Mill and Ruskin on the Woman Question Revisited," in *Teaching Literature: What is Needed Now*, eds. James Engell and David Perkins, Cambridge, Mass.: Harvard University Press.

*Notes of Ben Jonson's Conversations with William Drummond of Hawthornden* 1842, January 1619, London.

'Faolain, Julia and Martines, Lauro 1973, *Not in God's Image: Women in History from the Greeks to the Victorians*, New York: Harper.

Oliphant, M. 1900, *Queen Victoria: a Personal Sketch*, London.

Ormond, Leonee 1987, "'The Spacious Times of Great Elizabeth': the Victorian Vision of the Elizabethans," *Victorian Poetry* 25.

Ormond, Richard 1973, *Early Victorian Portraits*, vol. 1, London: Her Majesty's Stationery Office.

1977, *The Face of Monarchy*, Oxford: Phaidon.

"Our Foreign Gossip" 1855, Editorial, *Harper's New Monthly Magazine*, November.

Overbeck, Lois More 1992, "The Life of the Work: A Preliminary Sketch," in Bryant-Jackson and Overbeck (eds.) 1992.

Parry, Ann 1992, "Misses Victorier's Sons," in *The Poetry of Rudyard Kipling: Rousing the Nation*, Philadelphia: Open University Press.

Parton, James and Horace Greeley (eds.) 1869, *Eminent Women of the Age: Being Narratives of the Lives and Deeds of the Most Prominent Women of the Present Generation*, Hartford, Conn.: S. M. Betts.

Patmore, Coventry 1949a, *The Poems of Coventry Patmore*, ed. Frederick Page, London: Oxford University Press.

1949b, *Religio Poetae*, London. First edn 1893.

Paxton, Nancy L. 1992, "Mobilizing Chivalry: Rape in British Novels About the Indian Uprising of 1857," *Victorian Studies* 36.

Peel, Sir Robert 1899, *Sir Robert Peel: from his Private Papers*, vol. II, ed. Charles Stuart Parker, London: John Murray.

"The Performance of Obvious Duties" 1867, *The Queen, the Lady's Newspaper, and Court Chronicle*, 41. 5 January.

"A Pertinent Question" 1855, *United States Magazine and Democratic Review*, March.

Pizan, Christine de 1982, *The Book of the City of Ladies*, trans. Earl Jeffrey Richards, New York: Persea. First edn 1405.

Plowden, Alison 1981, *The Young Victoria*, London: Weidenfield & Nicholson.

*Poetry without fiction*, 1825.

Pomeroy, Elizabeth 1989, *Reading the Portraits of Elizabeth I*, Hamden, Conn.: Archon.

Ponsonby, Arthur 1942, *Henry Ponsonby: his Life from his letters*, London: Macmillan.

Poovey, Mary 1988, *Uneven Developments: the Ideological Work of Gender in Mid-Victorian England*, Chicago: University of Chicago Press.

Proust, Marcel 1987, *On Reading Ruskin*, trans. and ed. Jean Autret, William Burford, and Phillip J. Wolfe, New Haven: Yale University Press.

*A Puzzle for a Curious Girl* 1819, London.

"Queen Elizabeth" 1859, *Eclectic Magazine*, October.

*The Queen: a Memorial of the Coronation* 1838, London.

"Queen Victoria" 1852, *Southern Literary Messenger*, March.

"Queen Victoria" 1866, Editorial, *Ladies' Repository*, September.

"Queen Victoria" 1880, *Harper's New Monthly Magazine*, July.

"Queen Victoria's Private Character," *Appleton's Journal*, November.

Read, Benedict 1982, *Victorian Sculpture*, New Haven: Yale University Press.

Reid, J. C. 1957, *The Mind and Art of Coventry Patmore*, New York: Macmillan–Routledge & Kegan Paul.

Richards, Thomas 1990, *The Commodity Culture of Victorian England: Advertising and Spectacle, 1851–1914*, Stanford: Stanford University Press.

Ricks, Christopher 1987, "The Princess and the Queen," *Victorian Poetry* 25.

[Roberts, Mary] 1822, *The Royal Exile*, 2 vols., London.

Roediger, David 1991, *The Wages of Whiteness: Race and the Making of the American Working Class*, London and New York: Verso.

Rogers, Alexander 1895, *The Rani of Jhansi or the Widowed Queen: a Drama of the Indian Mutiny*, Westminster: Constable.

Rose, Phyllis 1983, *Parallel Lives*, New York: Knopf.

Rosenberg, John D. 1963, *The Darkening Glass: a Portrait of Ruskin's Genius*, New York: Columbia University Press. Reprinted 1986.

　1968, "Style and Sensibility in Ruskin's Prose," in *The Art of Victorian Prose*, ed. George Levine and William A. Madden, London: Oxford University Press.

Rowell, George 1978, *Queen Victoria Goes to the Theatre*, London: Paul Elek.

Royal Archives, Windsor Castle, journal entries referred to as QVJ and date of entry.

"The Rule of the English-Speaking Folk" 1901, *The World's Work* March.

Rushdie, Salman 1991, *Imaginary Homelands: Essays in Criticism, 1981–1991*, London: Penguin.

Ruskin, John 1865, "Two Lectures by Mr. Ruskin," Review of *Sesame and Lilies*, *The Nation* 1.

　1866a, Review of "The Queenly Power of Woman," *The Ladies' Repository*, March.

　1866b, Review of *Sesame and Lilies*, *North American Review* 102 (January).

　1969, *The Winnington Letters of John Ruskin*, ed. Van Akin Burd, Cambridge, Mass.: Belknap–Harvard University Press.

　1903–12, *The Works of John Ruskin*, 39 vols., ed. E. T. Cook and Alexander Wedderburn, London: George Allen. New York: Longmans Green & Co.

Russ, William Adam, Jr. 1959, *The Hawaiian Revolution (1893–94)*, Selinsgrove, Pa.: Susquehanna University Press.

Russel, William 1857, *Extraordinary Women: their Girlhood and Early Life*, London.

Said, Edward 1978 [1979??], *Orientalism*, New York: Vintage.

　1993, *Culture and Imperialism*, New York: Knopf.

St. Aubyn, Giles 1975, *Queen Victoria as an Author, Essays by Divers Hands*, 38.

　1991, *Queen Victoria: a Portrait*, London: Sinclair-Stevenson.

Sanford, Mrs. J. 1821, *Female Improvement*, London.

Sarkar, Sumit 1995, *Macmillan Modern India: 1885–1947*, Madras, India: Macmillan India. First edn 1983.

Sawyer, Paul L. 1985, *Ruskin's Poetic Argument: the Design of the Major Works*, Ithaca, N.Y.: Cornell University Press.

　1990, "Ruskin and the Matriarchal Logos," in *Victorian Sages and Cultural Discourse: Renegotiating Gender and Power*, ed. Thaïs Morgan, New Brunswick: Rutgers University Press.

Scanlan, Robert 1992, "Surrealism as Mimesis: a Director's Guide to Adrienne Kennedy's *Funnyhouse of a Negro*," in Bryant-Jackson and Overbeck (eds.) 1992.

Scholberg, Henry 1985, *Lakshmibai and the Captain*, Calcutta: Writers Workshop.

Seaton, Beverly 1985, "Considering the Lilies: Ruskin's 'Proserpina' and Other Victorian Flower Books," *Victorian Studies* 28.

Seligman, Daniel 1991, "Keeping Up: Exemplarism," *Fortune* 123.13 (17 June).

Sharpe, Jenny 1993, *Allegories of Empire: the Figure of Woman in the Colonial Text*, Minneapolis: University of Minnesota Press.

Shuman, Cathy 1994, "Different for Girls: Narrative Subversion as Social Containment in Ruskin's *Sesame and Lilies*, Mill's *Subjection of Women*, and Dickens' *Our Mutual Friend*," Ph.D. dissertation, Yale University.

Sigourney, Lydia 1849, *Illustrated Poems*, Philadelphia: Carey & Hart.

Simpson, Marc 1982, "The Dream of the Dragon: Ruskin's Serpent Imagery," in *The Ruskin Polygon: Essays on the Imagination of John Ruskin*, ed. Faith M. Holland and John Dixon Hunt, Manchester: Manchester University Press.

Sinha, Mrinalini 1992, "'Chathams, Pitts, and Gladstones in Petticoats': the Politics of Gender and Race in the Ilbert Bill Controversy, 1883–1884," in *Western Women and Imperialism*, ed. Nupur Chaudhuri and Margaret Strobel, Bloomington: Indiana University Press.

Sitwell, Edith 1936, *Victoria of England*, Boston: Houghton Mifflin.

Smyth, Sir John 1966, *The Rebellious Rani*, London: Fredrick Muller.

Sollors, Werner 1991, "Owls and Rats in the American Funnyhouse: Adrienne Kennedy's Drama," *American Literature* 63.

Sonstroem, David 1971, "John Ruskin and the Nature of Manliness," *Victorian Newsletter* 40.

    1977, "Millet Versus Ruskin: a Defense of Ruskin's 'Of Queen's Gardens,'" *Victorian Studies* 20.

Spear, Jeffrey L. 1984, *Dreams of an English Eden: Ruskin and his Tradition in Social Criticism*, New York: Columbia University Press.

"Speculations Upon the Consequences of a War with Great Britain" 1842, *Southern Literary Messenger* July.

Spielmann, M. H. 1901, *British Sculpture and Sculptors of To-Day*, London: Cassell.

Spiers, Edward M. 1992, *The Late Victorian Army, 1868–1902*, Manchester: Manchester University Press.

Spivak, Gayatri C. 1988, "Can the Subaltern Speak? Speculations on Widow-Sacrifice," in *Marxism and the Interpretation of Culture*, ed. Cary Nelson and Lawrence Grossberg, Urbana: University of Illinois Press.

Spurr, David 1993, *The Rhetoric of Empire: Colonial Discourse in Journalism, Travel Writing, and Imperial Administration*, Durham: Duke University Press.

Steele, Shelby 1987, "Notes on Ritual in the New Black Theater," in Hill (ed.) 1987.

Stein, Richard L. 1985, *Victoria's Year: English Literature and Culture, 1837–1838*, Oxford: Oxford University Press.

Stepan, Nancy Leys 1990, "Race and Gender: the Role of Analogy in Science," in *Anatomy of Racism*, ed. David Theo Goldberg, Minneapolis: University of Minnesota Press.

Stevenson, Sara and Helen Bennet 1978, *Van Dyck in Check Trousers: Fancy Dress in Art and Life 1700–1900*, Edinburgh.

Stoller, Paul 1989, *Fusion of the Worlds: an Ethnography of Possession Among the Songhay of Niger*, Chicago: Chicago University Press.

1992, *The Cinematic Griot: the Ethnography of Jean Rouch*, Chicago: Chicago University Press.

Stowe, Harriet Beecher 1854, *Sunny Memories of Foreign Lands*, 2 vols., Boston: Phillips, Sampson.

Strachey, Lytton 1921, *Queen Victoria*, New York: Harcourt Brace Jovanovich.

Strickland, Agnes and Elizabeth Strickland 1902–3, *Lives of the Queens of England, from the Norman Conquest to the Reign of Queen Anne*, 16 vols., Philadelphia: Barrie.

1851, *The Queens of England: a Series of Portraits of Distinguished Female Sovereigns. Drawn and Engraved by Eminent Artists, with Biographical and Historical Sketches, from Agnes Strickland*, New York: Appleton.

Strobel, Margaret 1991, *European Women and the Second British Empire*, Bloomington: Indiana University Press.

Strong, Sir Roy 1978a, *And When did you Last see your Father?: the Victorian Painter and British History*, London: Thames & Hudson.

1978b, *Recreating the Past: British History and the Victorian Painter*, London: Thames & Hudson.

1987, *Gloriana: the Portraits of Queen Elizabeth I*, London: Thames & Hudson.

Swinburne, A. C. 1987, "The Jubilee," excerpted in *Victorian Poetry* 25.

Swindells, Julia 1985, *Victorian Writing and Working Women: the Other Side of Silence*, Cambridge: Polity Press–Basil Blackwell.

Tahmankar, D. V. 1958. *The Ranee of Jhansi*, London: Macgibbon & Kee.

Tate, Merze 1962, "Great Britain and the Sovereignty of Hawaii," *Pacific Historical Review* 31.

1965, *The United States and the Hawaiian Kingdom: a Political History*, New Haven: Yale University Press.

Taylor, William Cooke (ed.) 1842, *Romantic Biography of the Age of Elizabeth; or, Sketches of Life from the Bye-Ways of History. By the Benedictine Brethren of Glendaclough*, 2 vols., London.

Tefft, Revd B. F. 1863, "Boreal Nights," *The Ladies' Repository* January–December.

Tennyson, Alfred, Lord 1898, *The Complete Poetic Works of Tennyson*, Boston: Houghton-Mifflin.

1987, *The Poems of Tennyson*, Christopher Ricks, Berkeley: University of California Press.

Thompson, Dorothy 1990, *Queen Victoria: the Woman, the Monarchy, and the People*, New York: Pantheon.

Thornton-Cook, Elsie Prentys 1927, *Her Majesty: the Romance of the Queens of England, 1066–1910*, New York: Dutton.

Tingsten, Herbert 1972, *Victoria and the Victorians*, London: Allen & Unwin.

Traylor, Eleanor 1987, "Two Afro-American Contributions to Dramatic Form," in Hill (ed.).

Trimmer, Mrs. 1794, *Fabulous Histories*, Philadelphia.

Trinh, T. Minh-Ha 1991, *When the Moon Waxes Red*, London: Routledge.

Trudgill, Eric 1976, *Madonnas and Magdalens: the Origins and Development of Victorian Sexual Attitudes*, New York: Holmes & Meier.

Vallone, L. 1995, *Disciplines of Virtue: Girls' Culture in the Eighteenth and Nineteenth Centuries*, New Haven: Yale University Press.

Victoria, Duchess of Kent 1830, "To the Bishops of London and Lincoln," 1 March.

Victoria, Queen 1868, *Leaves from the Journal of Our Life in the Highlands from 1848 to 1861*, ed. Arthur Helps, London: Smith & Elder.

   1884, *More Leaves from the Journal of A Life in the Highlands from 1862 to 1882*, London: Smith & Elder.

   1907, *The Letters of Queen Victoria*, vol. 1, *1837–1843*, ed. Arthur Christopher Benson and Viscount Esher, New York: Longmans, Green & Co.

   1930, *The Letters of Queen Victoria: Third Series. A Selection from Her Majesty's Correspondence and Journal Between the Years 1886 and 1901*, ed. George Earle Buckle, 3 vols. New York: Longmans.

   1964, *Dearest Child, Letters Between Queen Victoria and the Princess Royal, 1858–1861, a Selection from the Kronberg Archives*, ed. Roger Fulford, London: Evans Brothers.

   1985, *Queen Victoria in Her Letters and Journals*, ed. Christopher Hibbert, New York: Viking.

Victorian Collection, Special Collections, Brigham Young University, Harold B. Lee Library.

Walker, Susan Sheridan 1993, *Wife and Widow in Medieval England*, Ann Arbor: University of Michigan Press.

Ward, E. 1812, *The Reciter*, London.

Warner, Marina 1985, *Monuments and Maidens: the Allegory of the Female Form*, New York: Atheneum.

Washington, Mary Helen 1982, "Teaching *Black-Eyed Susans:* an Approach to the Study of Black Women Writers," in *All the Women are White, All the Blacks are Men, But some of us are Brave: Black Women's Studies*, ed. Gloria T. Hull, Patricia Bell Scott, and Barbara Smith, New York: Feminist Press. First edn 1977.

Weeks, Jeffrey 1981, *Sex, Politics and Society: the Regulation of Sexuality since 1800*, London: Longman.

Weinig, Sister Mary Anthony 1981, *Coventry Patmore*, Boston: Twayne – G. K. Hall.

Weintraub, Stanley 1987, *Victoria: an Intimate Biography*, New York: Dutton.

Welsh, Alexander 1971, *The City of Dickens*, Oxford: Oxford University Press.

West, R. 1993, *Narrative, Authority, and Law*, Ann Arbor: University of Michigan Press.

Whitman, Walt 1973, *Leaves of Grass*, ed. Sculley Bradley and Harold W. Blodgett, New York: Norton.

Wilkerson, Margaret 1992, "Diverse Angles of Vision: Two Black Women Playwrights," in Bryant-Jackson and Overbeck (eds.) 1992.

Williams, Mance 1985, *Black Theatre in the 1960s and 1970s: a Historical–Critical Analysis of the Movement*, Westport: Greenwood.

Woodham-Smith, Cecil 1972, *Queen Victoria: Her Life and Times, 1819–1861*, London.

Woolf, Virginia 1942, "Professions for Women," in *The Death of the Moth and Other Essays*, New York: Harcourt Brace Janovich.

Worsick, Clark and Ainslie Embree 1976, *The Last Empire: Photography in British India, 1855–1911*, Millerton, N.Y.: Aperture.

Wynn, Frances Williams 1864, *Diary of a Lady*, London.

York, Duchess of 1993, *Travels with Queen Victoria*, London: Weidenfeld & Nicolson.

York, Duchess of with Benita Stoney, 1991, *Victoria and Albert: a Family Life at Osborne House*, London: Weidenfeld & Nicolson.

Young, G. M. 1962, *Victorian Essays*, London: Oxford University Press.

"Zenobia" 1855, *United States Magazine and Democratic Review*, March.

# Index

CAMBRIDGE STUDIES IN NINETEENTH-CENTURY
LITERATURE AND CULTURE

General editors
Gillian Beer, *University of Cambridge*
Catherine Gallagher, *University of California, Berkeley*

Titles published